AF556821

TEACHING COMPUTING

A Practical Approach

ELEANOR BUJEA

STANLEY VOYCE

PRENTICE HALL, Englewood Cliffs, New Jersey 07632

Library of Congress Cataloging-in-Publication Data

Bujea, Eleanor.
Teaching computing.

Bibliography.
Includes index.
1. Electronic data processing—Study and teaching.
I. Voyce, Stanley. II. Title.
QA76.27.B85 1988 004'.07'1 87-18739
ISBN 0-13-891953-4

Editorial/production supervision and
interior design: **Marjorie Borden Shustak**
Cover design: **Lundgren Graphics, Ltd.**
Manufacturing buyer: **Margaret Rizzi**

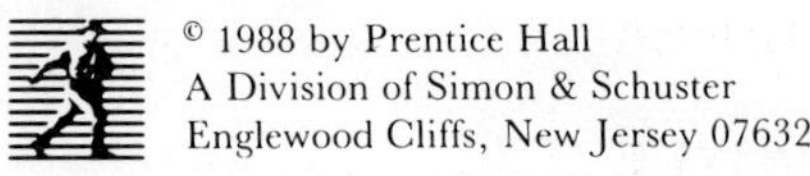

Printed in the United States of America

10 9 8 7 6 5 4 3 2 1

ISBN 0-13-891953-4 01

Prentice-Hall International (UK) Limited, *London*
Prentice-Hall of Australia Pty. Limited, *Sydney*
Prentice-Hall Canada Inc., *Toronto*
Prentice-Hall Hispanoamericana, S.A., *Mexico*
Prentice-Hall of India Private Limited, *New Delhi*
Prentice-Hall of Japan, Inc., *Tokyo*
Simon & Schuster Asia Pte. Ltd., *Singapore*
Editora Prentice-Hall do Brasil, Ltda., *Rio de Janeiro*

Eleanor Bujea

To my parents,
Pamfil and Maria Bujea,
and to my sisters and brothers,
Mary, George, Anne, Helen, and John.

Stanley Voyce

I dedicate this book in memory of my parents,
Nellie and William Ralph Voyce,
both of whom passed away while the manuscript was in preparation.
In this project, as with my other academic endeavors,
they offered unfailing support and encouragement.

Contents

Preface

Teaching Computing: A Practical Approach is designed to assist teachers of computer studies by making their instructional tasks simpler and more effective. It provides many suggestions and guidelines on how to improve the content and delivery of the introductory course.

The world of computing is changing and evolving almost daily, making the learning and teaching of computer studies both dynamic and challenging. Handling a course which is constantly evolving, and accommodating subject matter content spanning a wide range of student aptitudes, requires a variety of teaching methodologies and teacher competencies. This book provides the teacher with a useful guide to such methodologies and competencies.

The content of the book deals with information related to teaching the introductory computer studies course—the first course in the student's computing repertoire. In this context, it includes the teaching of computer literacy, computer awareness, and introductory computer science courses. In addition, it contains much useful information for instructing higher level courses, seminars, workshops, and in-service training sessions.

The book approaches the teaching of computer studies from the practical perspective and, as a result, includes topics such as how to:

1. Determine the content of the introductory computer studies course.
2. Set up adequate goals and objectives for such a course.
3. Order and pace the course correctly.
4. Make the most timely use of teaching methodologies such as lecturing, discussion, and question/answer.
5. Get the most use out of the vast collection of teaching resources which are available.
6. Teach various aspects of the course such as hardware, programming, societal issues.
7. Evaluate and test the computer studies student.

8. Set up the computer studies laboratory facilities.
9. Get further ideas and information on teaching computer studies.
10. Prepare the student for what comes after the introductory studies course.

The target population of readers of this book is broad. It is suitable for a wide variety of different instructors and educators, including:

1. The teacher who is just starting to teach computer studies.
2. The teacher who has had several years of related experience.
3. Instructors for all grade levels—elementary and secondary.
4. University professors, lecturers, and laboratory instructors.
5. Instructors of computer studies at community colleges and technical institutes.
6. Teacher interns and students studying methods of teaching computer studies courses.
7. School principals, directors of education, superintendents, and educational consultants.
8. Resource center librarians.
9. Individuals providing in-service education for teachers.
10. Directors and instructors of computer-related training programs in business and industry.

Although this book is crammed with useful ideas, we do not expect the reader to utilize every one of them; instead, we advise teachers to pick and choose those which are appropriate for their particular classroom environment. To assist in this selection process, the book has a modular design which allows the reader to start reading at any chapter without much difficulty. Each chapter of the book concludes with a set of *questions* which are designed to augment the content of the chapter by requiring the reader to either come to some conclusions about the various aspects of the chapter, or conduct research to obtain additional information necessary to answer the question. At the end of the book the reader will find a *glossary* of terms that the student would probably encounter in the introductory computer studies course; as such, it functions as a "mini-guide" to the content of the introductory course.

The book is *not* a computer science textbook, but rather a book on how to teach computer studies courses. Accordingly, it cannot—and should not—provide the in-depth coverage found in a computer studies or programming textbook; we expect the reader to have gained this knowledge separately—either before this book is read or at the same time. For those teachers who would like to research the topic in greater depth, we recommend that a current reading list of books be obtained from their resource center/library.

We, the authors, are well qualified to address its content. Together we have amassed a total of 30 years experience in education and 20 years in computer science. Dr. Bujea has degrees in accounting and administration, business education, and teacher education; Dr. Voyce has degrees in psychology, computer science, and educational theory. Dr. Bujea is an accountant and manager, and formerly an Associate Professor of the Faculty of Education at the University of Regina; Dr. Voyce was formerly an Associate Professor of the Department of

Computer Science at the same university and presently is working in the computing industry. We both have presented many papers, courses and workshops on the topic of education and computing.

ACKNOWLEDGMENTS

A number of people have been instrumental in the development of this book. We greatly appreciate the advice and helpful suggestions of John Bujea, who functioned as a most useful sounding board for our ideas. Thanks to Ben Wenzel, the original editor of the book in its early stages, for getting us started on the right track; and to Susan Willig, the current editor, and to Marjorie Shustak, production editor, for guiding the book to its completed form. We also acknowledge the three reviewers of the manuscript whose thoughtful comments and constructive criticisms were critical in shaping its content and direction, and those kind people who posed for the photographs.

Eleanor Bujea and Stanley Voyce

The preparation of the book often necessitated the sacrifice of precious time normally spent with my family on weekends, evenings, and holidays. I, therefore, owe an immeasurable debt of gratitude and heartfelt appreciation to my wife Colleen, my daughter Stephanie, and my son Derek, for their patience, understanding, encouragement, and love throughout the time spent working on this project.

Finally, a big thank-you to my co-author, Eleanor, who stuck with me through some trying moments, endured with the patience of Job all my shortcomings, and was altogether the best collaborator I could have had.

Stanley Voyce

1 Introduction

The modern educational system is in the midst of a revolution—the computer revolution—which is influencing every aspect of our society and our lives. Educators are particularly effected by this revolution, being entrusted with the responsibility to satisfy the demand for courses, workshops, and seminars about computing and computer studies. This demand comes from many quarters. Businesses need employees who are familiar with computing technology and/or are able to program. Laypeople are bombarded daily with products of the computing age (electronic banking, automated checkouts, "smart" microwave ovens) and must learn to understand and cope with them. Parents, realizing the importance of a computer education, insist that their children get exposure. Government officials, responding to the need for computer-literate citizens, are encouraging educational institutions to provide the necessary training. And many individuals are buying personal computers and seeking direction about their use. The result of this ever-increasing demand is a proliferation of courses on topics such as computer literacy, computer programming, and the use of computers in society.

In addition to stimulating the growing demand for computer instruction, the computer revolution is having another effect on education: The computer is entering the traditional classroom as a powerful teaching tool and tutorial aid. Over the past decade, many schools have begun using computing equipment to teach a portion of the content in mathematics, business education, English, social studies, and other classes. The computer programs needed to provide this instruction—called *courseware*—are currently available in such number and variety that it is now becoming difficult for the educator to make wise selections for any specific subject field.

The computer revolution has another major effect on education. Teachers are rapidly recognizing the advantages of using the computer to assist in teaching a variety of subjects. Thus, by learning to use word processors, students indirectly augment their writing skills; by using electronic spreadsheet software, they enhance their business education or mathematical knowledge; or, by writing programs to assist in solving mathematical problems, they learn more about the mathematics involved.

In summary, the computing revolution is having three dramatic effects on education by producing an increasing demand for instruction *about* computers; by providing an enormous potential for instruction *by* computers; and by providing the opportunity to teach other subject material *through* the computer.

Many educators are unprepared to meet these computer-related demands—the changes have come too quickly for them. Hence, they need information about how to use computers in their classrooms.

While much has been written on using computers as a teaching tool (instruction *by* computers) and as a teaching assistant (learning *through* computers), *little is available on how to teach about computers,* and thus help teachers provide courses in computer science or computer literacy. This book is designed to fill the gap for the educator; it will present an overview of how the schools are offering computer studies as a viable part of the curricula, what is actually happening in the schools, and how instructors may prepare themselves for teaching computer studies at all educational levels.

HOW THE SCHOOLS RESPOND TO THIS NEED

Since the turn of the century, when education became compulsory, it has been the task of teachers to prepare children for the society in which they live. Since the computer is playing an ever-increasing role in the lives of the students, computer studies is becoming an indispensable component of a student's education and many schools are making it mandatory.

Teachers offering courses about computers use a variety of terms to describe it, like computer awareness, computer literacy, data processing, computer science, computer education, information processing, and computer studies. The term used varies according to the perceived needs as identified by the educator.

Computer awareness. Many schools are responding to people's needs to cope with and to adjust to the computer and to be made "aware" of the role computers play in their lives. What is awareness? To be aware means that you are apprised, informed, cognizant or conscious of something. For the teacher concerned with computing, it means providing the student with some understanding of what the computer can do: its capabilities, limitations, and areas of application. In addition, the students are often informed about how computers affect them specifically and society generally. Thus in today's schools, we see an ever-increasing number of "computer awareness" classes designed to give the student background to discuss computers with their colleagues, and to cope with the effects of computing technology in their everyday lives.

Computer literacy. Computer literacy classes generally give the student all the content of a computer awareness class plus a little bit more—like an introduction to computer problem-solving and programming. The coverage is not intensive, but makes the student feel at home with a microcomputer, and may create a desire to learn more in future classes.

Computer science. Computer science classes are more intensive, and may prepare the student for a possible career in computing. They include the content of the computer awareness and computer literacy classes and go into greater depth with programming, offer one or more languages, develop familiarity with the inner workings of the hardware, and cover the theoretical and mathematical aspects of computing. Such detail does not come in a single course—in the university it requires three or four years. The beginning course in this sequence, normally known as the introductory computer studies course, is similar to the computer literacy course.

WHERE TRAINING IS AVAILABLE

Computer studies is being taught virtually everywhere and at every age level. In the *elementary schools,* small children are taught the basics of computer awareness and computer literacy; in many cases, they learn to write simple programs in languages such as BASIC and LOGO. In the *secondary schools,* older students receive more in-depth training, frequently including instruction in two or more programming languages. At the *universities,* course offerings vary greatly, ranging from introductory service courses to undergraduate and graduate degrees in computer science.

Community colleges and technical institutions provide specialized training in word processor operation, business-oriented programming, computer maintenance, and so on. *Extension departments and adult education institutions* provide an extensive variety of computer-related topics such as learning to use a microcomputer, using spreadsheet software packages, and setting up a small business operation.

Most companies and business organizations which require the services of computing personnel, supply in-house courses designed to upgrade their technical competence. All sections of the *military forces* are keenly interested in various aspects of computing software and hardware, supplying specialized courses to both officers and enlisted men and women.

Various *professional computer organizations* offer workshops, seminars, or "mini-courses" designed to either upgrade the computer professional or introduce the non-computing professional to various aspects of computing. *Computer stores and microcomputer dealerships* often deliver tutorials on the usage of their equipment and the basics of programming on their microcomputers.

Many *school boards and departments of education* offer introductory in-service courses on various aspects of computing.

Independent consulting firms frequently market seminars and short courses dealing with a wide range of computing concepts, including introductory material. And *mail order courses,* advertised in computing magazines, are also available.

QUESTIONS

1. What is the "computer revolution"?
2. How does the computer revolution affect the world?
3. How has the computer revolution affected education?

4. Why or why not is computer studies important for every individual?
5. How does computer awareness differ from computer literacy and computer science?
6. Provide evidence that a computer revolution is taking place.
7. How is your state or province responding to the need for computer education?
8. Define the following terms: computer literacy, computer science, computer awareness.

2

The Computer Studies Curriculum

Schools offering computer studies have a number of questions which must be answered regarding what must be taught and how it should be taught. Consideration must be given to what content should be covered; at what level should the specific content be offered; who should teach it; how it should be taught; and what equipment, if any, is needed. The first of these tasks, deciding on course content (curriculum), is very important.

To decide on content, the teacher must have a solid background in computer studies. Unfortunately, teachers' backgrounds in computing vary. The teacher with no experience in computing needs a crash course or courses before presenting the material; the teacher with adequate experience may only need a refresher course. However, *all* teachers must be involved in establishing the details of the computer studies program. For the inexperienced teacher, this means starting from scratch; for the experienced teacher, the main concern is refining the existing course content and improving its presentation. In many cases, a *curriculum guide* is available to give the teacher a framework within which to work; however, such guides do not prescribe the details required for the actual classroom presentation and the teacher must fill in many gaps, such as specifics of the course content, modifications dictated by the grade level, and specifications on the methods of delivery. These activities are called *curriculum development*.

WHAT IS THE COMPUTER STUDIES CURRICULUM?

At present, there is no agreement as to what constitutes the computer studies curriculum: what to call the course, the content to be taught, the number of courses to be included, and the time required to teach the subject matter. All vary from school to school. In some cases, primarily at the university level, the curriculum will include fifteen to twenty-five courses taken over a period of four or more

FIGURE 2.1 Extracts from a representative university curriculum offered by the Computer Science Department at The University of Regina.

The following table indicates the specific classes required for a degree with a major in Computer Science.

Degree Program	Required Computer Science Classes	Other Required Classes
B.A.*	Computer Science 200, 270, 300, 340, 400, 310 or 311 1 additional class in Computer Science numbered above 199	Mathematics 210, 211 and 222
B.Sc.	Computer Science 200, 270, 300, 340, 400, 310 or 311 4 additional classes in Computer Science numbered above 199	Mathematics 210, 211 and 222
B.A. (Hons) B.Sc. (Hons)	Computer Science 200, 261, 270, 300, 340, 375, 400, 440, 310 or 311 4 additional classes in Computer Science numbered above 199 at least one of which is above 399	Mathematics 210, 211 and 222

*A student majoring in Computer Science in the B.A. Program will register in the Faculty of Science. In selecting a program of study, however, the student may elect the major to be in one of the areas of the Faculty of Arts.

Students in an Honours Course are required to participate in the Honours Computer Science Seminar during the last two semesters of the program and to pass a comprehensive examination at the end of the program.

Course numbers and titles

COMPUTER SCIENCE 102
Introduction to Computers

COMPUTER SCIENCE 200
Introduction to Computer Science and Problem Solving

COMPUTER SCIENCE 203
Computer Science for Engineers

COMPUTER SCIENCE 230
Systems Software—An Application Perspective

COMPUTER SCIENCE 261
Methods in Numerical Analysis

COMPUTER SCIENCE 270
Business Information Systems

COMPUTER SCIENCE 271
Application Program Development

COMPUTER SCIENCE 300
Elements of Computer Hardware and Software

COMPUTER SCIENCE 305
Data Communications and Networks

COMPUTER SCIENCE 310
Discrete Computational Structures

COMPUTER SCIENCE 311
Finite Automata Theory

COMPUTER SCIENCE 330
Introduction to Systems Programming

COMPUTER SCIENCE 340
Programming Languages and Data Structures

COMPUTER SCIENCE 361
Numerical Analysis I

COMPUTER SCIENCE 374
Computer Methods and Modelling

COMPUTER SCIENCE 375
Information Storage and Retrieval

COMPUTER SCIENCE 381
Introduction to the Design of Digital Computers

COMPUTER SCIENCE 390–395
Directed Study in Computer Science

COMPUTER SCIENCE 400
Computer Systems Architecture

COMPUTER SCIENCE 405
Principles of Computer Graphics

COMPUTER SCIENCE 410
Formal Languages

COMPUTER SCIENCE 411
Computability Theory

COMPUTER SCIENCE 430
Advanced Topics in System Software

COMPUTER SCIENCE 440
Advanced Topics in Programming Languages and Data Structures

COMPUTER SCIENCE 461
Numerical Analysis II

COMPUTER SCIENCE 470
Database Systems

COMPUTER SCIENCE 471
Application Software Development Project

COMPUTER SCIENCE 476
Distributed Data Processing

FIGURE 2.1. (continued)

COMPUTER SCIENCE 371 Advanced Applications Programming	COMPUTER SCIENCE 490–495 Directed Study in Computer Science
COMPUTER SCIENCE 372 Advanced Systems Analysis and Design	COMPUTER SCIENCE 499 Honours Seminar
COMPUTER SCIENCE 373 Project Management for Data Processing Applications	

years. At the secondary level, the computer curriculum is frequently just three or four courses studied over a two-year period. At the elementary school level it could mean a single course taught in one semester.

These differences in course offerings are illustrated in Figures 2-1, 2-2, and 2-3, which present representative curricula at the post-secondary (university), secondary, and elementary school levels. Note the in-depth coverage at the higher level (see Figure 2-1)—courses offered range from introductory material dealing with computers in society and elementary programming to esoteric topics such as compiler construction and numerical analysis.

Coverage at the high school level (see Figure 2-2), on the other hand, is much more restricted—an introductory course plus several additional programming courses.

FIGURE 2-2 Representative High School Curriculum, Department of Education, Province of Saskatchewan

Grade 10 and 11: Computer Applications 10/20
Encourages an approach to learning that develops a sense of mastery in all students, in terms of specific knowledge and skills, as well as in developing a general sense of personal confidence in computer use.

Grade 10: Computer Science 10
Study and practice in problem solving, preparing algorithms, programming, and using the programming language BASIC. Emphasis should be on problem solving rather than the language.
Prerequisite: Computer Literacy.

Grade 11: Computer Science 20
Continuation and extension of the problem solving, algorithms, programming, and BASIC language syntax studied in Computer Studies 10. In addition, students experience some applications by working with a word-processing program and a spreadsheet program.
Prerequisite: Computer Science 10.

Grade 12: Computer Science 30
Pascal is considered at present the most appropriate language for Computer Science 30. Access to a computer is required for most homework assignments. Since this is the final high school class in a general introduction to programming/problem solving skills, a major project should be part of the course. The project provides an opportunity to synthesize the major components of the students' previous and current experiences.

FIGURE 2-3 Representative Elementary School Curriculum Department of Education, Province of Saskatchewan

Grades 7, 8, and 9: Computer Literacy
This 50-hour course entails study of applications, history, business and social impact, capabilities and limitations of computers, and nontechnical study of how computer systems work (25 hours). Also included are problem solving and programming (25 hours).

Grades K through 6
There is no formal curriculum guide in most schools. The computer is used for drill and practice in a variety of classes. Some programming instruction is given. Students may write simple programs, make software changes, and play games for instructional purposes. Time on the computer may be allotted to students as an award for work completion, as enrichment, or as members of a computer club. Time allotted is on a per-week basis rather than on a daily basis, unless the computer is utilized for tutorials.

The elementary level has the most restricted curriculum, with only one course dealing with the fundamentals of programming and computers in society (see Figure 2-3).

These three curricula are very different—which is to be expected since each institution caters to a different audience. However, examining the three curricula reveals common elements. These elements are the fundamental components of the computer studies curriculum and are taught regardless of age group or school level. When more than one course is included in the curriculum, many of these elements are usually dealt with in the *introductory course.*

THE INTRODUCTORY COMPUTER STUDIES COURSE

The introductory computer course may be known by several other names, like Computer Awareness, Computer Studies, Computer Literacy, Computing, Computer Science, and Introduction to Computers. Deciding which title to adopt depends upon the grade level and the school policies.

FIGURE 2-4 Major topics of the introductory computer studies content

History
Hardware
Programming and Problem Solving
The Computer Language
Software
Advanced Computer Concepts
Careers in Computing
Applications of Computers in Our World
The Effect of Computers on Society

The content of a typical introductory computer studies course varies from place to place and school to school. A typical, representative list of topics is shown in Figure 2-4 with sub-topics in Figure 2-5.

FIGURE 2-5 Sub-topics of the content

1. *History of Computers*
   - history before electronic computers—Babbage, and so on
   - generations of computers
   - development of software
   - appreciation of extremely rapid developments
   - the future

2. *Hardware*
   - computer systems
   - CPU and memory
   - auxilliary storage—tapes, disks
   - I/O equipment and media
   - printers, keyboards, CRTs
   - data entry
   - care of equipment
   - selecting hardware—evaluation, costs
   - number systems, binary arithmetic, character codes

3. *Programming and Problem-Solving*
   - algorithms
   - flowcharting and pseudocode
   - documentation
   - top-down design
   - modular programming

4. *The Computer Language*
   - syntax of language, statements
   - variables and constants
   - control structures—jumps, iterations
   - numeric and string manipulation
   - file handling
   - graphics
   - conditional branching
   - subprograms/modules
   - input/output
   - structures—arrays and tables
   - debugging and testing, error messages
   - style and documentation

5. *Software*
   - compilation/interpretation
   - fundamentals of operating systems
   - utilities

FIGURE 2.5. (continued)

comparison of programming languages
using software packages
electronic spreadsheets
word processors
editors

6. *Advanced Computer Concepts*
systems analysis
information retrieval and data base management
networks and telecommunication

7. *Careers in Computing*
kinds of jobs
training needed
job availability

8. *Application of Computers in Our World*
current and future
sample applications:
personal uses
business
government
military
entertainment, games
law
information industry
manufacturing
medicine
banking
transportation

9. *Effect of Computers on Society*
ethics of computing
unemployment
privacy and individuality
computer crime
attitudes to computers
effect on personal lives

The topics listed in the Figure 2-4 and 2-5 were derived by analyzing three major sources of information for the content of introductory computer studies courses: a survey of what many teachers of computer studies are currently teaching, curriculum guides from states and provinces throughout North America (see Figure 2-6), and introductory computer studies/science textbooks.

The topics presented in Figures 2-4 and 2-5 are not detailed enough to form the basis of a computer studies curriculum, nor should they be regarded as an ideal model of what to teach. They are only a cross-section of what typically oc-

FIGURE 2-6 Computing Topics Based on State and Provincial Curriculum Guides: High School Level

A research of fifteen state and provincial curriculum guides revealed a variety of topics taught in the school systems. Not all topics were found in every school; in fact, many were restricted to just one or two guides. These topics have been eliminated, leaving only those which were found in three or more guides.

List of Guides

Manitoba: CS205
Manitoba: CS305
New Brunswick: 112
Ontario: Sr. Division
Saskatoon: CS10
Saskatoon: CS20
Saskatchewan: C L
Saskatchewan: CS10
Saskatchewan: CS20
Saskatoon: Computer Literacy
Tennessee: classroom
Alberta: CS30
Oregon: K-12
Indiana: HS
Bellingham, WA: C L

List of Topics

accounting applications
algorithms
applications
arithmetic
arrays
branching
careers
commands
computer defined functions
debugging
decision-making skills
documentation
flowcharting
formatting
graphics
hardware
high level languages
historical background
I/O commands
I/O systems
language
library programs
looping
machine & assembly language usage
mathematical applications
problem-solving
program style
program systems
programming
searching
simulations
social impact
software
sorting
statistics & problems
string operations
subprograms
subroutines
terminology
"visicalc"
word processing

curs. An actual introductory curriculum in computer studies might ignore one or more of these elements—omission of operating systems and system analysis are good examples—or could contain additional features, such as the learning of assembly language. The choice depends upon the focus of the school and the background of the teacher. At the secondary level, computer studies may be included in the business administration course and may need to be adjusted to fit its overall objectives. At the elementary level, computer studies may be crammed into six weeks; or the course material may be imbedded in another course, such as mathematics.

THE COMPUTER STUDIES CURRICULUM GUIDE

The curriculum guide is a document, produced by state or provincial agencies, school boards, or groups of teachers, which outlines objectives to be met by students and prescribes the content to be used in achieving the objectives. An example of an abridged computer studies curriculum guide is given in Figure 2-7.

Usually, curriculum guides are very general, and rarely provide enough information. The guide needs some indication of resources, timing, and teaching style; furthermore, it usually must be modified to meet the unique goals of teacher, student, and school system.

The guide, then, must be expanded into the minute details of the actual concepts to be taught at the daily lesson level. Guides usually contain loosely defined goals and broad objectives. The teacher's task is to take the broad general objectives and formulate specific objectives so that the content of the course may be presented logically.

PLANNING THE COMPUTER STUDIES COURSE

When planning a computer studies course, the teacher must take the vague, original intention—such as, "We need a course for introducing computer science"—and convert it into the specific teaching activities which occur in each classroom period. Hence, planning consists of steps proceeding from the general to the specific. These steps can be classified into a series of specific activities.

1. *Setting the goals of the computer studies course.* Detail the goals and objectives of the course so that both teacher and student know what must be learned and can determine if and when learning has been accomplished. These goals also let students know what to study for tests.
2. *Refining these goals into instructional objectives.* Specify the content of the computer studies course and the procedures for evaluating the students so that important material is not omitted, and extraneous and irrelevant material is excluded.
3. *Determining the entering condition of the students.* Specify computer studies prerequisites so that students' background knowledge will meet minimum requirements.
4. *Deciding upon the order in which the objectives will be taught.* Make sure that the order of presentation is optimal so that simple material is presented before more complex concepts, and prerequisites are taught in the correct order.
5. *Estimating the time required to teach each objective, and deciding whether the overall time is appropriate.* Ensure that each topic of the computer studies course is taught in a suitable timespan. This means that concepts which are important and/or difficult to master will be given preference over unimportant or simple material.
6. *Dividing the course into units of instruction and determining the methods and resources required to teach each unit.* Select and order textbooks and supplementary readings well in advance to ensure their availability. Establish an adequate supply of reference materials in the library and resource centers.

FIGURE 2-7 Extracts from a representative grade school curriculum. From the Saskatchewan Department of Education Curriculum Guide for Division IV—Computer Science, 10, 20.

General Objectives: Computers in Society (Required)

Students will be able to:

*CA-GN-01A** Investigate and report on issues relating to the increased use of computers and the effects of technological change, e.g., threats to privacy, employment displacement and computer crime.

CA-GN-02A Report on trends and issues relating to computers.

CA-GN-03A Explain the impact of current technological change on the type of employment skills required in the future (new job skills, need for retraining, trends and opportunities).

CA-GN-04A Become aware of the potential jobs associated with computer use in a variety of fields by investigating job descriptions, salaries, working conditions and educational requirements.

General Objectives: Knowledge and Skills for Computer Users (Required)

Students will be able to:

CA-GN-05A Demonstrate confidence and resourcefulness in acquiring technical knowledge and proficiency in the use of applications software. (ongoing)

CA-GN-06A Demonstrate correct keyboarding skills when entering text. (ongoing)

CA-GN-07A Identify the major physical components of a microcomputer system (as locally implemented) and describe briefly the function of each.

CA-GN-08A Explain clearly the relationships among the hardware, system software, application software and the text or data used in applications programs.

AIMS

1. To develop an understanding of and appreciation for
   a. the historical and continuing evolution of computing technology.
   b. the powers and limitations of computers when used as problem solving tools.
   c. the continuing effects of computer technology on society.
2. To develop an understanding of the functions and interrelationships of the major components of a modern computer system.
3. To develop the ability to analyze a problem and prepare an algorithm leading to its solution.
4. To develop skill in applying standard programming techniques required in the design of a computer program.

*The 'A' suffix is used in this version to indicate that these objectives may be changed as feedback is received from the field.

7. *Determining the computing equipment required for the course.* Select and order any equipment or AV materials so that they arrive on time and are utilized at the appropriate point in the computer studies course.
8. *Ensuring adequate articulation has been provided.* Keep an accurate record of what is taught so that repetition at other grade levels is restricted to those points needed to reinforce knowledge.

Classification of Plans

The four plans necessary for the teacher of computer studies are year or semester plans, unit plans, sub-unit plans, and daily lesson plans.

The *yearly plan* involves determining what will happen in the course throughout the entire year or semester. A number of items need attention at this stage in the planning. The general objectives of the course are established or derived from a curriculum guide. The objectives are used to determine the division of the material into units. Units represent the major topics of the course; examples include history, hardware, programming, and flowcharting. The units of the computer studies course are typically associated with the individual chapters of the textbook.

A decision is made regarding the amount of time allocated to the course. This includes time for teaching, review, examinations, homework and study. The relative importance of each unit is estimated, based on its importance in achieving course goals. Preliminary estimates of the time required to teach each unit are made, based on the importance of the unit and its level of difficulty. Dates are determined for the completion of each unit. This estimate is used to help distribute teaching time, especially if team teaching is involved, and to firm up the dates for ordering materials and equipment.

Once a good yearly plan has been developed and estimates of the requisite units have been made, the *contents* of each unit are worked out. This stage of the procedure is termed *unit planning*. For each major unit developed, the following procedure is repeated. Establish the content of each unit; cite the objectives; estimate the preliminary time.

The unit is then divided into packages containing more specific portions of the course, known as *sub-units*. Each sub-unit is worked up in more detail: Objectives are set, content is determined, dates are set and further sub-units are derived, if necessary. Sub-units are separated into smaller and smaller parts until we eventually determine the specific goals to be reached each day—in other words, *the objectives for each lesson*. At the lesson level, only one or two concepts of the overall content will be taught.

Once the lessons have been planned, determine if the course coverage fits into the time frame. You might find that too much time was needed for the content identified, the time may be just right, or there might be more time than needed. Adjust the lesson plan to fit into the time period while still adhering to the major goals of the curriculum. The end product of this planning procedure is a detailed curriculum which lays out the *content, order,* and *pace* of the course.

The daily lesson plan When creating the daily lesson plan, the objectives are first laid out in terms of specific actions required of the student; these are termed *behavioral objectives*. The computer studies content required to fulfill these objectives is then selected. Each lesson consists of individual concepts—for example, the GOTO statement, the operation of the disk drive, or the effect of computers on employment. Two or three new concepts may be taught per day, but in most cases, one is sufficient.

Next ascertain if prerequisite knowledge has been acquired. This procedure, known as *vertical articulation,* will eliminate redundancies in the student's program; that is, those who learned keyboarding in a business administration course would not need to repeat it in a computer studies course. By pretesting the students, these redundancies can be ascertained and modifications to the proposed curriculum can be made. Vertical articulation should also be used to determine if there is any content overlap with courses that the student will take later. For example, binary arithmetic need not be taught in a subsequent computer studies course if it was covered in the introductory course. If overlap is found, either eliminate the redundant material from the course, or request that it is eliminated from the other course. The choice should be based upon the suitability of the material to the course and grade level. Problems may arise from overlap with courses that a student is taking at the same time. For instance, a student might be taking an introductory computer studies course along with a mathematics course which contains similar computing elements. The remedy to this problem, which involves dovetailing the two courses, is termed *cross articulation.*

Assuming that a good *textbook* has been chosen, the individual chapters or sections are allocated to the individual lessons or clusters of lessons dealing with a single concept. Supplementary reading material should also be indicated at this point in the planning.

The *resources* required to fulfill the objectives of each lesson also must be established at this time. This includes materials needed in class, in labs, and outside class. Imagine, for example, that we have a lesson to teach on floppy disks. A floppy disk system would be ideal for demonstration. A floppy diskette could be made available for the class. Brochures might be obtained for student reference, or a tour of a computer facility or computer store might be arranged so that the student could see the equipment.

The teacher also must decide how the material will be taught—the *methods and techniques* required to convey the material effectively. There are many ways of teaching the material—lecturing, discussion, show and tell, guest lecturing. The methods vary according to a number of criteria, including the nature of the material to be taught, and the ability level of the students. *Student activities* also must be determined for each lesson plan. Examples of student activities include small group discussions, individual programming, or interviewing computer professionals. The activity chosen depends on many factors, and therefore must be selected on an individual basis.

The nature of the *assignments* must be decided. Assignments are essays, projects, term papers, or programming problems. They allow the student to consolidate previous learning or effect new learning. For example if a student researches computer applications in medicine, he or she may also learn related material. Assignments help the student focus on important fundamental material, and serve to evaluate student performance.

Another activity of lessons planning is the specification of the evaluation procedures to be used. This activity, which involves the use of tests, quizzes, and questionnaires, serves to evaluate whether the student has mastered the concepts of the course, and whether the teacher is presenting material in the proper way.

QUESTIONS

1. What is a computer studies curriculum?
2. What is the difference between the computer studies curriculum in elementary, secondary, and post-secondary education?
3. Why is course planning so essential in computer studies?
4. Distinguish between student activities and teacher activities in computer studies.
5. Prepare a daily lesson plan for teaching the first lesson in "Keyboarding for the Computer" using the "touch method."
6. Using the chapter outline of a text in introductory computer studies, assume the chapter headings are the main topics of the course. Set up a plan estimating the time you would devote to each topic.
7. Define the following terms: articulation—vertical, articulation—horizontal, computer science, curriculum planning, student activities, teacher activities.

3

Setting Goals for the Computing Course

The initial stage in developing the computer studies curriculum is to establish goals which define the course direction. These goals help the teacher determine the content of the class, determine how the instruction will take place, and create tools for evaluating the students.

Setting up strong goals for the computer science curriculum is important because of the changing nature of the discipline. The teacher constantly must adjust the course content. Goals may differ from one semester to the next, from class to class, or from teacher to teacher. It is impossible to list the *definitive* set of goals for any introductory computer studies class. However, after such a course, students should be able to:

1. Be computer literate.
2. Operate a computer.
3. Write software.
4. Understand how computers affect society.
5. Write programs in BASIC or another language.
6. Understand the important components of a computer system.
7. Become familiar with employment opportunities.

These goals are not complete in themselves—they lack specific detail about lesson content. Furthermore, they fail to indicate what is expected of the student, and fail to provide insight into student evaluation to determine whether the goals have been achieved. There is no indication of how much time will be required to adequately master the content. Some goals take only a few minutes to accomplish; others will need weeks, months, or perhaps years to attain. For goals to be useful, they will need to be expanded into detailed instructional objectives which become practical guidelines for daily instruction in the computer studies classroom. These objectives define the required content, instructional methods, and evaluation procedures.

SOURCE OF GOALS IN COMPUTER STUDIES

How does one decide what is important and what is not? Here are some guidelines.

Interest and needs of the students. The teacher should give the students the opportunity to express their interests at the beginning of the course, rather than guess what they are. Typical students interests may be:

1. I would like to write computer programs.
2. Give me enough information so that I can buy a computer.
3. How do I run a computer?
4. What jobs are available in computing?
5. How do computers work?
6. I would like to write some computer games.

Requirements of the students' parents. While parents usually want what is best for their children, they may not be able to articulate what that is—especially with computers. A sampling of parent responses might be:

1. Make my son computer literate!
2. I want my daughter to know about computers.
3. We own a computer; my child should know how to run it.
4. Teach her to program a computer!
5. Let him play computer games!

Needs of the business community. Most students eventually will work in a job which requires some knowledge or expertise in computing. Consequently, it is wise to determine what skills are needed to prepare them for these vocations. While the teacher could directly interview persons from the business community, this information can also be obtained through an examination of job descriptions, surveys or interviews conducted in selected industries, telephone conversations with managers and directors, and informal discussions with members of professional business organizations.

Because of the variety of jobs requiring computer expertise, no attempt should be made to fulfill the needs of every employer. Select those skills which are common to many different jobs or tasks. Such skills include the use of a computer terminal, knowledge of computer terminology and jargon, and programming with a computer language such as FORTRAN or BASIC.

Needs of the community. Teachers should consider the overall environment in which students will spend their lives. They are increasingly bombarded by the products of computing technology in the home, school, stores, cars, hospitals, and just about anywhere. The challenges and demands of the changing world require everything from basic computer literacy to computer experts.

Student needs for further computing courses. Frequently the introductory computer studies course is the starting point in the long-term study of computing. In this context, one of the goals of the course will be to prepare the student for subsequent classes by including all material which is prerequisite for the more advanced course. A typical second-level course is assembly language programming. The teacher of such a course would presume that students had a background in working with the binary number system; previous experience with a high-level programming language; a basic knowledge of fundamental hardware components; knowledge of how to operate a computer; and knowledge of how to debug programs.

Another goal is to teach fundamental concepts needed in most other courses. These include operation of a computer keyboard; problem solving; researching computer science material; using a software editor; and familiarity with key terms and jargon, such as byte, microprocessor, iteration, data, secondary storage.

Subject matter experts. You may seek advice from computer experts—typically university professors—who are steeped in computer science. Unfortunately, these people may make decisions based on their own backgrounds rather than on current research. An expert whose specialty is system analysis would probably demand its inclusion in the introductory computer science course; another might promote database design.

The computer studies textbook. A computer book, especially the selected textbook, can be used as the primary guide for the course. This is tempting because the agenda is already set by the author, and little work is required to accommodate it into the course (Figure 3-1). Thus information about the history of computing, uses of computers in medicine, a comparison of programming languages, and an introduction to machine language programming, while worthwhile, may be inserted into a course because they are found in the textbook and not because they relate to the course objectives. The biggest problem with relying on textbook goals is that some of the goals might not match the students' needs.

Curriculum guides. Curriculum guides for computer studies, which specify what the teacher should include in the introductory course, are excellent. These guides, which are distributed by educational agencies such as the school board or a state/provincial body, are readily available.

When developing the computer studies curriculum for a specific school or course, obtain a number of guides from other states or provinces and use them to help refine your goals. Keep in mind that the needs and aims of these guides may be very different from those required and should not be adopted verbatim.

The local computer studies curriculum guide. A teacher may be required to follow the goals specified in the local/regional curriculum guide developed by the school board or state/provincial agency. Frequently these documents may be vague and general, and teachers will need to make the goals more applicable to their particular course. In other cases, the goals may be very detailed; they may even be written in the form of specific objectives. When using such a guide, teachers will have little input into their computer studies course. They will simply be expected to implement these goals in the form of specific classroom activities.

FIGURE 3-1 Typical table of contents and goals from introductory computer studies textbook

Table of Contents

1. An Information Processing Machine
2. Elements of Problem Solving
3. Other Planning Techniques
4. An Introduction to Programming
5. Peeking Inside the Processor Unit
6. Input into a Computer System
7. Output from a Computer System
8. Auxiliary Storage
9. The Microcomputer Revolution
10. Conversational Programming
11. Special Effects with Microcomputers
12. Computer Applications
13. Impact of Computers on Society
14. A Structured Approach to Planning Solutions
15. Structured BASIC
16. Structured FORTRAN
17. Controversial Issues Involving Computers
18. The Future
19. Glossary

Chapter 1 Goals and Objectives

—An understanding of the components of a computer system—hardware and software.

—An understanding of the five functions of digital computers—input, output, processing, storage, and control.

—A knowledge of the three types of computer systems and the four categories of digital computers.

—An awareness of the variety of computer-related jobs now available.

—An appreciation of the historical development of computers and the computer industry.

Rob Kelley, *The World of Computers and Information Processing* (Roxdale, Ontario: John Wiley & Sons Canada Limited, 1982).

Summary. When developing a program, consider using these nine suggestions, it would be unwise to use only one source. The typical computing classroom serves a variety of students who are taking the course for different reasons. Individual needs must be anticipated when designing the computer studies course. Thus, the course must cater to *every* student's needs.

COMPUTER STUDIES OBJECTIVES

After establishing goals for the computer studies curriculum, statements such as "to become computer literate" or "to write programs in BASIC" are too general. More precise, detailed statements are needed, such as:

1. To list three reasons for using computers in medicine.
2. To use the FOR-LOOP to implement algorithms which iterate.
3. To identify the major components of a flowchart by name.

Such statements, commonly called behavioral objectives or instructional objectives, are derived from broad goals which are refined until a set of objectives suitable for daily instruction is produced. Two additional components are necessary for behavioral objective to be useful. First, the *objective must be precise.* For example, an objective such as "To be able to identify and correct 'bugs' in a program" is incomplete because it does not answer questions such as: How large a program is the student expected to debug? In what programming language will the program be written? Will the program be fully documented so that the student has some idea about what the correct algorithm should be? Are the programs written by the student or are they written by another person?

Second, the *objective must stipulate the method for evaluating the student.* In the example dealing with program debugging, there are at least two ways in which the student might be evaluated. When handing in programming assignments, the programs are expected to work as originally specified and, therefore, contain no "bugs." The correctness of such programs is partially related to the student's ability to find and correct errors, hence marks would be allocated relative to how well the program works. Also, the student might be expected to find bugs in a prewritten program given on a test. In this case, the student has a time limit for finding the bugs and has to locate a certain percentage of them for a high score.

Examples of detailed objectives suitable for the introductory computer studies course are in Figure 3-2. The objectives must specify the expected behavior, the conditions under which the behavior occurs, and the evaluation process.

FIGURE 3-2 Example of detailed objectives

General Objective

To understand the two components of a computer system—hardware and software.

Specific Objectives based on the general objective

1. Name the two components of a computer system.
2. Name the devices which make up the hardware of a computer.
3. Define the processor unit and state its purpose.
4. Define "program" as used in computing.
5. State the difference between hardware and software.
6. Define the operating system of a computer.

Behavioral Objective for Specific Objective #1

a) The student shall name the two components of a computer system,
b) given the knowledge of what constitutes a computer system.
c) Both components must be correctly identified or no credit will be given.

The objectives shown represent only a fraction of the content of the introductory computer studies course. A full course will have hundreds, or thousands, of well-defined objectives. The production of a comprehensive set of objectives is difficult and time-consuming; it is not surprising that many teachers fail to produce them and rely instead on general course goals for content and instructional methods to be used.

The Importance of Detailed Course Objectives in Computer Studies

Better content coverage. A good set of objectives allows the teacher to pinpoint the content of the computer studies course down to the individual lesson or concept to be taught. In most cases, this content will have been determined before the course starts. With a complete list of objectives, the teacher will be able to make decisions about important and unimportant topics.*

By pinpointing the course content, the teacher can order the presentation of topics, determine the pace of instruction for each, and decide upon the methods and materials needed for teaching the content.

Improved evaluation procedures. A well-thought-out set of objectives usually results in a fair evaluation process. Many tests include questions unrelated to the course objectives. A typical example would be to ask the students to indicate the dates when certain computers (EDSAC, ENIAC, UNIVAC) were first introduced. Such a question would create problems for the students if they had learned the names of important computers and the order in which they appeared, but not the dates. Other faulty testing procedures concentrate on a few topic areas rather than providing a systematic, unbiased sampling. Frequently, programming questions on tests—account for 80 percent of the grade, though programming may not be that important in the overall course goals. By defining course objectives, the teacher can set up examinations geared precisely to the course goals (Figure 3-3).

FIGURE 3-3 Test questions based on objectives in Figure 3-2

Examination Questions

1. Name the two components of a computer system.
2. Name four computer hardware devices.
3. What is the purpose of the processor unit of a computer?
4. What is a computer program?
5. Using examples, describe the difference between hardware and software.
6. What is the purpose of an operating system of a computer?

*A common phenomenon in introductory computer studies courses is to devote almost the entire class time to teaching programming. While no one can dispute the importance of this, other facets of computing are just as important. Emphasis on programming is frequently the result of inadequate planning and poorly defined objectives. However, if appropriate goals are set and detailed objectives are derived, this does not occur.

Clearer student expectations. Another reason to establish objectives is that students know precisely what to expect: they know what to treat as important, what to dwell on in reading, and what to skim over. As a result, students can budget time wisely (devote more time to the important objectives) and are motivated to learn since they are clear on the goals. Students should be aware of the objectives from the beginning of the course. Thus the wise teacher will distribute and discuss a syllabus in the first or second class period.

Less dependency on the textbook. Following the textbook too closely in the computer studies class will result in a rigidity in the content of the course. The textbook approach appeals to neophyte teachers because of the simplicity required to plan the course; however, it fails on many counts. The students may dwell on irrelevant details in the textbook since there is no way for them to gauge their importance. Students may have difficulty preparing for examinations since they don't know what to study. Also, important objectives may not be included in the textbook. Therefore, computer studies textbooks should never be the focal point, for defining the course objectives, but rather the main resources for achieving the objectives of the course.

Better control of course content. One by-product of maintaining a detailed set of objectives is that the objectives can be utilized as a checklist by the teacher. By ticking off each objective as it is fulfilled, the teacher is assured that no key concepts have been omitted.

CREATING OBJECTIVES FOR THE COMPUTER STUDIES COURSE

Once the teacher has decided to utilize objectives in the computer studies class, he or she must generate a comprehensive list. A representative example is shown in Figure 3-4. The goal is for the student to know how to program using the language BASIC.

In the example, evaluative criteria (usually included with the specific objectives) have been omitted. Secondly, only a few course objectives have been generated. Hence, only a limited set of detailed objectives, centered around the syntax of the language, has been shown.

Note that the objectives fall into several groups ranging from *general* restatements of the original course goals, to *specifics* dealing with individual concepts and skills which might be taught in a single lesson.

A well-defined set of objectives forms a *hierarchical structure* beginning with broad goals and ending with the detailed individual objectives. For example, to be able to use the BASIC language means that the student must know the syntax of the language. And knowing the syntax of the language means that the student must know the keywords, identifiers, concepts, statements, and line numbers.

This structure affects the ordering of the subject matter; each objective in a grouping must be achieved before the student has completely attained the parent objective. For example, in Figure 3-4, it would be necessary to know what a program is, be able to identify and fix bugs, and be able to document programs in order to know all the facets of writing BASIC programs.

FIGURE 3-4 Generating the course objectives

I. Programming in BASIC.
  1. Know the parts of a program.
    a. Use the syntax (grammar) of the language properly.
      i. List the valid keywords of the language.
      ii. Identify and construct valid examples of identifiers and constants for both numeric and string values.
      iii. Define the concept of a statement.
      iv. Use line numbers correctly.
      v. Know the format of FOR, PRINT, NEXT.
      vi. Identify and create valid examples of arithmetic expressions.
      vii. Identify and create valid examples of logical expressions.
  2. Use the BASIC language.
     Explain the meaning of various constructs of the language.
     For example: "To write statements in BASIC which are grammatically correct."
  3. Transcribe algorithms into BASIC code.
  4. Run BASIC programs on the computer.
  5. Identify and fix bugs in the BASIC program.
  6. Create logical readable code.
  7. Read the algorithms of prewritten programs and explain what the program does.
  8. Document programs.
  9. Produce BASIC programs for assignments and run them.

Developing the hierarchical structure of objectives results in a built-in design of the course in terms of the units, subunits, and lesson plans. Another important feature of hierarchic structures is that they allow the teacher to filter out extraneous material. Consider the following example. An ambitious teacher might decide to show the students the principal components of another programming language after having covered the details of a language such as BASIC. While such an endeavor might enhance the students' knowledge of computer studies, the teacher must ensure that it is a reasonable objective. In most cases, it is not. For example, if the goal is "to learn how to program," the coverage of the second language will add nothing to achieving this goal and may even confuse the student. However, if the goal is "to evaluate the relative merits of different programming languages," the inclusion of a second language would be justified.

Sources of Ideas for Objectives

Teacher's background knowledge. Many teachers have good intuition about what should be taught in the introductory computer studies course. This knowledge may come from their practical experience with computers; courses they have taken; readings in computer studies journals; attendance at conferences; or their experience in the field.

Textbooks and other documents. Textbooks are filled with concepts and skills which the student is expected to master. The information in the table of contents, the index, and the text itself can be useful when deriving the list of objectives. The list should be subdivided into three groups: Topics which were anticipated in the original list of objectives; topics not anticipated but that should be included; and topics which should be omitted from the original list. If a topic in the textbook was not an original course objective, the teacher must decide if it is worthwhile. If so, it should be incorporated into the class objectives; if not, the topic is discarded.

Computer studies textbooks sometimes provide lists of objectives at the beginning of each chapter, intended to help the student organize the reading material. Unfortunately, these objectives rarely are adequate for the teacher, since they lack detail and comprehensiveness.

Lists of objectives also can be found in the instructor guides which accompany many computer studies texts. These objectives usually are more detailed than those in the textbook. Detailed explanations frequently are included.

USING TAXONOMIES OF OBJECTIVES IN THE COMPUTER STUDIES COURSE

Different levels of behavior required in a computer studies course should always be considered. Some objectives require only memorizing factual information or definitions.

1. to know that a byte is composed of eight bits.
2. the definition of a CPU is. . .
3. a microsecond is one millionth of a second.

Other objectives require more thought and action, such as calculating the number of bytes on a disk given the sector size and the number of sectors; categorizing a new peripheral device as either input or output; and identifying the syntax errors in a given piece of programming code. These require the manipulation of information, rather than the regurgitation of facts.

Some objectives require complex thought processes, such as solving a problem by implementing a computer program; or determining whether a specific microcomputer would be suitable for handling word processing. These objectives rank at the highest level of behavioral classification.

Although most objectives in the computer studies curriculum are cognitive (all the preceding examples fit into such a category), a subset are not. In particular, a few motor skills are necessary, such as correct fingering on the keyboard and inserting diskettes into disk drives. Some objectives require the development of attitudes and values with respect to computers, such as those dealing with societal issues, privacy, and unemployment.

Thus, the content of computer studies encompasses a range of objectives requiring different *levels* of cognitive functioning, learning of psychomotor skills, and development of values and attitudes. Hence, it is good practice—and in many cases, mandatory—for the teacher to provide a mixture of different kinds of objectives in the computer studies course rather than focusing on one level. When generating a wide range of objectives, it is helpful to categorize them. Such a classification scheme is commonly called a *taxonomy of objectives.* A number of researchers have developed taxonomies which are widely used in education; Bloom and Gagne, for example, have proposed general-purpose classification schemes.

If teachers use a taxonomical classification scheme in the introductory computer studies course, they begin by examining each objective and identifying it according to the categories of their taxonomy. The resulting categorization can help a teacher ascertain whether the objectives cover all levels of behavior rather than just the lower levels. Objectives at the higher level may be more difficult to phrase and to teach, and therefore may be lacking in teachers' lists of objectives.

The categorization can help with decisions about the best resource materials and teaching methodologies to use. For instance, lecturing is a good way to convey factual knowledge to the student; reading the textbook is another way. Unfortunately, neither of these methodologies is suitable for the development of attitudes towards computers. A teacher cannot lecture an attitude to students—the one-way, forced situation could even breed an undesirable attitude. Thus, students must manipulate, compare, and contrast the components of an attitude themselves. Discussion is more suitable to good attitude formation.

The categorization can help determine the order in which the content will be covered. For instance, since factual information forms the foundation for other kinds of learning, this information must be taught first. The categorization can also help create test questions which cover the full range of behaviors required by the student. Objectives which are well stated may easily be converted into test questions.

A Classification Scheme for Computer Studies

After examining the computer studies content in detail, we recommend the following classification scheme.

Knowledge of facts
Finding information
Learning concepts
Transferring learning
Analyzing information
Evaluating information
Developing skills in predicting
Detecting and correcting errors

Knowledge of facts. By far one of the most important behaviors required of the computer studies student is the learning of specific facts, jargon, terms, and definitions. When learning such material, memorization is all that is required.

The importance of such learning for computer studies should not be underestimated: Factual information forms the foundation for all higher-level learning. For example, a student cannot decide whether a computer has enough memory to hold a program without knowing what a byte is. A student cannot learn to properly insert a diskette into its drive without first learning the sequence of actions which are required. And using programming statements such as A = B + C * D in a program would be folly unless the student had first learned the fact that multiplication is performed before addition.

While learning facts is very important in the introductory computer studies class, many teachers overemphasize this behavior to the point of ignoring more important higher-level activities. This happens because facts are easy to teach, and the textbook usually concentrates on factual information. Also, tests which measure the retention of factual information are easy to create.

The biggest problem with teaching facts in the computer studies class is that in reality, even the brightest students cannot hope to memorize all the factual information of computer studies, since the volume increases daily. Hence the teacher should emphasize fundamental facts. Fundamental information forms the basis for learning higher level behavior. If a fact is not necessary for any subsequent learning, then it is best to omit it.

Tips on Teaching Factual Information. Always present factual information *before teaching the higher-level objectives.* Facts are easily forgotten unless they are presented in a *meaningful context* and are subsequently used. Therefore, memorizing that a byte contains eight bits is not as meaningful as learning that characters are stored inside a computer's memory as individual codes which require 8-bits to represent the character. Thus 8-bits is a fundamental unit of computer memory and is given a special name—a byte.

Whenever possible, encourage the students to *rephrase factual information in their own words* rather than repeat it verbatim from the textbook. Thus if the student has learned that "flowcharts are used to express an algorithm in 2-D form," the teacher would be happy if the student, when asked to define the term "flowchart," rephrased it into a form such as: "A flowchart is a graphical representation of the steps leading to the solution of a problem." Use *lectures,* augmented with transparencies and/or the blackboard, as a major vehicle for introducing factual information.

Finding information. Since a teacher should not demand that students memorize a lot of facts, another approach is to require students to discover this factual information when it is needed. For example, instead of asking the class to memorize the actual storage capacities of different brands of disks, the teacher could require the students to look up these numbers in the manual or text when doing assignments. And rather than making the student learn every detail of a programming language, the teacher could have them keep a copy of the programming language reference manual handy for reference. This is done by computer professionals; a competent computer scientist can find information quickly. Not everything need be memorized.

Tips on Teaching Information Finding. *Teach generalities* (concepts) in the classroom and ask the students to research specific details. For example, when teaching about microcomputers, the teachers may spend most of the time talking about the fundamentals of a microcomputer and ask the student to research the details about a specific piece of hardware.

Teach fundamentals, and ask the class to research additional information. For instance, when programming in BASIC, the beginning student must know how to use the simple PRINT statement for producing output on the terminal. On the other hand, more advanced constructs, such as the PRINT USING command for creating nicely formatted output, are not essential for the beginning programmer, and could be located in the programming manual by students who are interested in furthering their knowledge.

Allow the class lots of *practice at finding information* in various sources. Exercises include using the computer manual to find out how to delete a file, print a file or format a disk. Show the students how to use the command employing each instruction on the keyboard. Also, magnetic tapes come in a number of densities. Ask the students to find out what the common densities are and compute how many bytes would be on a magnetic tape at each density.

Provide the class with guidelines on where to find the information they need. Examples of information sources are textbooks, computer manuals, software manuals, glossaries of computing terminology, computer-related journals, and computer magazines. Teach the students how to use these sources of information properly.

Use *open-book exams* where appropriate. By doing this, the teacher encourages the practice of looking up information rather than memorizing it. A good example of such a practice is to allow the student to use the programming manual when writing a programming assignment or examination. Constantly remind the students that it is perfectly acceptable to not know everything.

Learning concepts. By emphasizing generalities rather than specifics, the teacher avoids reams of factual information and intricate details. These generalities are commonly termed *concepts* and represent groups of objects, ideas, or terms which share some common features. In computer science, for example, there is the concept of *memory,* an entity which subsumes many different kinds of storage such as RAM, ROM, primary memory, secondary memory, and so on. All of these share the common feature of being able to store binary information which is the key characteristic of the *memory* concept.

Another useful concept is that of the *algorithm*—a series of instructions which leads to the solution of a problem. There are thousands of specific algorithms which the student might study. Examples include algorithms to tie one's shoelace, bake a cake, sort numbers, convert Celsius to Fahrenheit, or find the largest number in a collection of numbers.

Another important concept is the *central processing unit* (CPU). This describes microprocessors such as a 6502 chip, the processing unit inside a large mainframe, or the specialized processor inside a hand calculator. In spite of their differences, all these devices can execute programs, and have internal components such as an ALU, busses, controller, and registers—key characteristics of the CPU concept.

Since everything about a concept can be applied to any of the specific objects which it subsumes, much irrelevant or redundant learning can be avoided. This statement can be best explained with the following example: If the student has mastered the concept of a CPU he or she realizes that it must execute programs and contain an ALU. So if the teacher introduces a specific example of a CPU—a Z80 for instance—the student need not be told that a Z80 executes programs and contains an ALU. Such information is redundant since it is implicit in the concept CPU. Hence, the teacher can spend time concentrating on those features of the Z80 which are unique to this particular processor and which sets it apart from other examples of CPUs. Learning any factual information is enhanced if the student can first classify it into a higher-level concept, for example,

1. the teacher states that a VT96 is an example of softcopy printer and assumes that the students will therefore realize that it will not produce output on paper but on a CRT.
2. the teacher informs the class that a drum is a form of secondary storage and, therefore, assume that the students will relate this information to their knowledge of secondary storage and come to the conclusion that drums are similar to discs and tapes.

Tips on Helping the Students Develop Computer-Related Concepts. Learning a concept requires the student to note *similarities* that exist between the different instances of the concept. Hence, it is imperative to give the student lots of practice at identifying similarities between different items, for example.

Q: In what ways are a light pen, keyboard, card reader, and joy stick similar?
A: They are all used to enter information into a computer.

Note that the similarity that the student has noted turns out to be the definition of the concept *input*. The teacher may show the class examples of programming errors, all of which produce an error diagnostic when they are typed in. The teacher then points out that all these errors are instances of *syntax* errors.

Learning concepts requires the ability to distinguish *differences* between things. Students must become aware of how various items subsumed by a concept differ. For example, a student could be required to ascertain how various input devices, such as card readers and keyboards, actually differ from each other; or how various storage devices, such as floppy disks and hard disks are discriminated.

When learning a concept, students should be required to develop their own ideas about it. This is done by giving the student examples of items which fit the concept and examples of those which do not. Thus a teacher might present a session on disks by first showing examples of the concept such as various kinds of floppy disks and hard disks. This is followed by a demonstration of devices which are not disks, such as cassettes and memory. The students would be required to identify the common characteristics of the concept by noting the similarities and differences of the devices.

Finally, the teacher should avoid using *definitions* to teach concepts by making statements such as: "Memory is any device which can store binary information." Although such an approach is easy, the student may simply memorize the definition without knowing what it means. It is better to let the student formulate the concept and produce the definition to see if the concept has been mastered.

Transferring learning. Transfer of learning occurs when the teacher takes advantage of similarities which exist with previously learned material. Such a procedure, for example, might be employed whenever the students learn a second programming language. Many of the concepts covered in the first case will be applicable in the second. For example, the teacher might point out that the arithmetic operators have the same precedence values as they have in BASIC. Therefore, multiplication and division are done before addition and subtraction.

Or, in FORTRAN, the DO-LOOP is used for implementing iterations. This is similar to the FOR-NEXT in BASIC. In both cases, previously learned material can be used as a reference point for learning the new material. Here are some other examples. The student learns how to operate a microcomputer—how to use the keyboard, turn on the machine, and insert disks. This knowledge is useful when learning to operate similar equipment. Or, the student learns about the operation and functioning of floppy disks and transfers this learning to the operation and functioning of hard disks.

The ability to transfer previously learned information into a new learning situation is a critical skill for the computer studies student. Teach representative instances—for example, one programming language—and then make sure that the student transfers this knowledge to learning similar material—for example, a second programming language.

Transfer of learning is particularly relevant in developing algorithms for solving programming problems. An experienced programmer or analyst who is developing an algorithm does not work in a vacuum. Algorithms are typically related to each other: the experienced programmer has worked on many problems, and has studied examples of solutions in books or journals. Thus, when confronted with a new programming problem, the programmer will compare it—in whole or in part—to similar ones which have been successfully solved.

This skill of transferring learning will be particularly useful to the student who pursues a career in computing. When someone is hired to a computing position, it is unusual that he or she possesses all the necessary skills. Thus on-the-job experience will be required, where unique knowledge specific to the job requirements is acquired. The student's previous computing background can be used as a springboard for the job-specific training.

Tips on Teaching Students to Transfer Learning. When the teacher has a group of topics which are similar in content, just one of the topics should be taught in detail. The students should then be given practice exercises dealing with transferring their knowledge to learning about the others. For example, if the overall lesson is about printers, teach the operation of a specific printer—like a line printer—in detail. Mention the other kinds of printers and then ask the students to research the details on their own.

When teaching a topic in detail, try to get the students to focus on the points which can be transferred. For example, when the teacher discusses FOR LOOPS in BASIC, a wise practice would be to focus on their role in implementing iterations because the concept of iterating will be valuable in learning a new language.

Train the students to relate new situations to something which they have encountered previously. Thus, if a student were confronted with a programming problem which required printing a table of square roots and had never done this before, the automatic reaction should be for the student to think about previously-completed problems which involved the printing out of tables. For instance, if a program was previously written to print out the squares of numbers, the similarity between it and the problem in hand should be recognized—both solutions require the printing out of a table of numbers.

Analyzing information. Analysis is the process of breaking down an object, idea, or system into its components. This is necessary to understand the organizational structure of an object and perceive the relationship between its components. Having such a facility is important to the computing studies student. For instance, when solving a complex problem, it is much easier for computer scientists to break it up into smaller sub-problems which are easier to solve than the large complex one. When trying to understand how hardware functions, it is necessary to first understand the building blocks of the equipment. And when trying to understand other people's software for maintenance or for pedagogical purposes, the skilled programmer breaks up a long program into smaller chunks and, given adequate documentation, examines each.

Evaluating information. The ability to evaluate is one of the highest-level behaviors required of the computing student. While only a moderate amount of evaluative skill is required in the introductory computing studies class, it becomes particularly important in some of the higher level classes.

Evaluation involves being able to form a judgment—good/bad, faster/slower, better/worse, "I would buy it"/"I would not buy it"—and to justify this decision with objective evidence. Thus, an evaluation is based on rational and logical thought rather than on emotions or values. Knowing how to evaluate properly is critical to the computer scientist who is faced regularly with decisions like which brand of computer is the "best" for word processing; which software to obtain for writing CAL courseware; and which algorithm to employ for a problem solution.

Tips on Getting Students to Analyze and Evaluate. Before making any kind of evaluation, the problem must be analyzed into its component parts. This process allows each component to be separately evaluated, then an overall conclusion is based upon these individual evaluations.

The student must have practice in analyzing the subject matter which is to be evaluated. For example, suppose the student were asked to evaluate a computer system and decide whether or not to buy it. Making a sound decision requires analyzing the system into individual parts which will be separately evaluated—processing unit, storage, software, or network hardware. The student then makes a judgment on the merit of the computer system with respect to each point. Lastly, an overall evaluation is derived by applying subjective weights to each point relative to its importance.

Practice is necessary in *gathering the facts* to apply these criteria. Thus, in our example, the student should learn how to find the speed at which the computer operates; documentary evidence on the ease of its use; and statistics on reliability—average down time, mean time of repair, and so on.

Learning to *compare and contrast* is critical for making evaluations and should be made a course objective. Knowing whether one computer is better than another depends upon seeing similarities and differences between the two machines and making judgments upon the degree of difference. Thus an exercise such as "Indicate, with factual evidence, the differences (or similarities) between structural programming and unstructured programming," is excellent for facilitating this skill.

Developing skills in predicting. The field of computer studies is evolving so rapidly that it is important for the practitioner to be skilled at looking into the future and making predictions with some degree of confidence. Thus the student should get some practice in the area of prognosticating.

Tips on Teaching Predicting Skills. Fostering the ability to predict is somewhat difficult since the student will not get feedback about whether the predictions are on the right track or not. Asking the student, "What do you predict the number of microcomputers will be in five years?" presents the obvious problem of waiting five years to see. Therefore, we suggest that the teacher utilize situations for which the answer is already known—*but of which the student is unaware.* Thus, we could give the student data on the state of computing five years ago, ask for predictions up to the present day, and then allow the student to verify the answer with the actual data.

More emphasis must be placed on the method of forming predictions rather than actually making a successful prediction—the means rather than the end. Mastering a good methodology means that the student can gather adequate background information on which to make a valid prediction based on information from the past; and that he or she has a sense of where changes are heading and how long they will take. Any prediction, especially those involving computer studies, can be off target. Actual examples of good and bad predictions from computing literature can be analyzed by examining and having the student examine reasons for successful or unsuccessful predictions.

A by-product of this activity should be a student who looks skeptically at journals which contain articles involving computing prognostication. The literature—especially the current literature—abounds with writers who comment on the future of computing. Often the author's decision is based on opinion, not on factual evidence. The critical student will be able to reject such articles while at the same time accepting—still with some reservations—those which have a solid foundation.

Detecting and correcting errors. An important skill for the computer scientist is to diagnose and rectify problems arising when working with hardware or writing software. This ability, which is called *trouble shooting* in the case of hardware and *debugging* in the case of software, is composed of a rather complex set of component behaviors.

A typical example of trouble shooting which students might encounter is a terminal that doesn't work properly. Although the student could run to the teacher for help in this situation, such behavior should not be encouraged. Instead, the students should be urged to try solving the problem themselves. One way of attacking the problem would be to systematically check all the possible causes and eliminate each one until the culprit is found. The student might check to see if the terminal is turned on or plugged in, the computer is running, the baud rate is correct, and the terminal is hooked to the computer.

An example of debugging a program is a little more complex than the one for trouble shooting. However, the procedure is essentially the same—the student methodically eliminates possible causes until the right one is found.

Tips on Teaching Error Detection and Correction. There are many skills to be taught about debugging and trouble shooting. First, the student needs to look for the *diagnostic symptoms* whenever a piece of equipment or a program is not working properly. For a piece of equipment, symptoms might be that it is not working at all, buzzers may be blinking or lights flashing, or it may be responding, but doing the wrong thing. The symptoms depend upon the equipment. Since one would not necessarily expect the student to memorize such symptoms, the class should know how to look them up in the hardware documentation.

Similar diagnostic symptoms occur with software. There may be syntax errors, the program might not run, or the program might run but not do what it is supposed to do.

The next skill is learning how to *track down the problem,* once the student recognizes it. In other words, diagnosing the difficulty and determining the probable causes of the malfunction. With hardware, it is usually necessary for the student to be aware of probable causes—either by knowing what they are or by accessing a manual which lists the potential problems. Suppose, for example, that a student is confronted by a terminal which is not working properly—it does not type at all. The student probably is aware of some of the causes for such malfunction, and each of these should be checked out. However, the solution might not be simple—for example, the baud rate might be incorrectly set—thus the student should know how to discover the potential causes in the appropriate systems manual.

Diagnosing software errors is a little different. Because there are so many possible causes of malfunctioning, especially in a long program, it is often difficult to pinpoint the error. Nevertheless, it is worthwhile to learn some frequently occurring symptom-cause relationships which can be employed to assist diagnosis. For example, whenever a program fails to read in the correct number of values during an iteration, it is recommended that the student check the controlling variable of a loop to see if it counts the right number of times. Or when a program results in a "floating-point overflow," it is valuable to check the instances of division in the program and see if any of them might be dividing by zero.

Any trouble shooting procedure or debugging session should always be *systematic* rather than hit-or-miss. The students will need to practice attacking the problem in a systematic way, with the most likely cause first. At the end of such a procedure, the student would be satisfied that the list of possibilities has been exhausted.

Finally, the students must realize that the first attempt to detect and correct a problem might not succeed—especially in the case of software—and other approaches should be attempted. Thus, the capacity to adapt is necessary. Going hand-in-hand with this is the development of a high level of *tolerance to frustration,* since the solution may sometimes take a long time to find.

QUESTIONS

1. What is the one most important source of goals in computer studies? Justify your answer.
2. The teacher must consider the needs of all involved parties before developing the computer studies curriculum. Identify the parties. Identify the two most important needs of each party. Support your choices.
3. Using the objective "To know how to debug," set up objectives similar to those in Figure 3-4.
4. What is meant by "the hierarchic structure of objectives"?

5. What is the difference between trouble shooting and debugging?
6. Write an objective for each of the taxonomies for each of the following topics:
   a. programming
   b. hardware
   c. computers in society
7. Find an example of an article on a prediction in computing and comment on it.
8. Define the following terms: behavioral objective, curriculum guide, general objective, objective, specific objective, successive refinement, taxonomy.

4

Ordering and Pacing the Course Content

Once the teacher has decided the objectives and content of the computer studies course, it is time to generate both the order and the pace in which the topics will be presented.

SPECIFYING THE ORDER OF THE COMPUTER STUDIES CONTENT

Decisions must be made about which course objective is to be achieved first, which one next, and so on. Since there are a variety of ways to impose such an ordering, the teacher will need to decide on the one which is best. The instructor might consider a number of criteria which can be utilized when arriving at this decision.

Order in Terms of the Subject Matter Structure

The most important influence on the sequence of instruction is the hierarchical structure of the computer studies content where the material taught first is *prerequisite* for the material which follows. The prerequisite nature of computer studies content can be best understood by looking at some examples

A case in point is that PRINT statements, when learning BASIC, must come before the learning of other statement types, such as the FOR LOOP. This ordering is mandatory because the students will need to include output instructions in all the programs they write—hence, the PRINT statement must come first.

Another programming example is the learning of systematic techniques for finding and correcting errors in a program by working through the code and removing the bugs. Since this skill depends on understanding the meaning of the code, the student first must have written some successful programs, even if they are simple.

When the teacher decides to introduce advanced details of computer architecture—such as the operation of the fetch/execute cycle—it is wise to have first covered the basic concepts such as the CPU, stored programs, and computer memory.

Before using a computer terminal or microcomputer keyboard, the student must learn how to turn the equipment on and off, and how to utilize the special function keys. To learn details of character codes such as EBCDIC and ASCII, one must first understand the basics of the binary number system. The details of I/O devices such as printers and card readers cannot be properly understood without a fundamental knowledge of the concepts of input and output, and the basic elements of systems analysis are difficult to understand without prior experience with program design tools such as flowcharts or pseudocode. Finally, the uses and applications of disk technology must be preceded by an introduction to the operation and other important characteristics of disks.

While other factors might also influence the order in which the topics are presented, adhering to the prerequisite structure of the material is essential for developing a successful course. If the teacher neglects this structure, the class may be in the situation of learning something without having the background necessary to do it.

Ensuring a Properly Ordered Course

First, the teacher must be thoroughly familiar with the prerequisite structure of the computer studies content to be taught, and *second,* the teacher must use this structure to build the course.

The latter activity, transforming the subject matter structure into the ordered course, is not very difficult. It requires patience and sufficient time to work through the content methodically. It is the first condition—knowing the subject matter structure—which creates problems for many teachers since they are not sufficiently versed in the structure of the material to properly create a well-ordered course.

Understanding Computer Studies Subject Matter Structure Facilitates Proper Course Ordering

To understand the subject matter structure, the teacher must thoroughly *understand the content* itself. Hence, the teacher should have taken at least one course in computer studies, have read a number of texts on the topic, and feel adequately prepared to teach the content of the course.

Assuming that a solid background in computing studies has been obtained, teachers should not be surprised if, on the first pass through the course, there are still some weak areas in sequencing. The structure will invariably need refining as they discover that their preconceived notions of the prerequisite relationships are not verified when actually teaching the class.

Another problem may arise if the beginning teachers use the sequence presented in their own computer studies classes in college. They should be wary because problems will arise if the original college class was poorly organized. And even if an excellent structure for the course was used, this structure may not be appropriate for their students whose needs and goals are different.

The second possibility for structures may be the *curriculum guide.* If a detailed curriculum guide has been prescribed for the course, it may specify the order in which the topics should be covered. Since typical guides have probably been developed by subject matter experts, it is advisable to heed its recommendations when creating the course, especially for the first run through (Figure 4-1).

The third method for structuring an introductory computer studies class is examining the ordering of the topics in suitable *textbooks.* If a book is well written and readable, the author should have ensured that material is not introduced in one chapter of the book without having covered the necessary background material in earlier chapters.

After the teacher has incorporated the prerequisites into the computing course, sequencing is not necessarily finished. Since little of the curriculum will fall into the "teach-this-first-so-that-the-student-will-understand-this-next" paradigm, the teacher will still have to shuffle the order. For example, suppose the course objectives include societal issues and computer programming. Since the teaching of programming does not depend on the teaching of societal issues, either one can be taught first.

Similar flexibility can occur when teaching how disks work versus how tapes work, or the history of computing versus the application of computers. If there is

FIGURE 4-1 Sample ordering of topics based on curriculum guide

Topics	Subtopics
1. Attitudes	anxiety fear of computers freedom from fear and anxiety
2. Applications	where how why
3. History	devices people
4. Impact on society	issues future
5. Systems	hardware software languages industry careers
6. Problem solving	analysis algorithms
7. Programming	style system commands coding in BASIC

no prerequisite relationship with such topics and the teacher could teach either one first, how is the actual order decided? While a toss of the coin would work, it is better if the teacher takes into account other factors.

Order for Motivation and Interest

While maintaining interest and motivation is important throughout the entire computer studies course, it is especially significant at the beginning and end. Getting off to a good start is critical. It is necessary to capture the attention of the students right away by presenting material which is thought-provoking, challenging, exciting, and interesting. A good starting point would be to involve the students on the first day by showing them, right on the computer, what it can do, followed by some simple hands-on interaction. Alternatively, the teacher might start off by showing an interesting movie on computing applications which will capture the students' imagination and set the stage for other topics throughout the course.

Order to Accommodate Teaching Resources

The teacher must take into consideration the presence or absence of teaching resources when deciding on the order of content (Figure 4-2). There is a great variety of resource material available for possible adoption in the computer studies classroom: books, films, slide shows, exhibits. Some of these resources are available throughout the year—a school-owned videocassette for example—and thus can be utilized at any point in the course. These resources have no effect on the ordering of the content of the course because they are immediately available. On the other hand, if the resource is not going to be available throughout the

FIGURE 4-2 Resources affecting the order of course content

Topics	Resources
Applications	speaker from government speaker from business community computer system in school
History	books in school library books in classroom speaker from university
Impact on Society	speakers from business community school magazines in library financial news local newspapers students' experience and attitudes
Systems	tours of businesses speakers from business community computer career choice programs
Programming	computer manuals tutorials on diskette

entire semester, then the course content must be ordered according to availability. For example, a movie on making microcomputers might be available only on a certain date. In this case, schedule the coverage of topics dealing with the content of the movie when it is available.

If a teacher arranges for a speaker on how a business uses computers in the office, background material should be covered beforehand so the students understand the topic. Likewise, when computing equipment is only available for a portion of the semester, it would then be mandatory to schedule the programming part of the course, especially the hands-on portion, for the period when the machines are present. (Such equipment might be shared with other schools and, therefore, be located in each school for only a few weeks.)

Order from Easy to Difficult

A rule of thumb is to teach easy material before teaching more difficult concepts. A teacher should not present examples of complex programming problems without having worked through a series of increasingly difficult problems. Starting out with a difficult example of programming breeds confusion and creates an attitude that the material is harder than it really is.

Proceeding from easy to difficult is an approach which can be adopted throughout the computer studies curriculum; for example, the teacher might have the students write 5-line programs before they write 100-line programs, or get them to play computer games before requiring them to write software for games. Students should write programs which have a linear structure before they write ones which require decision making and branching. A teacher should explain how to use a diskette before discussing the theory behind disk operation, and how a simplified hypothetical machine works before looking at the details of a real one.

How can the teacher decide which material will be easy and which will be difficult? In many cases, the distinction is obvious: 5-line programs are easier to handle than 100-line programs. However, some relationships are harder to see: Is learning about adding binary numbers easier than subtracting binary numbers? This is harder to decide unless the teacher has already taught the course and realizes that students generally have no difficulty with binary addition but can get into all kinds of problems with subtraction.

After teaching the course once, the teacher gains insight into the relative difficulties of the topics. By having students report about the difficulties they encounter with each topic, or by using test results as a measure the teacher can adjust the content ordering for the next semester.

Of course, when using the easy-to-difficult criteria, the teacher must accommodate the natural structure of the course. A teacher, for example, would not mindlessly order the course from simplest to most complex—a jumbled mess could result because, after one topic is covered, the class might proceed to an entirely unrelated topic. To illustrate, consider a hypothetical course ordered in terms of increasing difficulty without paying attention to continuity. This listing might be:

1. What is a computer? (**least difficult**)
2. Write a short (5-line) program.
3. How are computers used in society?

4. How do computers work?
5. Evaluate the societal effects of the computer.
6. Write a long (100-line) program. (**most difficult**)

By following this order, the result would be a haphazard coverage of the content—jumping from hardware to software, to applications, back to hardware, back to applications, and finally back to software.

Obviously, the order must be reworked so that similar materials are grouped together and taught contiguously. Thus the material could be reordered:

1. What is a computer?
2. How do computers work?
3. Write a short (5-line) program.
4. Write a long (100-line) program.
5. How are computers used in society?
6. Evaluate the societal effects of the computer.

This process yields three sub-areas—hardware, software, and applications—which encompass the original six topics.

Order to Generate Variety

There is value in grouping related topics together and teaching them as a unit; the subject matter is then cohesive and contiguous. Although such an approach is generally acceptable, sometimes it may have to be modified, particularly if the unit covers an extended period of time for topics such as the teaching of programming or the uses of computers in society. In these cases, the extended coverage of one topic can result in a reduction in interest. Students usually prefer variety, which stimulates interest and attention.

To avoid extended coverage of the same topic, intermix the programming sections of the course with nonprogramming material. For example, early in the year spend several periods teaching the fundamentals of beginning programming. Then ask the students to write a small program as an assignment. While they are writing this program in the laboratory, in the regular classtime introduce a topic like the use of computers in everyday life. By the end of this unit, the programming assignment is finished and the students can spend several more periods on more advanced programming. Then, another assignment is given, and some more nonprogramming material is covered while the students work on it.

Switching from one topic to the other throughout the semester has two benefits. First, the students are constantly stimulated by different material—there is no time to stagnate. Second, the time required to cover the programming part of the course is extended—if it would have needed three weeks to cover as a contiguous unit, it will now require six weeks since other material is being interspersed. This extension allows the students more time to work on their assignments—an activity which usually requires as much time as possible. The student better understands programming because the time pressure is lessened. In addition, student demand on the limited equipment is reduced, allowing more students to be enrolled in the course every semester.

Here is another example of intermixing topics to generate variety: If the teacher were to teach a number of peripheral devices like line printers, card readers, optical character readers, and joysticks, the logical approach would be to present them as a contiguous unit. However, the students could lose interest by the time the last one is taught. To foster interest and attention, a better approach might be to intersperse the discussion of each device with examples of application areas of each in the real world. Thus, the discussion of the technical details of the line printer would be followed by a description of how, where, and when it is used. After doing this, another device is taught in a similar fashion. By the time the teacher has finished, two topic areas have been covered—I/O devices and application areas—without subjecting the student to a drawn-out discussion of either one.

Order to Accommodate Teacher and Student Preferences

Two other factors—teacher and student preferences—should be taken into consideration when determining the course order. The background and attitude of the teacher will usually influence the way the course will be taught. The instructor might feel more comfortable with the simpler topics first. Starting with easy material gives the teacher time to bone up on the more difficult material. He or she might present material which students find enjoyable and thus benefit from their enthusiasm at the beginning of the course. Or an instructor may have a preferred teaching methodology. Such as the "example-rule" approach for introducing concepts, and do things like show examples of bugs (errors) commonly found in programs before discussing the classification scheme for identifying them: syntax errors, the run-line errors and the logic errors.

The background and needs of the student also have to be accommodated when sequencing the course. Thus, the teacher might ask the students, at the beginning of the course, what interests them and work through some of this material first. As long as the overall structure of the course is not upset, this approach is recommended because it generates interest and motivation. It also leaves students with the feeling that the teacher is responsive to their wishes. On the other hand, if the content suggested by the student will not be understood without first providing certain prerequisite material, then it will be necessary to defer the topic until after some groundwork is laid. A teacher could start by reviewing materials which the students have covered in previous courses to determine what the students already know.

Order Based upon the Textbook

Probably the most widely-used—though not necessarily the best—technique for sequencing the topics of the computer studies course is to use the order specified by the textbook assigned to the course. Hence, the table of contents becomes the chronological outline for the course. Two sample tables of contents (Figure 4-3) illustrate how easy it is to adopt this topic order for teaching purposes.

There are several motivations for using the textbook to establish course order. First, it is easy. Second, *not* following the textbook might breed confusion on the part of the students, since the teacher might be covering topics in a different order from the text.

Although the teacher could pay close attention to the textbook sequence,

FIGURE 4-3 Two different tables of contents which may be used to determine order

Table of Contents

1. Introduction
2. Computer Jargon
3. The History of Computing
4. Computer Applications
5. Computers in Government
6. The Value of Information in Society
7. Computer-Related Occupations
8. Computers and Humans
9. Computer Systems
10. Computer Components
11. Algorithms and Flowcharting
12. Computer Programming and Design Logic
13. Beginning BASIC

Table of Contents

1. Introduction to Computers
2. Computer Applications in a Modern Society
3. Evolution of the Computer
4. How a Computer Works
5. Input/Output Concepts and Devices
6. Storage Concepts and Devices
7. The Program Development Cycle
8. Flowcharting
9. Introduction to Computer Programming
10. Programming Languages
11. Processing Methods and Applications
12. Computer System Management
13. The Future

there is no need to be a slave to it. Here are some ways in which the teacher can deviate:

1. If the teacher will be covering content in Chapter 3 before Chapter 2, have the students read both chapters for continuity but tell them that Chapter 3 will be discussed first.
2. Have the students read Chapter 3 and discuss its contents before they even read Chapter 2. If Chapter 3 depends upon understanding the concepts from Chapter 2; an overview session should be provided in which the necessary content is taught. *Choose a textbook that is fairly modular so that not too much prerequisite material is needed for each chapter.*
3. If the teacher assigns textbook readings for homework, it is not necessary to cover the material in class in the same order. For example, if a chapter contained the following topics: mainframes, minicomputers, microcomputers, and computer systems, and the teacher assigned the whole chapter as reading, then other orderings are possible when the topics are covered in the class. For example, the topic order—

computer systems, microcomputers, minicomputers and mainframes—is just as acceptable.

Build in Flexibility

Regardless of the initial ordering, situations will arise when reordering becomes necessary. Reordering may be necessary due to a break-through in computer technology; an important TV broadcast on some aspect of computing; a computing innovation adopted by the community; or the acquisition of new or additional hardware or software. Accommodating such reordering requires a great deal of flexibility.

SETTING THE PACE FOR THE COMPUTER STUDIES COURSE

Once the topics of the computing course have been determined and an order has been established, the next step is to estimate the pace at which each topic will be presented. Setting the pace involves many factors. For example, an instructor can go at a faster rate with brighter students or in the higher grade levels, but proceed more slowly with students of average or below average ability, younger students, and students in a lower grade. A fast pace is desirable if the teacher is to fulfill as many course objectives as possible—there is so much to learn in a typical computer studies course.

The hardest part of pacing a course is making reasonable estimates about how long each topic will actually take to teach. It is especially difficult with computer studies courses, since it is hard to allocate time limits to programming assignments.

One way for the teacher to improve accuracy in pacing is through experience. Of course, accurate records will be necessary if this experience is going to be useful. As each topic is covered, the teacher should write down the time it *actually* takes along with a notation about whether the pace seemed too fast, too slow, or just right.

Unfortunately, even the most experienced teachers cannot depend entirely on their backgrounds to gauge the pace of the course since factors vary from one semester to the next. The students change, the content changes, and student interest and motivation change. In computer studies, the discipline is evolving rapidly and the pacing of the content will also be affected by these changes.

Estimating Time

How does one estimate the amount of time for each topic? Here are some guidelines.

1. Allocate more time to topics which require in-depth coverage. As a case in point, to talk about *all* the features of a programming language—in-depth coverage—will require much more time than coverage of just the *essential* features of the language.
2. Allocate more time to those topics which are perceived, by the teacher or by others, to be difficult to master—such as flowcharting, binary subtraction, and file manipulation.
3. Allocate more time for topics that are *fundamental* and thus of prime importance for

understanding the rest of the course: for example, the concept of program iteration or an understanding of input/output.

4. With lower-grade or slower learners, more time is needed to cover each concept. It might take several weeks to teach the meaning of the special function keys on the keyboard to third graders, for example, while tenth graders could be taught the skill in less than a week.
5. Spend more time on content which interests the students—gaming, programming—as long as the other topics are not jeopardized.
6. Devote a lot of time to content taught at the beginning of the course. Remember that computer studies material is foreign to most students, and they easily become lost unless they get off to a good start.
7. Since difficult material will probably be deferred until the end of the course, allocate sufficient time for its coverage—teachers typically leave difficult topics like systems analysis and database management until the end. These topics need a lot of time but are generally rushed if insufficient time remains.
8. Reserve a generous block of time for programming content. The teacher could write the program beforehand, then multiply the observed time by a factor of four or five. The result is a good estimate of the time needed for the average student to accomplish the same task.
9. Allow ample time for activities such as writing tests and taking up the answers; reviewing material at periodic intervals throughout the semester and before examinations; answering students' questions; attending to administrative details such as handing back assignments and signing out materials; and the loss of class periods because of school participation in field meets, films, fire drills, etc.

Adjusting the Pace Daily

The preceding guidelines can be undertaken before the class commences in order to get accurate estimates of the time. However, once the course is underway, it may be necessary to make adjustments to the pace on a day-to-day or week-to-week basis because of inaccurate time estimates or when the course gets out of step.

Inaccurate estimates. If the estimates are off, parts of the course will be covered too quickly or too slowly. Let us presume that two class periods were reserved for teaching flowcharting, while in reality the topic needs at least four class periods. As a result, the teacher's presentation will be hasty, superficial, or both. Fortunately, the teacher who perceives this problem early adjusts by immediately adding two more class periods to the topic and revising the schedule for the balance of the semester.

When making revisions, teachers rely primarily on feedback from their students to indicate whether the pace is too fast or too slow. If the pace is too fast, students may have no idea what the teacher is talking about, be unable to answer questions, or ask many "silly" questions. The drop-out and absentee rate may increase, or the test results are worse than expected.[1]

Some indicators of a pace which is too slow are that students become bored and inattentive, start dropping the class, and have a high absentee rate. Note that

[1]Weekly quizzes are better than monthly exams when using exam results for feedback on course revision. The teacher should pay attention to apparent difficulties with individual items on an examination rather than using the overall results.

these symptoms also may occur because the subject matter is uninteresting, the presentation is poor, or the order is bad. Like any good diagnostician, the teacher will have to look beyond the symptoms to the cause.

Getting out of step. Getting out of step can result from unforeseen circumstances causing periods to be lost or shortened: teacher sickness, professional development days, special meetings, or student activities are examples. The teacher might not be starting the class on time, or may be ending the class early due to inadequate planning. The four or five minutes lost from each class period accumulates to an entire period every two or three weeks. Or, the students may be asking too many questions or getting the teacher sidetracked on other topics. Whatever the reason, if the teacher is to successfully adapt, it will be necessary to make frequent modifications. Making modifications requires that the teacher gauge where the class is at any given moment. This is where the original lesson plan can be useful by comparing it to the daily log. By performing this chore daily, discrepancies will be noted immediately.

If a discrepancy should appear, how can it be accommodated? Make sure that a degree of flexibility has been built into the course; in other words, the course is designed to be altered without causing other problems. Try leaving a week or two of *free time at the end of the course* as a safety factor in case the schedule starts to slip. Some expendable activities, like playing computer games, should be planned for this time period in case the course finishes too soon. Plan to *omit certain topics* in case time becomes tight. The topics omitted should be of secondary importance and must be optional to the fulfillment of the objectives. Areas of fundamental importance required for later learning should never be omitted. Expendable topics might include a field trip to a computer store, a movie on how chips are made, the discussion of systems analysis, binary arithmetic, and programming of file handling. Topics selected for possible exclusion should be interspersed throughout the course, and thus the importance of day-to-day monitoring should be obvious.

Teach some topics in less detail than was originally intended. For example, in discussing I/O devices, it is not necessary to cover the whole list of peripherals. In order to convey the essential aspects of I/O, only a subset is necessary. Therefore, if time gets tight, a number of these peripherals can be omitted without causing a detrimental effect on its objectives.

Move some of the material out of the formal classroom periods when time is at a premium. A teacher might provide CAI lessons on BASIC programming which the students can run anytime they wish. He or she could ask the students to read the chapter in the textbook on computer applications and then review the reading in the class period rather than lecturing. Videotapes of lectures and demonstrations can be examined in the resource center. A videotape on the techniques of using the diskette drive might fall into this category. And tutors can be used to work with students who are having problems. In all these approaches, the goal is to save the formal classroom periods for activities which can only be done in that setting, and shift material which can be learned in other ways into more flexible time slots.

Make sure that the course components are *modular.* Modularity means that each section of the course is an entity unto itself and has few, if any, connections to the other modules in the course. Thus modules can be left out or moved around without disturbing the flow of the course. Sample modules might be "Computers in Society" or "BASIC Programming."

QUESTIONS

1. Why is the order of topics in computer studies important?
2. What are some of the exceptions to the rule of teaching "easy-to-difficult" in the computer studies curriculum?
3. Pacing content delivery is a problem to teachers, especially new teachers. One of the problems in making adjustments is that teachers are unwilling to make alterations in their original course plans. How can administrators help teachers become more flexible?
4. Is the teacher justified in putting the onus on the students to work on their own outside the classroom on CAI programs or in the computer laboratory? Why or why not?
5. Define the following terms: CAI, computer applications, modularity, order, out-of-step, pace, prerequisite, teaching resources.

5

Individualized Instruction in the Computing Class

Individualized instruction implies one teacher/one student, rather than group instruction. With individualized instruction, the learning environment can be optimized for each student in the class. Individualization helps maximize the potential of each student; it is especially important among students with different backgrounds and varying abilities.

There are three fundamental ways to individualize the computer studies curriculum. First, *vary the pace of instruction.* Some students learn about computing faster than others, and the best way to treat these differences is to allow students to proceed at their own speed. This variability in learning rate is most pronounced when students are learning to program—some students "catch on" right away while others succeed only after much repetitive practice.

Second, *vary the content of the class.* In this form of individualization, no two students are taught exactly the same material. Instead, the computing course is divided into sections based on core, enrichment, and remediation material.

Core material is what everybody learns because it is important or essential for the mastery of more advanced material. When the student comes into the course having already mastered the core material, the teacher who is interested in individualization will not force that student to study such material again. In this case, the student could either work ahead or be given enrichment material. An example is the student who has already learned to program—the teacher would assign this student more challenging programming problems in lieu of the simple problems other students are assigned.

Optional enrichment material is for the advanced student who deals well with the core content and takes advantage of extra instruction. This material is based on the core but is in greater depth. Remediation material is for the student who has difficulty and needs extra work in order to master the core content. This material is in the area in which the student is experiencing difficulty.

Another technique of individualization is to *vary the method of instruction.* No two students learn in exactly the same way. Some learn best by listening to lectures; others prefer reading; some like to discuss and ask questions; others like to watch movies or listen to tapes; still others like to research relevant topics. The instructor can take advantage of such preferences and tailor the method of instruction to the student, ideally this is done without altering the content of the course.

Can Individualization Take Place in the Computer Studies Class?

The first reaction of a person who is responsible for teaching computer studies to a group of about 40 students might be that any attempt to individualize by varying the pace, content, or method of instruction is impractical. The teacher would have to spend an inordinate amount of time working with each student on an individual basis. However, there are many ways to augment and vary *group* instruction in order to achieve a considerable degree of individuality.

Individual Differences of Students

Before looking at the techniques for achieving individualization, consider some of the ways in which students differ. Knowing these differences is important if we wish to match the method of instruction to each student's optimal learning environment. Students might differ in these ways:

1. Their *experience* with various aspects of computer studies. Some know nothing at all; some have had previous computing courses or learned a programming language; a growing number have a computer at home.
2. Their *motivational level and interest* in the topic. Many students are eager to take computer studies; some have learned the basics and are interested in learning more; a minority have no desire to take the subject but are in the class because of external pressures.
3. The capability to *work alone.* Some students work well by themselves and prefer doing so; some will not work unless constantly supervised; others have to be spoon-fed. Teaching the latter two groups can be difficult when dealing with content that is naturally self-learned; programming is a skill that partially falls in this category.
4. The capacity to deal with *ambiguity and abstractions* and the ability to *tolerate frustration.* These characteristics can have a major bearing on learning problem-solving/programming skills where making mistakes should be accepted as part of the learning experience.
5. The *natural ability* of the student to learn the material. This has to do with the student's level of intelligence plus a specific aptitude for learning computer studies. A student's ability to use logic in problem-solving is one example of a useful aptitude.
6. The existence of a *physical handicap* (Figure 5-1). Students who are blind, deaf, have cerebral palsy, are paraplegic, or have one of many other physical handicaps present a special challenge to the teacher.

WAYS OF INDIVIDUALIZING

Using the Computer to Individualize

The computer is an ideal tool for accommodating individualization in the classroom. There are two ways it can handle students on a one-to-one basis.

First, when writing and correcting programs, the student can work alone.

FIGURE 5-1 The teacher will need to accommodate the handicapped student in the computer classroom.

The computer does not require teacher supervision in order for the students to run software and develop programs. This means that students can use the machine whenever they want to, progressing at their own pace. This advantage is often countermanded by some teachers when assigning programming material. They place a deadline on completion of the program—such as by the end of the classroom period—and force the students into a lock-step approach. This rushes slow students and bores brighter ones. The computer studies teacher should instead assign programming material with a reasonable deadline which will easily accommodate every student in the class.

Second, the computer can be used to take over some of the teaching responsibility. This can be done by having the computer perform some of the classroom management functions such as testing, record keeping, and prescription. This approach, known as *Computer Managed Instruction* (CMI), facilitates individualization in a number of ways. For example, examinations can be tailored to each student. Each student gets a different exam—where the order of the questions is changed or the questions are different. It may also be possible to select the difficulty level of test questions. Also, CMI allows the teacher to spend more time with students individually.

The computer can also perform some of the pedagogical functions normally done by the teacher, such as drill and practice, remediation or one-to-one tutoring of the student. This approach, known as *Computer Assisted Instruction* (CAI), allows individualization in two ways.

First, the computer interacts with the student on an individual basis—through the computer keyboard—and the pace, duration and time of instruction can be adjusted to each student.

Second, a well-designed CAI package will have different paths available through the computer studies content. Based on the interaction with the students, the CAI program will select those paths which provide an optimal learning environment by adapting to their needs. There are a number of CAI packages available for teacher usage in computer studies.

Individualizing by Selecting Reading Material Wisely

Reading material such as textbooks and journals can be an ideal vehicle for individualization. Reading materials can be tailored to the needs of each student by varying the pace. Some students read quickly and with good comprehension, while others take their time and reread some passages two or more times. A student shouldn't be required to complete reading during a specified length of time, such as by the end of the class period (Figure 5-2). Permit the students to decide when they wish to read the material.

Suggest that the student *reread the material* if there has been difficulty with the original reading. Allot *supplementary reading materials* to the student who is ahead. This material should provide enrichment and be motivational and interesting; examples include articles on robotics or books on advanced programming techniques. Assign supplementary readings to match individual areas of interest. For instance, a student might be interested in medicine, the teacher would prescribe additional reading materials on computer applications in medical practice. Or,

FIGURE 5-2 Reading Assignments for Computer Studies

Reading assignments for this course are given below. All readings are to be completed by the dates listed.

Reading Material*	Date Completed By
Chapter 1	September 7
4	22
3	27
5	October 12
6	17
2	November 7
7	15
8	22
9	December 1
11	5

*In addition, supplementary readings should be included for each chapter from journals such as *BYTE*, *Business Week*, the computer manual, and other journals in the library.

assign supplementary readings to the student who is having difficulty with specific topics. For instance, if the student is struggling with writing programs in BASIC, a book containing lots of sample program problems along with their solutions might be ideal for helping the student. *Reading lists* of books and articles on computing may be of interest to students. Allow the students to choose which they want to read (Figure 5-3).

An instructor may offer an *individualized reading course* in which the student reads a number of books and discusses their content with the instructor. This technique, in which no other teaching strategies are used, is normally employed only at the university/post-secondary level.

Use *programmed textbooks* in computer studies if they are suitable. In a programmed text, the student reads several pages of the book, answers questions based on the content, and gets immediate feedback on whether the answers are right or wrong. Also, use *student workbooks,* if available. These workbooks contain summaries, examples, problems, and self-administered tests based on the content of the primary textbook.

Use *job-instruction sheets.* These instructions are designed by the teacher to guide the student through an activity or procedure, such as storing a program on a diskette or running software packages on the computer (Figure 5-4). Job instruction sheets may be supplemented by directed readings from a variety of textbooks, manuals, or other materials, and include drill and practice exercises.

Individualizing Through Differentiated Assignments

Another excellent way to individualize the computer studies instruction is by giving assignments. Not only can the students progress at their own pace, but

FIGURE 5-3 A Sample Supplementary Reading List

Are You Computer Literate? (Billings and Moursund)
A Basic Approach to BASIC (Mullish)
The BASIC Handbook (Lien)
BASIC and the Personal Computer (Dwyer and Critchfield)
BASIC Programming Primer (Mitchell and Parodie)
Computer Graphics Primer (Mitchell)
Computer Programming in the BASIC Language (Golder)
Introduction to Computers and Data Processing (Shelly and Cashman)
Introduction to Computers and Information Processing (Cassell and Jackson)
Learning BASIC Fast (DeRossi)
The Mind Appliance: Home Computer Applications (Lewis)
The Most Popular Sub-routines in BASIC (Tracton)
A Structured Approach to Programming (Hughes)

Machine specific books such as:

Pet/CBM Personal Computer Guide (Osborne)
Radio Shack BASIC Computer Language (Lien)

FIGURE 5-4 Job Instruction Sheet

Using the PRINT Statement

Student's name____________________Evaluation____________________
Period____________Date started____________Date finished____________
Approved____________________ ____________________
(Instructor) (Person for whom work was done)

Equipment and Materials: A computer keyboard and monitor

Introduction: The computer has some basic commands and statements: PRINT STOP RUN NEW SAVE LOAD INPUT GOTO READ DATA LET FOR...NEXT RETURN RESTORE IF...THEN. This lesson deals with the PRINT command.

Example:

Your instruction	Computer prints
PRINT "HI"	PRINT "HI" HI

Steps	Key Points
1. See what happens when you key the following commands into your computer.	1. You may have to use the shift key to print the quotation (") mark.
2. Key PRINT "HELLO"	2. Press RETURN/ENTER after each line.
3. PRINT "HELLO	3. Although some computers may not require the closing quotation mark, get into the habit of using it to keep you out of trouble with more complicated commands.
4. PRINT "3+4"	4. Notice, when quotation marks are used with a mathematical expression, the computer does not perform the arithmetic.
5. PRINT "HELLO THERE" Press DEL key to move back as many spaces as necessary so that you will print "HELLO ELEANOR"	5. DEL stands for delete. On your keyboard, you may find the key INST DEL which means instant delete.
6. Use the DEL key to correct any keying errors in the future.	6. Deleting on the computer keyboard is eliminating the impression completely.

FIGURE 5.4. (continued)

7. Key in 10 mathematical questions such as: PRINT 1+5	7. Do not use the quotation marks for these statements.
8. With similar mathematical expressions, use the following: * for multiplication 20*5 / for division 20/5 — for subtraction 20−5	8. Remember to press RETURN/ ENTER at the end of each line. Use DEL key for making corrections.

Question: Perform 5 mathematical problems using 3 digits for each problem and using +, *, /, and −. Copy the questions and the answers on a sheet of paper and hand in to the instructor. When finished, you will have 20 questions.

different assignments can be provided for the students based on their needs and abilities. In addition, the teacher can allow students a choice among assignments of equal difficulty. Assignment materials which can be individualized include essays, research projects, and programming.

Essays allow students to work on topics which interest them. Essays can be assigned on broad topic areas such as the student's favorite computer application; the characteristics and merits of a particular kind of computing equipment; or the effects of computing on an individual student's lifestyle. The students would be asked to narrow the scope of the essay by writing about those aspects of the topic that interest them.

Research projects are more ambitious than essays, but they also allow students to pursue a personal area of interest. The research project provides practice in finding and assimilating computer and computer-related materials in the resource center, and generally requires more in-depth research and better documentation than does an essay.

The *programming assignment* allows considerable latitude for individualization. Programming is an activity that must be done on an individual basis. The students work on designing the problem solution alone, write the code, key the program into the computer, and finally correct and debug the program themselves. Because of the solitary nature of this activity, there is no reason to specify when or how long the students should work on the problem; instead, they should be allowed to proceed at their own pace. Neither is there any need to specify how the student should write the program. There are many ways to attack the problem to find an acceptable solution in the form of a program, and individual approaches should be encouraged.

Another way to individualize programming assignments is by having each student work on a different program, rather than having everybody write the same one. There are several ways to accomplish this. First, permit each student to select a programming problem from a master list of possible programs. Make sure that all the problems have approximately the same difficulty level. Second, give extra assignments to ambitious students who need more challenge or to the ones who are having difficulty and need remediation. Third, allow students to suggest their own programming problems on topics of interest: computer games, personalized accounting systems, robot-controlled software. Ask the students to hand in a short proposal so that programs which are too hard or too easy can be screened out.

Individualizing by Using Extra-curricular Activities

Individualization can result from activities occurring outside the classroom. The only problem is that the teacher has limited control over the quality or type of activity.

Work experience with computers can be beneficial. Students sometimes get summer jobs which involve working with computers; since no two jobs are the same, each experience will be unique. Some educational institutions, especially universities, have formalized this procedure and offer degrees which include work experience as part of the curriculum. These programs, known as *co-operative work programs* or internships, typically involve alternating semesters of study with work in the computing industry. By the time a degree is obtained, the student will have a few years of valuable experience plus formal schooling.

By joining a *computer club,* either in school or in the community, the student can benefit from valuable experience which is not available in the classroom. Clubs provide the opportunity for students to talk to other interested computer buffs, operate a variety of computing equipment, share computer software, and read the magazines and journals to which the club may subscribe.

Introducing Individualization in the Classroom

Although the classroom is normally viewed as a place for housing group learning, there are a number of ways in which the teacher can introduce a certain amount of individualization:

By limiting *class enrollment,* the teacher will have more time to interact with each student. One-to-one interaction is very important in computer studies, especially when discussing the problems a student might be having with a computer program. Therefore, the school administration might consider keeping the class size small.

A teacher can still make a class *seem* smaller by *grouping students* with similar abilities and interests. Instead of talking to the entire class, address individual groups while other groups work on their own tasks. Also, whenever possible, use *student assistants.* They could counsel students on computer problems, lead seminars, demonstrate equipment, and direct small group discussions.

Individualization can be achieved when *lecturing* to the students, repeating the material at least once so that the students who are having difficulty receive some extra instruction. However, in order not to bore the advanced students, rephrase the material, embellishing it with interesting anecdotes. Or have the students start on assignments or projects if they understood all aspects of the lecture. Spend ten to fifteen percent of the lecture talking to the bright students who may need this extra attention to stimulate their interest. And answer as many student questions as time permits, both on an individual and group basis.

Get the students to *relate their experiences* and knowledge. Have them lecture on their experiences with computing applications; give presentations of student-owned equipment; report on recent computing contacts; or work programming problems at the chalkboard.

Individualizing Using the Media and Resource Center

The resource center provides an ideal environment for individualizing instruction in computer studies. Not only does it house the books, manuals and programmed texts, but it is full of audio-visual materials such as audio cassettes, games, filmstrips, software packages, kits, taped lectures, movies, videocassettes, narrated slides, and video disks. All these can contribute to individualization of learning when the student works alone. The student can determine the pace of instruction; decide when to view the material; decide which material to access; and choose an instructional package which is more interesting or more suitable to their own learning style.

Using One-to-One Student Contact

The best type of individual instruction in the computer studies class is when the teacher interacts with the student on a one-to-one basis. While the teacher may be able to do very little of this during normal class periods, he or she could arrange for after-hour *tutoring* for students experiencing difficulties with the course. If the teacher does not have time to do this personally, student assistants can be employed.

Keeping *office hours* can also be beneficial. During office hours, the teacher can answer questions, clarify points of confusion, go over programming assignments, counsel problem students, and counsel students on course options or job possibilities in computer studies.

A teacher may opt to stay for a while after each class period to answer individual questions. By terminating each class session early, there is some time for talking to individual students. Students may also be invited to talk to the teacher during the assignment period or the latter part of the class period.

Individualizing by Distance Education and Self-study

Many students are unable to study in the normal classroom environment because they are sick, are handicapped, live in a place where there are no schools, or are working at full-time jobs. Instruction for these students is partially individualized since they must work on their own and at their own pace.

There are three major ways for these students to work by themselves and complete an introductory computer studies course.

Correspondence school. The correspondence school enables students to interact with their instructors by mail. The student does most of the work at home, like reading, writing programs, and taking tests. Computer studies materials are sent to the student by the educational institute and the student returns completed assignments, program listings, and examinations for evaluation and feedback. Within this framework, students work at their own pace.

Distance education. Distance education uses media such as the telephone and television to set up a communication link between the instructor and a number of geographically dispersed students. The teacher talks on the telephone and all students listen; or there may be a live TV broadcast of the teacher lecturing. While this procedure is an excellent way to get the computing course into remote areas, it does not allow much individualization of instruction. Most of the interaction is one-way, and the teacher can't respond to different student needs. Recognizing this deficiency, some institutions offer distance education classes which allow two-way communications between students and teacher. This is done by using the telephone to ask the teacher questions, melding correspondence school techniques into the distance education class; by the students visiting the teacher or vice versa.

Self-study. Self-study is the perfect vehicle for individualization—students pick their own computer studies material, determine when to study, decide how fast to go, and even administer their own self-testing and evaluation. When used wisely, it is probably one of the better ways to learn. Unfortunately, for the young student or the person who is just beginning to learn a new subject area, this method may not yield optimal results.

IMPLEMENTING INDIVIDUALIZED INSTRUCTION

How does the teacher decide to have one student read a certain book, another work on remedying a program problem, a third work on enrichment material, and another—with computing background—skip a section of a course?

Making such decisions is not easy. However, there are many books that suggest ways to match the individual student to specific instruction. This discussion will be restricted to one technique—modularization—which has proven to be successful for individualizing the computer studies curriculum.

By breaking up the content of the computer studies courses into *independent modules*—for instance, one module on computer applications, one on hardware, another on programming—and teaching these as separate mini-courses, the teacher can match the content of the course to individual student needs. For example, the student might have a sound programming background but no experience with computer applications. If a modular system were used, the student could omit the programming module but take the remaining modules. Another student might have taken a computer literacy course in a lower grade and, therefore, be allowed to omit the computer applications module after satisfactorily answering a basic set of questions.

The division of a course into modules has two requirements. The content of each module must be independent, and there must be an *objective* procedure for deciding whether a student will take or bypass a particular module.

With *independent modules,* it is necessary that if one is omitted, the student is able to move to another without losing continuity. This means that one module should not be dependent on another module in any way.

Decision-making is based upon giving two kinds of tests with each module: the pretest and the posttest. The pretest is used to determine whether the student should take a module of instruction. If the student scores well on the test, he or she can skip the module. If this score is not achieved, the module becomes mandatory.

Posttests determine whether the student has achieved the objectives of the module. If so, the student progresses to another module; if not, remediation or repeating of the module is necessary.

The finer the division of the subject matter into smaller modules, the better. However, carrying it to an extreme becomes an administrative nightmare for the teacher. This is where computer assistance in the form of CMI and CAI can be invaluable, since CMI systems can keep track of student progression through each module, administer tests, and recommend prescriptions to the teacher. CAI systems provide the opportunity to divide the subject matter up into very small modules—even to the level of the individual concept—and to work the student through this content in a systematic way. This can only be done when the student and teacher are in a one-to-one teaching situation.

QUESTIONS

1. Create a job instruction sheet for:
   a. Using the cursor—in all directions.
   b. Logging on/off a time-sharing computer.
   c. Utilizing a diskette.
   d. Developing a checklist for why computers or terminals are not working.
2. If individualized instruction in computer studies is so important, why is it not implemented by all teachers? Give your reasons and justify them.
3. What is the difference between correspondence courses and distance education? Which is the preferred method, and why?
4. Suppose a student is having difficulty learning to program. Indicate the ways that instruction might be individualized for this student in order to provide assistance.
5. Suppose a student has already taken a computer literacy course, but must take your computer literacy course because it contains content which is mandatory (e.g., programming) and was not included in the earlier course. Indicate how to accommodate this student on an individual basis without requiring the student to redo course work.
6. Some CAI programs teach a course by dividing it into modules, giving a pretest before teaching the module, and then skipping that module if the student shows mastery on the test. Modules are small so that the mastery test is only examining one topic. Suggest the modules which might be found in a CAI lesson on:
   a. Learning to use a microcomputer
   b. Learning binary numbers
7. What fundamental knowledge would be downplayed or omitted by persons who are teaching themselves to program?
8. Create a differentiated assignment (essay) for a discussion of the uses of a particular input device.
9. Create a reading list of articles on the following topics suitable for the introductory computer studies class:
   a. Computer networks

   b. Computing jobs
   c. Personal computers
   d. Database systems
   e. Storage technologies

10. Define the following terms: aptitude, CAI, CMI, computer club, core material, distance education, enrichment material, individual differences, individualized instruction, individualized reading, job instruction sheets, learning modality, modularization of content, pace, programmed text, reading course, remediation, self-study, student workbook.

6

Methods of Teaching Computer Studies

The effective computer science teacher uses a *variety of teaching methods* like lectures, discussions, films, or demonstrations. This policy is better than using a single favorite method and sticking to it regardless of its suitability to the subject matter. For example, research shows that lecturing is the most frequently used teaching method. But this method may be boring, and may not be the best tool for teaching the specific subject matter. Teaching about computer hardware, for instance, realistically cannot be accomplished by the lecture method alone—an effective teacher might introduce the concept of computer hardware by means of a lecture, then show a film on how computers work, followed by a demonstration of their operation.

A variety of teaching methodologies generates more student interest and is better suited to achieve the goals of the course. A few of the methods suitable for use in the computer studies class include lecture, demonstration, discussion, gaming, and question and answer.

Figure 6-1 lists some of the factors which influence methodology. The teacher should select the technique or method which would be most effective in any given teaching situation.

LECTURE

The lecture is considered to be the best way of communicating large amounts of information quickly to large groups. The lecture is probably the most widely used teaching technique in the computer studies class. Virtually every instructor employs it, and some use it almost exclusively. Unfortunately, much of the computer studies content is ill suited to this technique.

Lectures are frequently augmented by audiovisual aids such as chalkboards, transparencies, and slides which are used to help present the information in a

FIGURE 6-1 Factors Influencing Teaching Methodology in Computer Studies

What are the student's needs?
What is the student's age level?
What is the student's intellectual ability?
What are the student's physical and mental characteristics?
What is the student's need for practice and drill?
What is the student's need to verbalize the knowledge?
What is the student's attention span?
What are other identifiable needs?
What is the purpose of the learning?
What are the needs of the program?
What is the subject matter content?
Is the content inherently interesting?
Is abstract learning necessary?
Is there need for memorizing facts?
What is the student's interest in the topic?
How relevant is the topic to the student?
What is the transferability of the topic to other courses?

second modality. In addition, students can usually ask questions either during or after the lecture.

A typical lecture in computer science combined with other techniques would be a lecture on the manufacture of silicon chips. To facilitate the delivery of this lecture, the teacher gathers slides depicting the various stages in the manufacturing process. Transparencies can be prepared listing things such as the kinds of chips, their costs, manufacturing time, and so forth. These materials are brought to the classroom, where the teacher briefly introduces the topic—"Today we are going to talk about the manufacture of silicon chips"—and then describes the procedure while showing the slides and the transparencies. When finished, the teacher answers student questions. If there are none, the teacher poses a few questions to start the students thinking about the concept presented.

Advantages of Lecturing in the Computer Studies Class

Lecturing is probably the easiest teaching technique for the instructor to use; not much preparation is required, especially if the teacher uses the chalkboard, writes on transparencies, or is willing to ad lib. A person with a good computing background could easily give a fifty minute lecture with little preparation. Even if preparation is necessary, lecture notes and materials frequently can be reused.

Another advantage of the lecture is its suitability for large classroom situations. Some computer science classes, particularly in universities, have hundreds of students crammed into one room. In such a situation, the lecture is the only feasible way to deliver the material; techniques like discussion and debate are unrealistic when the class exceeds standard size. Sometimes the disadvantages of the large group classroom situation may be reduced by regrouping the students for laboratory or discussion sessions following a large group lecture. Where feasible, large groups should be subdivided for problem solving and question-and-answer sessions at least once a week.

Criticisms of Lecturing

A major criticism of the lecture is that it is a one-way communication between teacher and student leading to a somewhat impersonal setting. However, a more serious problem is that it tends to produce a passive attitude because the student partakes minimally in the learning process.

Also, the spoken word is not a good media for conveying the content of computer studies efficiently. Compared to other techniques, the amount of information retained by the student will be relatively small. The student will get much more out of fifty hours of reading the computer studies text than listening to fifty hours of lecturing.

While low student involvement may be acceptable in some subject areas, active student participation is necessary for learning much of the content of introductory computer studies.

Learning to program the computer is a problem-solving activity which cannot be learned passively; the student must practice the technique until it is mastered. If a teacher depends solely on lecturing, not much retention will occur, and there will be little or no hands-on experience with the computer.

Learning how to operate equipment can be best accomplished by an expert demonstration followed by practice, rather than simply telling the student what to do. Learning about the societal effects of computers can be best taught by having the students reach their own conclusions about the merits of computing—for instance, by debating or role playing, rather than by simply incorporating the instructor's opinions and values extolled in a lecture.

When to Lecture

The lecture is best used for relatively short periods of time rather than full class periods; intersperse lecturing with other teaching techniques. The lecture is effective in presenting factual material rather than material requiring critical thinking or practice; hence, lecturing is good for introducing a topic, defining concepts, reviewing material at the end of the class period or before an examination, and clarifying difficult concepts. Some of these activities may require five to ten minutes at the most; others may require more time. Thus, a fifty minute class period can be divided up into a number of short lectures, with the rest of the time devoted to other teaching techniques.

Mini-Lesson Plan for a Lecture

Let us set up a mini-lesson plan on the manufacturing silicon chips. Suppose the plan calls for two fifty-minute periods to teach this topic. As a guide for teaching the lesson, the subdivision of the unit might be:

Day 1

1. Overview the topic—10 minutes*
2. Show a film on chip manufacture—20 minutes
3. Discuss the film—15 minutes
4. Review and assign a reading from book—5 minutes*

Day 2

5. Review previous day and overview what will happen today—10 minutes*
6. Demonstrate a silicon chip—10 minutes
7. Discuss and answer questions from readings—15 minutes
8. Clarify difficult points through question-answer—10 minutes*
9. Windup—5 minutes*

*Denotes activities where the teacher is lecturing.

This plan uses lecturing where it is needed, yet relies on other techniques to augment the learning—namely, film analysis, discussion and demonstration. Only two-fifths of the time is devoted to the actual lecture; the rest of the period allows students to take a more active role.

Variants of the Lecture

Now examine some of the variants of the lecture which may be used in computer studies. Five variations are discussed: textbook lecture, prerecorded lecture, lecture by distance education, student lecture, and guest lecture.

Lecturing from the textbook. Lecturing from the textbook is perhaps the most widely used teaching method in computer science. The lecture content is usually based directly upon the textbook material, progressing from chapter 1 to the end of the book without deviation as illustrated in Figure 6-2. The reason for the popularity of this method is that the textbook provides a predefined structure to the course; very little preparation by the teacher is required if the order and content of the text is strictly followed. Textbook teaching is generally used by the teacher who lacks confidence in subject matter mastery. The teacher does little or nothing in lesson plan preparation.

FIGURE 6-2 Sample Table of Contents Used in Textbook Lecturing

Chapter 1	Introduction
Chapter 2	History and Evolution of Computing
Chapter 3	Data Processing and Data Entry
Chapter 4	The Central Processing Unit
Chapter 5	Secondary Storage
Chapter 6	Input and Output
Chapter 7	Programming Languages
Chapter 8	Programming in BASIC

As a teaching methodology, textbook lecturing suffers from all the problems of lecturing, but has several other *disadvantages*. The content of the course becomes rigid. For example, if the teacher wanted to discuss programming languages first, the student would have to read that chapter without reading the intervening chapters; this would be impossible with most textbooks, where one chapter builds upon the next.

The lectures can get extremely boring, since the students are usually asked to read the chapter before the class is held. If the lecturer adds no new content, students tend to either read the text or listen to the lecturer—seldom both.

The quality and content of the course depends solely on an external author whose approach might not be entirely in harmony with the needs of the school. For example, the teacher may want to teach more about societal issues; the treatment of systems analysis may be too complex; the chapter on data communications may be unnecessary; and material dealing with computer applications in society and business may be missing altogether.

Prerecorded lecture. In the prerecorded lecture, the presentation is put on *tape* or *film*. A number of prerecorded lectures are commercially available on different topics in the computer studies curriculum. In addition, many schools make their own tapes of individuals speaking on selected topics in computer studies.

The prerecorded lecture has several *disadvantages* compared to the live lecture: a) there is no personal contact between the lecturer and the student; no questions are possible, and therefore minute-by-minute alterations of the lecture are difficult if not impossible; b) the style of the lecturer, if the tape is purchased, may not be suitable for the audience; c) the attention span of the student lags much more quickly than if the person is "in the flesh"; d) it requires considerable time to record a good lecture, making the commercially prepared lectures expensive; e) tapes generally quickly become obsolete because of the rapid changes currently occurring in computer technology. Tape revisions require commitment of time and energy.

In spite of these difficulties, the prerecorded lecture has some merits. For instance, the product can be slick and have fewer errors than a live performance. Individualization and modularization of instruction is also possible, since the tape can be played back at any time.

Lecture by distance education. Normally, the lecturer is in the same room as the listeners. However, with the marvels of modern technology, it is possible to transmit the lecture to other locations by means of written materials, telephone, radio, cable, TV broadcasts, or computer tutorials. This permits people who are not in the classroom—such as students in business and those who are in remote communities or who are ill—to hear the lecture. The students may talk to the lecturer and ask questions by means of a long distance telephone link. Several computer studies courses—introductory computer studies and others—are taught in this manner in many universities across the nation.

Student lectures. In this variation of lecturing, students spend part or all of a class period talking about an aspect of computer studies in which they are interested. While this procedure should not be used on a daily basis, when used judiciously it provides a change of pace for the class, a change for the instructor, and—what is most important—it actively involves the student in researching and presenting the subject matter. Ideal topics for presentations include computing equipment; a student-written program; new equipment; a computer application of particular interest to the student; software packages; an article on computers; or a report on the computing job of a family member.

Although the student lecture has advantages, it also has some *drawbacks.*

1. It works best in small computer studies classes (fewer than twenty students). In a big class, there is not enough time to accommodate all the students unless the presentations are very short—five to ten minutes each.
2. Everyone suffers from a student lecture which is poorly researched or delivered.
3. There may be a break in continuity, since the subject matter of students' lectures may not fit well into the plan.
4. If the student lecture becomes lengthy, the teacher may decide to cut off the presentation, leaving the lecture unfinished.

Guest lecture. In guest lecturing, a knowledgeable person is invited to give the lecture at the school, or the students attend a seminar or conference elsewhere. This practice adds variety to the class sessions, and can be a great motivator. Guest lecturers should have specialized knowledge to share with your students. Persons capable of giving such lectures in computer studies include other teachers; persons using computers in business or industry; visiting computer experts; or computer dealers.

One problem with the guest lecture program is that it may be difficult to provide continuity between the normal class material and the material covered by the guest lecturer. Also, the lecturer may use unfamiliar computer jargon or assume background material that the students do not have. These problems can be circumvented, however, by suitable pre-briefing of the lecturer who can adjust the content of the lecture to satisfy the needs of the students; alternatively, the students can be prepared for the technical vocabulary the speaker may use.

How to Lecture Well

What can the instructor do to maximize learning during lectures? Here is a checklist of things to consider. The points are geared to one major tactic; they try to involve the audience as much as possible in the lecture.

1. *Know the computer studies material.* A good background enhances the instructor's capacity to adjust to audience response during the lecture and also to answer questions intelligently.
2. *Plan* each lecture well. The computer studies materials should flow smoothly, and relate to both previous and future learning; do not jump from topic to topic.
3. Avoid using computer *jargon* that the students don't understand.
4. Make abundant use of *teaching aids* such as props, materials, and transparencies. Use any media which can be used to help convey the computer studies material; they should stimulate student interest.
5. Maintain *eye contact* with the students. Eye contact gives each listener the feeling that the speaker is addressing him personally. It also allows the instructor to gain valuable feedback on how the material is received.

6. *Encourage questions* throughout the lecture, and if possible, let other students answer the questions to encourage student interaction.
7. *Adjust* the lecture whenever necessary. Do not stick to a prepared script when the students have lost interest in what is being said, or if the students' questions necessitate a change of direction in the presentation.
8. Capture the *student's attention* at the start of the class period. If student attention is not received from the start, there is a good chance that it never will be.
9. Provide the students with a written or oral summary of the *instructional objectives* of the lecture. Do this either at the start or at the end of the period—preferably both.
10. Make sure the lecture is delivered at a *moderate tempo*. Going too slowly generates boredom; going too quickly frustrates the student who learns more slowly or wants to take notes.
11. Ensure that each student realizes the *importance of the computer studies content* of the lecture. This can be accomplished by basing an assignment on the lecture material or by having a discussion of its content after the presentation.
12. Continually ask the students *questions* based on the lecture. This keeps their attention, and involves them in relating the contents of the lecture to their own experiences in computing.
13. Use personal *anecdotes* when they will improve the presentation. Students thrive on such material; it gives them insight into the practical aspects of the computer studies content.
14. *Humor* is always welcome. Humor reduces anxiety, but be careful to make it fit in with the computer studies material.
15. Let the students know what is *opinion* and what is *fact*. Where possible, provide other opinions as well, so that the students have information for comparison purposes and can make their own judgments.

DEMONSTRATION

The demonstration is an excellent teaching technique to use in the computer studies classroom. The teacher or student shows the class how something works or how to operate a piece of equipment, rather than just talking about it. The method requires that a real object be manipulated as the teacher describes what is happening. Real objects include hardware items such as computers, diskettes, or modems. Examples of software, such as programs or flowcharts, are also excellent for demonstrations.

Some Example Demonstrations

Diskettes. The teacher holds up a computer diskette, commenting upon its size, its flexibility, how it revolves, and so on. The diskette could even be passed around to permit closer inspection. If it is no longer usable, the diskette can be ripped open to reveal what is inside.

Next the teacher demonstrates the operation of the disk drive, describing the purpose of the various switches, latches, and indicator lights. A diskette is inserted and removed from the drive several times; if time permits, the students do this as well. When inserting the diskette, the teacher stresses the importance of placing it in the correct way (there are eight possible orientations, but only one is valid).

Finally the class is shown what happens when the diskette drive is actually operating—when the user is loading a program or printing a disk directory, for example.

Software packages. Before allowing the students to use a software package—such as a word processor—first show what it does and how it works. Exercise caution to avoid presenting the full complement of features, thereby overloading the students. First, demonstrate a few of the main features of the software package and allow the students to consolidate this information by using the software; then present more features and have the students practice again, and so on.

Additional topics suitable for the demonstration. Here is a short list of additional topics which the teacher could present in the form of a demonstration. Refer also to the section on props and real objects in Chapter 7 for a longer list of suitable items.

Hardware

1. Inserting paper into the printer
2. Using the computer keyboard
3. Connecting the parts of a computer system
4. Utilizing a small robot attached to the computer
5. Inserting and removing tapes from a cassette drive

Software

1. Writing small BASIC programs using a display monitor at the front of the classroom
2. Walking through a flowchart step by step
3. Using a spreadsheet package
4. Learning about the function of individual BASIC statements
5. Debugging programs

Why Use Demonstrations?

There are at least four cogent reasons for using the demonstration to teach computer science content. The demonstration brings the student closer to the *real-life world of computing;* for example, seeing a piece of computing equipment in actual operation is much more realistic than just hearing the teacher talk about the device. Also, the technique provides much-needed *variety* to the teaching methodology.

The demonstration can *save* a lot of class *time.* Showing the students how to connect a modem to the microcomputer requires less time than a verbal description of the operation.

The teacher can easily *alter the presentation* to suit the needs of the moment. This capability is particularly useful for demonstrating the entry of a small program into the computer. When typing in the code, the instructor can introduce errors, correct them, and show the results of the updated program. Changes also can be made in response to student questions or suggestions.

Variants of the Demonstration

There are at least five variations to the teacher-centered demonstration.

The on-site demonstration. The class takes a field trip to a computing center in some local business or visits an industrial establishment which manufactures computer hardware, and is given an actual demonstration by the company.

Job instruction sheet. The steps of the demonstration are itemized on a handout and the student works through the instructions, thereby giving the demonstration to himself.

Show and tell sessions. The student demonstrates to the rest of the class a personal item which incorporates (directly or indirectly) some aspect of computing technology. Good examples are a digital watch, computerized toy, or a program the student has written.

Guest demonstration. A person from outside the school—an industrial representative, banker, politician, data processing manager, or scientist—comes into the classroom and demonstrates hardware and/or software.

Student evaluation. The teacher can use a demonstration to test the student on some practical aspect of the course. The student is asked to demonstrate mastery of a particular skill such as using the keyboard properly, retrieving files from the disk, or finding information in a computer manual. Giving a test in this fashion circumvents the problem of trying to adequately measure the mastery of these skills with the traditional pencil and paper test.

CLASSROOM DISCUSSION

An important—but infrequently utilized—teaching methodology in the introductory computer studies course is the classroom discussion. By discussion we do not mean an informal group discussing the latest computer game, but a carefully structured exchange of ideas which is directed towards a specific goal.

Computer Studies Topics Suited for Discussion

Topics which harbor some aspect of controversy, require the formulation of opinions or attitudes, necessitate the development of a plan, or call for the exploration of some hypothesis are the best candidates for discussion. The students could discuss the *social effects* of computers. Divide the class into two equal groups, with each group pursuing the question of whether computers are creating jobs or generating unemployment.

The students could attack a *programming problem* by actively cooperating on the solution and exploring which alternatives are better. The teacher mediates the procedure, writes the solution on the board, and intervenes only if the students are stymied or get off on a tangent.

The teacher could describe an *industrial or business application* of computers and ask the class to decide upon the "best" computer system to accommodate this application. The students are required to suggest the hardware and software necessary to support an airline reservation system, for example.

Students may debate the *advantages and disadvantages* of various pieces of computer equipment (like tape vs. disk) and recommend applications for which each device is best suited. They could discuss the *ethics* of some aspect of computing, such as the effects upon an individual's privacy caused by having personal information stored in huge data banks.

The class might be asked to *evaluate* a software package which the teacher has just demonstrated, commenting on its potential usefulness, cost, and ease of use. Or the students could exchange ideas about the *future* of the computing industry and predict what might be the most likely trends in both hardware and software developments.

Why Use the Discussion Technique?

The discussion technique is an excellent way to introduce *variety*. It provides a stimulating change from the lecture. The discussion format forces the student to *actively participate* in the learning process—thinking and reflecting—rather than simply regurgitating facts.

Some computing topics are particularly suited to the discussion technique. For example, the development of positive or negative attitudes towards the use of computers (like, "Computers are bad because they are dehumanizing our society"; "Computers are good because they are revitalizing the economy") cannot transpire by "telling" the students what to think; the evolution of attitudes takes place only if the students come to their own conclusions. The classroom discussion is an excellent environment for the student to formulate opinions.

The classroom discussion allows the students to develop and practice their *interpersonal communication skills*. Some examples of interpersonal interaction in the world of computing include: co-operating with colleagues when working on a large software project; dealing with customers or users; and explaining a programming task to subordinates.

Finally, the classroom discussion provides an opportunity for the students to practice the complex vocabulary and *jargon* of computer science in situations which demands clear and precise utilization of the terminology.

Format of the Discussion

The discussion can take place with the class as a *single unit* or divided into *small groups*. While either format is acceptable, the small group technique is favored because it fosters more participation of the individual student.

Basically, the following steps are recommended to set up and administer the small group discussion:

1. Divide the class into groups of four to six students.
2. Appoint individual responsibilities to each group member.
3. Assign to each group a question to answer or theme to pursue. The question or theme might be the same for all groups (e.g. "How are computers enhancing our way of life?"); or might be different in each case:
   a. Group 1: "How are computers enabling us to be realistic?"
   b. Group 2: "How are computers increasing our standard of living?"
   c. Group 3: "How are computers allowing us to be better informed?"

4. Allow the students time to do any background research necessary to fulfill the goals of the discussion.
5. When this research is completed, have the groups discuss the topic.
6. After twenty to thirty minutes, ask the groups to wrap things up.
7. Finally, ask the groups to report their conclusions to the rest of the class and, if necessary, combine all the findings into an overall conclusion.

Responsibilities of group members. Normally, the individuals within a group will be allocated specific roles to play. For instance, a typical group might have a *group leader,* who keeps the discussion moving and steers it in the right direction when it strays. The leader will occasionally pose questions to the other group members. These questions are designed to get individual members to participate if they are not contributing enough, or make sure that alternative viewpoints are adequately represented.

The *resource person(s)* act as subject matter experts (specialists) on the topic. In this role, they provide the factual information for the group. Since these students are required to do research, prepare handouts, and gather materials, their active participation in the actual discussion should be downplayed.

The *recorder* (or secretary) keeps notes on the progress of the discussion, jotting down key points, creating a summary of the results, and presenting the group's conclusion to the class.

Remaining group members are expected to be the major participants in the discussion. They must be prepared, and peruse the materials provided by the "resource" members.

The teacher's role. The teacher should adopt a relatively passive role in the discussion. The teacher should appoint students to individual groups and select the leaders, establish goals for each group, and keep track of the time.

The teacher must maintain a suitable environment within the room, keeping down noise and minimizing interruptions. He or she monitors all the groups, checking on the progress of the discussion and arbitrating if disagreements arise; fosters a congenial, friendly atmosphere, ensures that disagreements do not get personal, and encourages the acceptance of divergent points of view. The teacher lets the students work independently, but functions as the group leader if the class is discussing a topic as a single unit. The instructor summarizes the overall results of the discussions at the end of the exercise. And finally, he or she encourages individuals to participate by giving each person a specific responsibility which will be called on at some point in the discussion; assigning grades for participation in the discussion; and selecting an interesting topic.

Variants of the Discussion

There are a number of variants to the discussion which immerse the students in an interchange of ideas. In the *debate,* a competitive discussion takes place between two sides. The participants in the debate present forceful arguments in support of their viewpoint with the objective of "winning" the debate. Examples of debating topics include:

1. computers will "take over" the world;

2. FORTRAN is the best programming language; or
3. Commodore microcomputers are the best.

With a *case study,* students are asked to solve a computer problem cooperatively. Normally they will need to do some background research first. An example of a case study topic follows.

> A small company (50 employees) which manufactures and sells soft drinks has decided to computerize its operation. Since the company has no computer expertise, it has opted to retain some computing consultants to set up the system. The class is divided into 2 halves. One half will play the role of the soft-drink company executives, while the second half will act as the consultants. The two groups work together to investigate those tasks performed by the company which would derive the most benefit from the introduction of computers and to subsequently make recommendations as to the kind of hardware and software which would be needed.

Film analysis is another discussion technique. The students watch a film dealing with some aspects of computer science. The teacher might ask them to pay particular attention to certain aspects of the film. (e.g. "Observe what computer devices are portrayed in the film" or "Notice that this movie was made 10 years ago and will contain examples of outdated technology") At the end, the class is asked to discuss the key points and arrive at some conclusion with respect to the impact of the computer.

Task groups are small student committees which occupy the members in some ongoing work activity. For example, a committee is organized to run a "computer fair" for parents and other interested adults. The committee would normally be split into subcommittees responsible for booths, advertising, refreshments, equipment, and so on. Or, a task group is established to investigate the job situation in the computer industry. Subgroups are assigned specific tasks to pursue in depth, such as monitoring newspaper advertisements, retrieving resource information from the library, talking to industry representatives, and tracking down tables of job descriptions and job classifications.

GAMES

Games, simulations, and other play activities can be most fruitful for teaching computer studies. Although their use is more widespread in the lower grade levels, certain kinds of games are beneficial at all levels.

Games in computer studies can provide a variety of learning opportunities for the educator. They are valuable because they are *fun* to play and relieve student tension and anxiety. Such tension relievers would be beneficial as distractors during the stressful activities of programming or debugging.

Games can *create an interest* in certain aspects of the curriculum that might be difficult to generate otherwise. Learning the binary code for letters of the alphabet is not an exciting experience; however, introducing a game in which students send each other secret messages written in binary can foster interest. Games can also function as *motivational devices* if the teacher turns the opportunity to play a game into a reward for doing work.

What kinds of games are appropriate for the computer studies class? There are many possibilities, but we will mention only a few. These games contain computer content to be learned—the following crossword puzzle falls into this category—or require the students to utilize computing equipment and thus learn about computers as a by-product.

Crossword puzzles. Crossword puzzles can be adapted to computer studies jargon (Figure 6-3). When this is done, the educational objective of the puzzle is to provide practice at identifying and defining computer terms. The difficulty level of the puzzle could be adjusted for the grade level in which it is to be used.

Word games. In a word game, the student has to discover computer terms which are imbedded within a jumble of letters. The educational goal is to learn to identify and spell computer terms. Figure 6-4 illustrates an example of a word game to help learn the parts of a computer. The game can be competitive by awarding prizes to the student who can solve the puzzle the fastest or find the largest number of terms.

Computer games. Computer games are familiar to everyone; they can be played on either a home computer or an arcade machine. They come in a myriad of formats, the majority involving either hand/eye coordination (like PAC-MAN) or problem-solving abilities (like *Dungeons and Dragons*).

Many have questioned the educational merit of computer games, arguing that they are simply pastimes designed to while away the hours and liberate players of their money. However, even the most trivial has some degree of pedagogical value, and some of the better designed games are excellent teaching tools. With this in mind, examine some of the possible merits of using computer games in the computer studies class:

1. They can act as an icebreaker for the student who is unfamiliar with or afraid of computer equipment—the fear of computers is a prevalent phenomenon. By playing a game, the student can learn to use a computer in a nonthreatening environment.
2. Because they require the user to manipulate or attend to one or more computing devices, games can be used to help teach certain aspects of computing such as computer graphics; the manipulation and operation of the joy stick, the mouse, and other pointing devices; the proper utilization of the keyboard; the correct methods for using cassettes and diskettes.
3. Games can also act as a model for student programming problems. This is accomplished by having students play a computer game, then asking them to write a program for a game which is similar to the one just played; the students could also be asked to improve the original game by modifying the program.

Control of the Use of Computer Games. The use of computer games in the classroom could quickly get out of hand. Moderation and judicious usage is recommended. Limit the game playing activity to a specified time of the week, such as Friday afternoon when motivation may be low. Permit students who have completed their day's work to have access to a game as a reward. Or, use the game only when it has pedagogical advantage over other teaching techniques.

FIGURE 6-3 Computer Crossword Puzzle

1 I	N	I	T	I	2 A	L	I	3 Z	E			4 C
N					L			E		5 C		A
6 P	7 A	8 G	I	N	G		9 E	R	10 R	O	R	S
U	N	I			O			O	O	B		S
11 T	A	G			12 L	E	13 D		14 M	O	V	E
	15 L	O	16 G				17 I	C		18 L	E	T
	O		19 E	20 D	P		21 S	O	S			T
	22 G	O	T	O			K		23 T	R	E	E
24 K				25 S	E	N	S	E				
26 C	27 O	28 D	29 E		30 N	S						31 I
	R	R	O		32 I	N	T	E	G	E	R	S
		U	M	33 W		34 C	A	M				A
35 C	O	M		P		36 A	C	R	O	N	Y	M

Computer Crossword Puzzle

ACROSS

1. To preset a variable to a proper starting value.
6. Programs are divided into fixed sizes or segments.
9. Deviations from correct values.
11. A portion of an instruction.
12. An acronym for light emitting diode.
14. To transfer form one location of storage to another.
15. A record of operations.
17. An electronic circuit fabricated on a single piece of material.
18. A BASIC command assigning a value to a variable.
19. An acronym for processing performed largely by electronic digital computers.
21. An acronym for silicon on sapphire.
22. A command changing the direction of a program, given certain circumstances.
23. A special kind of linked list.
24. An abbreviation for kilo.
25. To read holes punched on a card.
26. To write a program or routine.
30. One-billionth of a second.
32. Whole numbers which may be positive, negative, or zero.
34. An acronym for computer-assisted manufacturing.
35. An acronym for computer output to microfilm.
36. A word formed from the first letter or letters on words in a name or phrase.

DOWN

1. The introduction of data from an external storage medium into the computer.
2. An acronym for an algorithmic language.
3. A numeral normally denoting the lack of magnitude.
4. A magnetic tape storage device.
5. An acronym for common business oriented language.
7. Pertaining to representation by means of continuously variable physical qualities.
8. An acronym for input data that is bad resulting in bad output data.
10. Non-erasable permanently programmed memory.
13. Low cost storage media used widely on microcomputers.
16. To obtain a record from an input file.
20. An acronym for disk operating system.
27. An alternate step.
28. A peripheral storage device consisting of a cylinder with a magnetized surface on which data is recorded.
29. An acronym for the end of a message.
31. An acronym for indexed sequential access method.
33. The use of computerized equipment and systems to facilitate the handling of words and text.

FIGURE 6-4 Word Game

This word game is made up of computer terms. Circle each letter of the words you find. Some letters are used more than once. With the 6 letters remaining, make up the mystery word.

```
M I C R O C O M P U T E R
I A N R G N I G G U B E D
N N I I A S T I U C R I C
I A N N T S T U N H F F O
C L T D F I H O R P D C M
O O E R I R A D R T U N M
M G G D R G A L R A L T A
P M I O O A I M I O G E N
U A R T N C R T E Z C E D
T R B L A N G U A G E E T
E S U O M P E N I L M O R
R E Q U E U E T U P T U O
S T G N I M M A R G O R P
```

Words

analog	debugging	integer	mouse	RAM
and	digital	language	off	record
circuits	error	line	output	ROM
code	get	mainframe	port	set
crash	initialize	microcomputer	programming	storage
CRT	input	minicomputer	queue	tape
				turtle

QUESTIONING PRACTICES

The use of questions and answers, in which the teacher asks a question and one of the students verbally attempts an answer, is the second most popular teaching strategy, superseded only by the lecture.

Ways to Use the Questioning Method

There are a number of different ways of employing this strategy in the computer studies classroom.

Questions and answers are most frequently employed as a *companion to the lecture method.* Either the teacher lectures first and then has a question/answer session at the end of the period, or the questions are interspersed throughout the lecture. In the former case, the questions summarize the contents of the lecture and help the students consolidate the material. In the latter case, the questions add variety to the lecture and maintain the students' attention.

Student questions, on the other hand, help to clarify the content and provide immediate feedback to the lecturer on how well the content is understood. The students are no longer passive participants in the classroom interaction, but have an active role in the teaching-learning situation. Teacher questions keep students on their toes, attending to the lecture content, since they may be called upon to give an answer at any time.

Questioning can be used as a *pre-testing screening tool* to determine whether a particular topic should be taught. There are two reasons for this. First, it may be necessary to ascertain whether the class wishes to study an *optional section* of the course. For example, it may not be practical to cover all the possible application areas of computers. The teacher can give the students a feeling of responsibility by having them select those topics which should be taught. Ask questions such as: "What computer applications do you want to learn about—sports, government, law? You choose the topics." Or, ask an open-ended question: "What are some of the computer application areas you wish to discuss this semester?"

Second, the teacher may need to determine what the class *already knows.* The decision can be based on a short verbal test given at the start of the topic, or on a pretest. Because of the consequences of making an incorrect conclusion, the test must accurately examine the students' knowledge of important aspects of the area, as well as assess the depth of that knowledge. Also, there must be enough questions to get an adequate sampling of all the students in the room. A single question, "Do you know how to draw flowcharts?" is not enough. It requires merely a yes/no answer, and the students could avoid doing the work by falsely answering "Yes." A better approach is to draw a flowchart on the chalkboard and ask different students to explain portions of it; what they know about flowcharting will quickly become apparent. If the teacher is uncertain about the validity of such verbal testing, a pencil and paper test can be used instead.

Questions play a key role in *student discussions* about computers. They are usually the starting point of a discussion, and thus set the theme for the rest of the session. Questions such as "Are computers making us less human?" or "How have computers changed our lives?" are used to get the ball rolling. In addition, they could be used in the middle of the discussion to stimulate student thinking or to get the discussion back on course if it has been sidetracked.

Questions are the main vehicle for learning about the computing *backgrounds and personal lives of the students.* In the early stages of the course, questioning should be used to find out if the students own computers; why they are taking computer studies; and whether they intend to become computer scientists. The main goal is to get to know the students better and make them feel that the instructor is interested. The process also allows class members to get to know each other.

Questions can be used to obtain *feedback* on *how well the students are doing.* If a student consistently is unable to answer the teacher's questions, additional questioning can be used to pinpoint the problem. Unfortunately, in-depth questioning of every student is difficult if the class size is too large. Thus, only gross measures of student behavior—such as identifying pupils who are not working or who are having difficulty understanding the computer studies material—can be obtained by verbal questioning.

Another goal of question-and-answer sessions is to gain *feedback on the quality of the course*—to appraise both the content and the method of delivery. If the students consistently answer the questions correctly, then the instructor probably is teaching well (or the questions may be too easy). On the other hand, if questions are consistently answered incorrectly, then something is wrong and a change is warranted.

Questioning allows a forum for the students to *express their opinions* or to *relate their experiences.* Such activities make the students feel that they have something to contribute and that their ideas are worthwhile.

To get students to offer an opinion, ask questions like "Are computers intelligent? Why or why not?" and "Does the latest type of disk drive have any advantages over its predecessor? If so, what are they?"

To get students to relate their experiences, ask questions such as: "What did you see on TV this week pertaining to computers?" or "If you were in a computer store recently, what new thing(s) did you see?"

Getting Students to Participate

In the computer studies course, the primary motive for using questioning techniques is to increase student participation. The goal is to create an atmosphere in which all the students are eager to answer questions, even those students who are shy or uncertain of their expertise. However, unless the teacher makes an effort to involve everyone, the situation quickly arises in which only a few individuals answer the questions—probably those who have a computing background. The teacher must strive to include everyone, using the following suggestions.

At the beginning of the school year, sit down with the class and explain carefully *what is expected of them,* pointing out that everyone is expected to answer questions and that if they don't volunteer, they will be asked directly. Set the stage for maximum participation by using questions that have *many valid responses.* For example, the question "What is an example of a microcomputer which can be bought in a computer store?" has a number of correct answers. With such questions, there is an excellent chance that all the students will be able to give a correct answer, and the probability is increased that students will volunteer an answer the next time.

An example of a question which has many possible correct answers follows.

Q: Now that we have covered the ways in which disks are used, can you name an application area for which they are suited? (pause) Bill?
A: Airline reservations . . . since they need to keep data on flights.
Q: That's good. How about you, Sandra?
A: In a personnel office, they keep track of employees' names on a disk.
Q: Fine. Any more, Edward?
A: In the school here, to store all our programs.

The teacher could involve several more students with this particular question, there are so many possible answers. Note that although this question is not thought-provoking, it did achieve its primary goal which was to produce student participation. Note also that the teacher did not respond to or discuss the student replies, other than to make a favorable comment such as "good" or "fine." The same question was simply redirected to another student.

Another example of *question redirection* follows:

Q: Now that we have discussed software packages in class, name some packages which you have used recently. Joanne?

A: The game we were playing yesterday—Asteroids, I think.
Q: Good. Any more? Tony?
A: PAC-MAN!
Q: That's right. Those are both games. Are there any software packages other than games? Stan?
A: The word processing package on your computer.
Q: Good, what's the name of that package? Anyone?
A: WORDPRO!

In both examples, except for the last question in the second example, the teacher did not ask for volunteers but directed the question to specific students. This approach is good because it spreads the interaction throughout the classroom, keeps the students alert, and is so open-ended that anyone will be able to come up with a reasonable answer.

Another way to encourage students to participate is to provide *clues* on either the way the students are expected to respond or what the answer actually is. This approach is invaluable when dealing with students who are unsure of their answer but realize it is correct when they receive the clue. It is also recommended practice when asking questions at the beginning of the course when it is desirable to get off on the right footing.

There are several ways to provide clues when asking questions. First, *indicate what not to include* in the answer. Say, for example, "Besides disks and tapes, what are examples of magnetic storage media?" In this case, students are led to zero in on the correct answer. By supplying the hints "disks and tapes," the respondent is reminded of what the term "magnetic storage media" means.

Another technique is to *use leading questions.* For example, "Disks are relatively slow compared to primary memory. How fast can they store data?" Here we establish a frame of reference with respect to disk speeds. If the students know the speed of memory access, they have a clue as to the speed of the disk.

Provide the *right answer as one of several alternatives* and ask the student to select the correct one. For example, "Which one loses its information when the power is turned off—ROM or RAM?"

Provide an indication of the *form of the correct answer.* For example, "What word beginning with *a,* stands for a series of steps leading to the solution of a problem?" "What is the term used for the sending of money electronically? Its abbreviated form is 'EFTS.' " "Paper output is called hardcopy. Output which is destined for a VDU is known as (the teacher writes _____ copy on the chalkboard). "What is the four-letter word which means an 8-bit group of adjacent bits?"

Students will be more likely to respond if the teacher allows the class *time to think* about the question. At least three seconds should elapse between the end of the question and the solicitation of the response. Three seconds is the lower boundary for simple questions; harder ones will require more "think time," especially if calculations or problem-solving are necessary. For instance, questions like, "What is the command used in BASIC for branching to a subroutine?" will not need more than three seconds. However, if a flowchart is displayed on the overhead projector and the students are asked what the algorithm represents, a much longer time interval is necessary.

Plan to have a few questions *designed for certain pupils.* These may include difficult and challenging ones, like "Sam, what do you think is the reason for requiring one-sided diskettes to always be placed in the drive in the same way?" and simpler ones like: "Gerrard, which way do we insert a diskette into the drive?" In addition, make sure to include some questions that a particular individual—especially the reticent one—will be able to answer.

Dealing with Student Answers

Sometimes the answer to a question is *perfect;* more often, the teacher will not be this lucky. Sometimes the answer is *totally wrong;* sometimes it is *partially correct,* but insufficient because it lacks depth; or, if one asks for volunteers, there may be *no answer* because no one is willing to try.

When the student gives a correct answer, the teacher's role is straightforward. Acknowledge the response so that the individual is rewarded for the effort and the rest of the class knows the answer was right. Dealing with answers that are less than perfect is more difficult. It does not suffice to say "wrong" or "that's not it" and then turn to another student for the answer. The actual approach taken by the teacher depends upon the nature of the incorrect response: whether it is totally wrong, partially correct, or silence.

Wrong answers. If the answer is totally wrong, do not go on to another student; instead, try to elicit the correct answer—or at least a partially correct one—from the student. The intent here is to avoid leaving the student in a state of failure.

In order to help the student get on the right track, prompts and clues are necessary. Here are two examples.

Q: What is a disk used for, John?
A: Don't know.
Q: Could you use it to store your program?
A: Yes.
Q: That's right. In what other ways can it be used?

or

Q: What is the CPU's function in the computer, Alex?
A: To store your program!
Q: That's the memory's job. What about the CPU? Perhaps if you think about its name, it will help. What does CPU stand for?
A: Central Processing Unit.
Q: Right, now try again. What do you think the CPU does?
A: Processes.
Q: You've almost got it. But we need to know what it processes. Do you remember?
A: Oh yes! It runs the program.
T: That's right! Remember, class, the CPU executes the program which is residing in the memory of the machine.

In both cases, the teacher helps the student come up with a suitable answer. In the first example, this is accomplished in a direct fashion. The student is given the simple choice of responding "yes" or "no"; the teacher supplies the rest.

In the second example, the approach is more complex. Instead of giving the answer, the teacher gets the student to generate an answer—at least a partially correct one—by a series of well-placed clues and prompts and then sums up with a complete answer. The role of the student is more active than in the first example; more student thinking is accomplished.

In some situations, no matter how hard the teacher tries, the student cannot be coaxed to offer a correct answer. When this occurs, take time to explain what the answer should have been, both for the individual's benefit and for the rest of the class. Ascertain the reasons for the student's difficulty so that appropriate remedial actions can be taken.

A student's failure to answer could be because he or she has not done the homework and doesn't know enough to give an answer. Or, the student finds it difficult to understand the topic on which the question is based, and therefore cannot produce a suitable answer. In this case, remedial assistance is warranted.

Partially correct answers. If the student's answer is partially correct but lacks substance, the approach is to work with the student until a satisfactory answer is obtained. This is necessary so that neither the student nor the rest of the class is left with the impression that the first answer was a good one. It also benefits the student, who feels capable of more than just the first simple incomplete answer.

In developing a better student response, a good technique to use is *probing*. Probing requires the student to further explain or justify the original response in some way. Examine the following interaction.

Q: Do you think that well designed programs are easier to debug than poorly designed ones? . . . Stan?
A: Yes.
Q: Why, Stan?
A: Because they have fewer errors.
Q: Why would that be?
A: Well, the programmer takes more care in deciding what he is going to do; there is less chance of errors because he understands the program better.
Q: Do you mean all kinds of errors—syntax, run-time, logic?
A: No, the major kind would be logical; a well-designed program would have fewer logical errors.
Q: Very good! So what you are saying is that a programmer who takes care with the program design will ultimately have fewer logical errors and an easier task of debugging.

Here the teacher gets the student to explain the answer until the final response has more substance. Observe that the student really knew more than was originally revealed with the first responses. Teacher probing helped reveal additional knowledge.

Lack of response. Finally, we have the case in which no answer is forthcoming—silence reigns in the room. At this point, there is a great temptation for the teacher to take the easiest route, which is to answer the question.

Q: Who knows what bubble memory is?
A: (Fidgeting, silence)
Q: No one knows? Didn't you do your homework last night? Oh, well! I'd better tell you, because you need to know what it is for the next topic.

The teacher has made a mistake by answering the question. The effect is to reward students for inactivity. What can be done instead? The technique which is adopted depends partly on the reason for the lack of an answer: the students know the answer but are reluctant to cooperate; the question may have been poorly worded and hard to understand; perhaps the students understood the question but do not know the answer; or maybe the teacher gave insufficient think-time.

In the first case, the teacher needs to develop a more *positive attitude* to question-answering. In the second case, a *rewording or rephrasing* of the question is necessary. For example:

Q: Why is non-destructive reading of a tape desirable?
A: (No response; no one knows what the term "non-destructive" means)
Q: Let's try again. When you read information from a tape into memory, the original data on the tape is not destroyed but remains intact. Why is this desirable?

In the third case, where the students do not have the background to answer the question, it is necessary to *backtrack* and teach the necessary material. The only other alternative is to retract the question; unfortunately, this will make the students wonder why the question was asked to begin with. Here is an example of backtracking in response to student difficulty with a question.

Q: Now that we have studied output devices, perhaps someone can tell me why companies use computer output microfiche as an alternative to printed copy.
A: We haven't covered that topic, sir.
Q: I haven't? I guess you're right. Well, we had better do something about that right away.

A mini lecture may follow, or the teacher might direct the class to the necessary background material by stating: "Well, there is a good description of it in the textbook, Chapter 6. Read it tonight and we will pick up from there."

Some Other Tips for Good Questioning

Observe good questioners in action and see how they elicit responses from their classes. There are films available depicting the proper techniques for question-and-answer sessions.

Avoid using question-and-answer sessions in a *large class.* It is hard to get everyone to participate, for large audiences are intimidating to some students. The physical characteristics of a large room also work against the teacher; many times the students are unable to hear each other.

Do not ask *too many questions;* this is easy to do when quizzing students on computer studies jargon. Some teachers have been known to ask two or three hundred questions a day—or, approximately one question a minute! The number of questions asked should depend on the level of the class, the subject matter, and the detail required in the answers.

If necessary, prepare some of the *key questions* before entering the classroom; a question may require intricate wording, or it may need exactly the right phrasing. Make up the rest of the questions during normal classroom interaction.

An important key question might be, "In what ways did you interact with a computer over the weekend?" Suppose that the teacher is using this question as the focal point of a discussion on personal computers where the purpose is to motivate the students to reflect on how they could use the computer. The question therefore is critical to the ensuing discussion.

Suppose a five- or six-line program segment is displayed on the overhead. The teacher asks this intricately worded question: "What do you think this short program does?" Such a question must be prepared in advance so that it is free of errors or examples of poor programming.

The instructor should word questions in language which the students *understand;* avoid using unknown computer science *jargon;* keep the *grammar* and *format* of the questions simple; and keep the questions *short* so that the students can remember them. Here are some examples of badly-worded questions. Try to turn them into well-worded ones. The question "Why do common carriers have different tariffs for wide-band data communication links?" involves too much jargon; at least four terms must be understood in order to comprehend the question. In the question "What effectuates the displacement of the read/write contrivance?" the vocabulary is too difficult; furthermore, the big words are unnecessary—the question can be rephrased.

Questions are sometimes too wordy and complex: "When is the hardcopy printer used, and when would you use a softcopy? There are some application areas that are better-suited to using printed output—getting listings of a program, for instance; on the other hand, CRT's have their advantages. So why would you use one rather than the other?" If the students haven't fallen asleep by the time the question is asked, they will probably be dazed trying to figure out what the question really is. Keep it short and simple.

Be certain to *reinforce correct answers* to questions. Give a positive response, and then add a favorable comment. This will indicate that you were listening to the student's answer. You might also add a short comment, giving new information to enrich the topic for the entire group. New interest may be stimulated and any errors in knowledge and thinking clarified.

Questions that are too *indefinite* are not good. For example, "What do we know about computers?" is too open-ended. The class may not have a clue on what is expected for an answer. To ask "In what ways have computers improved our daily lifestyle?" is superior because the question now has a definite focus.

Do not ask *two or more questions* at the same time; confusion will invariably result. To ask, "Why are low-level programming languages different from high-level languages, and under what circumstances would a programmer use a low-level language?" requires two different lines of thought. Split the question into two parts and ask them consecutively.

Don't *repeat* the student answer to the *rest of the class.* This encourages the student to address the teacher and not the classmates. It also encourages the rest of the students not to pay attention to the answer, since they know the teacher will repeat it.

Categories of Questions

There are many kinds of questions that can be asked in the computer studies classroom. They range from the simple, easy-to-answer variety to those requiring much thought and high-level interpretation.

Low-level questions. Low-level questions involve recall of information and regurgitation of facts. They are the most frequently used questions—not necessarily because they are an example of good teaching practice, but because they are easy to formulate. Low-level questions typically request the student to define, state, list, identify, or describe—for example:

1. *Define* what a program is.
2. *List* three kinds of errors.
3. *Who was* Herman Hollerith?
4. *Identify* two kinds of storage media.
5. *What is* the technical term for the blinking dot on the screen?
6. *What was* the first computer ever built?
7. *State* the two reasons for using a parallelogram in a flow chart.

Some key words which generally indicate low-level knowledge questions are: *understand, recall, recognize, acquire,* and *outline.*

Making up low-level questions is usually straightforward. However, if problems arise, consult the questions found at the end of the chapters of most computer studies texts; many of them are low-level.

Higher-level questions. On a slightly higher level are questions which ask the student to explain material in their own words. By doing this, the student shows a better understanding of a topic. Examples follow:

In your own words, tell me how a computer executes a program.
Prepare a simple flowchart.
Distinguish between a flowchart and pseudocode.
Demonstrate by example which works faster—the tape or diskette.
Summarize the textbook section on the diskette.
Are tapes superior to disks? *Why? Why not?*
Differentiate between input data and output data of a computer system.
Defend the "cashless society" by giving pros and cons which can be substantiated.

In all these examples, knowledge on a low level is still required by the student; however, now the students must describe this knowledge using their own words rather than those dictated by the teacher or listed in a textbook.

Thought-provoking questions. While low-level questions are necessary to learning, they must be accompanied by more thought-provoking questions to get the students thinking rather than merely memorizing. The following are examples of categories of high-level questions.

In the first category, the teacher asks the students to use the information which they possess to solve problems, predict events, or seek relationships.

1. *What is the future* of the tape drive in business?
2. Given the following arithmetic statement, *what would it produce* as output?
3. What *predictions* can you make based on your readings regarding future input devices in computing?
4. Describe how you would *use* the computer to solve a problem in business mathematics.
5. How do you *maintain* a good log of the programs you need?

The next category requires the students to make an analysis, categorize, or choose between two or more items.

1. Here are two solutions to a problem to be solved on the computer. *Select* the one you consider to be the better solution.
2. *Analyze* a given program and *make modifications* which will make it run more efficiently.
3. What are the *bugs* in this program?

The next level requires the students to create, plan, design, or integrate information. They must visualize or compile information into a newly organized pattern.

1. From the discussion on documentation, what *conclusions* can you draw?
2. *Relate* your own experiences—such as you have acquired on your latest field trip—to what you have read in this chapter.

The highest level questions require students to appraise, compare, and make judgments or evaluations upon which decisions are made. They are usually expected to justify their answers.

1. Do you think computers are harmful to society? From your *research* on the topic, *justify* your response.
2. Now that we have looked at various kinds of computer equipment, what would you *consider* buying for your home? Give the reason for making the choice.
3. How do microcomputers *differ* from mainframes? How are they the same? Which would have the greatest benefits for *use* in business and *why?*

REWARD MECHANISMS

Getting students to work in the computer studies class can sometimes be frustrating and time consuming. Merely telling them that they must work or they will fail is frequently an unfruitful approach. An interest in learning the material—either an intrinsic liking of the subject matter or one instilled by the teacher—is a necessity in overcoming the motivational problem. Even so, students can lose interest if they are not rewarded and encouraged to be industrious.

The teacher can provide reward mechanisms to get students to work. A particularly effective *award* might be the presentation of a "certificate of achievement" to students who reach certain goals.

Grant *special privileges* to students who work hard. Such privileges might include access to computer games or other software; access to the computer during special and additional times; and the honor of working as an assistant doing minor equipment maintenance such as paper changing, dusting, or ribbon replacement.

Praise and encouragement are always worthwhile motivators when appropriate. Remember that many aspects of computer science can be frustrating, especially certain phases of programming. A lot of students find programming difficult and often become negative when they are unable to solve a problem or debug their software. Encouragement to keep on trying or praise for past accomplishments can work wonders for maintaining student self-esteem. It is also important for students to realize that encountering problems is a normal phenomenon when writing programs.

Similar encouragement can be achieved through *peer recognition.* Most students thrive on acknowledgment by their fellow classmates. The teacher can easily set the stage for this by displaying good work on the bulletin board, leaving copies of well written programs for the perusal of other students, or handing copies of this work around the class.

QUESTIONS

1. Develop a mini lesson plan for a three-day session on the history of computing, and show which parts would be best conveyed by the lecture technique.
2. Make a videotape of your own lecture on a computer studies topic; then critically analyze it with your peers.
3. Outline the instructions you would give a student lecturer in order to optimize the quality of the student's presentation.
4. Make up a crossword puzzle using the jargon on input/output.
5. Visit a video arcade or game store and find examples of games which:
   a. have little pedagogical value.
   b. could be used for teaching purposes.
6. Define the following terms: computer games, demonstration, gaming, leading question, lecture, lesson plan, low-level question, methodology, probing, question-and-answer, small group discussion, strategy, technique.

7
Teaching Resources for Computer Studies

This chapter details the vast amount of teaching resources available to the teacher of computer studies. Such resources typically are used to augment teaching methods, strategies, or techniques, although some of the resources can be used alone and become methodologies in their own right. Figure 7-1 lists the resources available to computer studies teachers for classroom use.

BOARDS

The board is one of the oldest and most widely-used tools found in the classroom. In one form or another it has been around for thousands of years. The traditional format involves a green or black slate board on which the teacher writes with chalk. Such chalkboards are used by the majority of computer studies teachers.

Categories of Boards

The covered chalkboard. The covered chalkboard is used to hide pre-written materials such as programming assignment solutions, flowcharts, tests, assignments, or drills so that the students cannot read the material in advance. This can be accomplished by placing cardboard or paper over the board, or by having a sliding chalkboard where one of the boards can be moved in front of the other. By preparing the computer program in advance, the teacher can ensure that the presentation is neat and accurate. Furthermore, valuable class time is not wasted. With the sliding chalkboard, the area is effectively increased by 50 to 100 percent, allowing the production of larger programs and flowcharts.

The white board. The white board (Figure 7-2) uses an erasable felt pen; hence it is free of dust—a dust-free environment is recommended for computing

FIGURE 7-1 Teaching Resources

boards	chalkboards	bulletin boards
	magnetic boards	felt boards
	white boards	flip charts
transparencies	diazo film	photocopy film
	picture lifts	thermal film
still projection	filmstrips	microfilm
	slides	opaque projection
	videodisks	videotapes
motion pictures	films	videodisks
	film loops	videotapes
	television	
audio techniques	tapes	disks
real objects	mockups	working models
	models	real things
	props	static displays
reading/pictorial	books, textbooks	flash cards
	brochures	handouts
	cartoons	journals
	coloring books	magazines
	comic books	manuals
	diagrams	newspapers
	dictionaries	photographs
	drawings	posters
	encyclopedias	wall charts

FIGURE 7-2 The white board and flip chart are excellent visual media for augmenting or replacing the chalkboard. They are especially useful in a computing laboratory environment.

equipment. *Chalk dust* can get into a keyboard and cause it to malfunction; if it settles on a diskette surface, it damages the disk head or the surface of the disk.

White board pens come in many colors. Flowcharts, programs, and computer logic diagrams can be easily and attractively color coded to separate the sections visually and make them easier for the student to understand.

The magnetic board and felt board. The magnetic board is a steel board to which magnetic-backed objects can be attached. Metal boards and white boards can be used as magnetic boards. A variety of computing materials can be fastened to the board with a magnet, or a magnetic strip can be attached to the back of the object. Examples include cutouts of equipment from computer magazines, posters obtained from computer vendors, photographs of appliances in the home which contain microprocessors and block diagrams of the components of a computer.

One advantage of the magnetic board is that objects can be moved around or replaced easily; this is not possible with the ordinary chalkboard.

Felt boards are covered with felt or flannel. These can be used as a substitute for the magnetic board. The objects are backed with flannel, felt, sandpaper, or garnet paper which adheres to the felt board. It is used primarily with small children, but can be used with all grade levels.

The flip chart. The flip chart is a pad of large sheets of paper, generally inexpensive newsprint, which hangs on an easel (Figure 7-2). The easel can be moved around so it can be seen from anywhere in the room. This mobility can be useful in a room full of microcomputers if the chalkboard or white board is not conveniently placed. The flip chart, like the white board, is dust free.

Bulletin boards. Bulletin boards come in all sizes, shapes, and materials. All kinds of things can be attached, including three-dimensional objects made of paper, metal, fabric, or yarn. Examples of materials which can be displayed are journal articles, templates, small robots and examples of student work.

When to Use Boards

This media may be used at any level and for most computer studies content. The chalkboard is a good *aid to lecturing*—for displaying key points, to help organize the material, and to keep the teacher on topic. All boards can help in giving *demonstrations*—such as the correct way to start up a computer or guidelines for handling and storing diskettes.

The contents of the board can be used effectively as an aid to the *discussion* method. Material is placed on the board and used as a guide or focus for subsequent discussion; or the board is used to summarize key points made by the students as the discussion progresses. A particularly useful application is in discussing flowcharting or programming.

How to Use the Board Effectively

Write in a *straight line.* Make the letters big enough to be seen from the back of the room. Before the class comes in, write on the board, then walk to the back of the room and determine whether the student sitting in the back row of the classroom can read what has been written and, at the end of the class period, check to see how visible and organized the chalkboard work actually was. Don't write on the entire span of the chalkboard. Instead, *divide* the board into "*pages*" by drawing vertical lines and always work from the left edge of the chalkboard to the right. Never jump around erasing a portion of the board to insert extra material. If the teacher wishes to keep a permanent section—one used only for key points developed throughout the class period—it should be placed in one of the "pages" at either end of the board and labeled appropriately.

To draw diagrams and other illustrations, consider projecting the image on the board with an overhead projector or a slide projector, and trace the outline of the picture on the board (Figure 7-3). Use *templates* (wooden or plastic) for drawing the boxes of a flowchart or the shapes of equipment such as disks, tapes, terminals. These keep the work neat and speed up the production of diagrams (Figure 7-4).

Don't talk to the board; that is, avoid speaking with your back to the class. Write on the board, then turn around and begin talking.

FIGURE 7-3 A good way to draw diagrams on the board is to trace the image projected by an overhead.

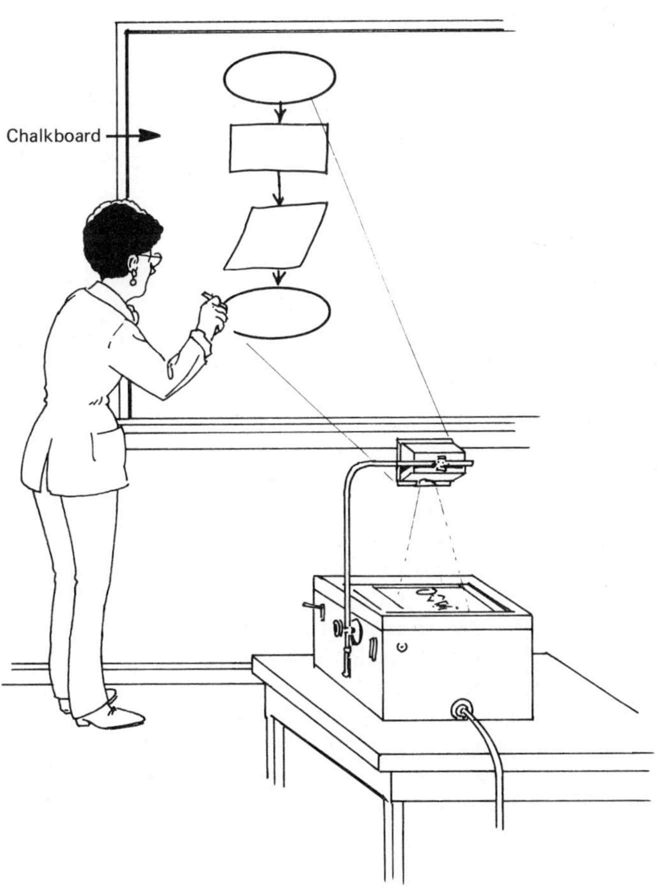

FIGURE 7-4 Wooden flowcharting templates can be used to draw large flowcharts on the chalkboard or flip chart.

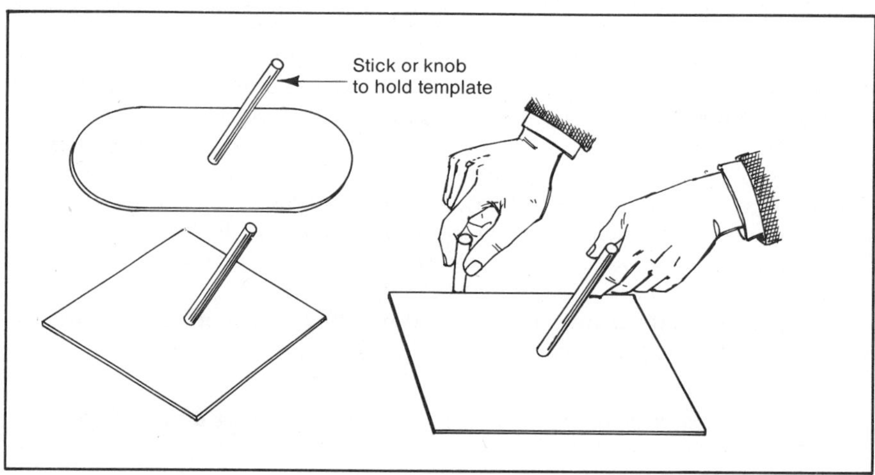

Expect the students to take notes on what is written on the board. Make it relevant and legible. The teacher should not prepare material beforehand for *verbatim* copying onto the board—programs, for example. Creating *handouts* saves valuable class time; however, bringing prepared material to class limits flexibility and the ability to adjust to changing conditions.

TRANSPARENCIES

The transparency (sometimes referred to as a *foil*) for the overhead projector is one of the most useful media for displaying textual information and drawings. The standard transparency consists of a clear plastic (acetate) sheet or continuous role of acetate film. The teacher writes information on this acetate sheet, which is then projected onto a screen or light-colored wall. Teachers use special permanent or water-soluble pens or wax pencils to write on the plastic. Another way to make transparencies is to copy handwritten or photocopied documents directly on the transparency by using one of several techniques.

If the teacher does not wish to use homemade transparencies, previously prepared material depicting computing content—usually in the form of *transparency masters*—is available from many publishers. In fact, many introductory computer studies textbooks have a selection of transparency masters; the master is simply copied on to the acetate sheet by using a thermal or photocopier.

A special form of transparency, the *overlay,* consists of more than one sheet of plastic, joined together at one edge and layered (Figure 7-5). Each transparency has a small portion of the image on it. As the teacher folds each transparency into place, talking about each new section as it is presented, the image develops until it reaches its completed form. Such overlays are extremely useful for successively presenting the lines of a program, for systematically displaying the parts of a flowchart, or for developing diagrams of the operation of computing equipment.

FIGURE 7-5 The transparency overlay. This is used in teaching about the functional components of a computer system.

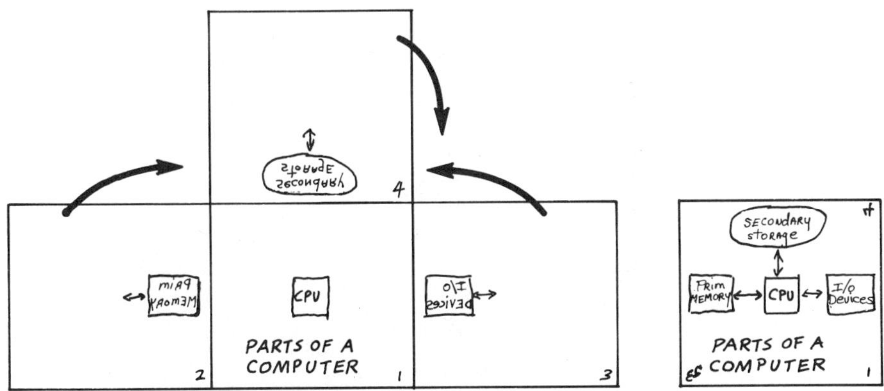

How are Transparencies Used?

The transparency can be used as an aid to the lecture. As the lesson progresses, the teacher either displays prepared transparencies or develops an outline on a blank transparency. The contents of a transparency can be used as the focal point for student discussions by either displaying a controversial issue for the students to examine or by itemizing the points that the teacher wishes to be discussed.

The overhead projector can be used to display copies of examination questions, student programs, and any material that is difficult or expensive to duplicate.

Transparencies can be used by students in their "show and tell" seminars. Transparent objects, such as flowcharting templates, may be displayed effectively on the overhead projector (Figure 7-6). Since the transparencies act as a record of a teacher's lecture notes, students can review the material independently. Continuous-roll transparencies serve this function best.

Ways to Make Transparencies

There are several ways to make a transparency, depending upon the kind of material to be copied and the quality of reproduction desired. The simplest way is to write or draw directly on the acetate sheet with either *marker pens* or *wax pencils.* The pens and pencils come in many colors and the pens can be either water soluble or permanent.

A *picture lift* is the simple process of taking a photograph or text from a computer magazine or journal and transferring it directly to an acetate sheet. There are commercially prepared materials to assist you in transferring the image, or you may use mac-tac, con-tac, or other transparent adhesive shelf paper (Figure 7-7). *Diazo film* utilizes a "blueprint" process to transfer the images onto the plastic sheet. Multicolor products are possible with this process. The *thermal technique* is the most popular way of producing transparencies. In using this method, an origi-

FIGURE 7-6 The overhead projector can be used to display real objects which are placed directly on the stage of the projector. The teacher uses a pencil to direct student attention to the area of the flowcharting template which she is describing.

nal or master of the image first must be prepared; the original is then transferred to the acetate sheet. Most *photocopiers* can be used to make transparencies directly onto mylar film. The toner is fixed onto the film in the same way photocopies are made on paper.

Comparison of Chalkboards and Transparencies

Of all the media available for use in the computer studies classroom, the two most commonly used are the overhead projector and the chalkboard. They provide moment-to-moment adaptability, allowing the teaching materials to be created as the educator talks. Programs can be developed or altered, flowcharts can be adapted, parts of a piece of hardware can be drawn or described systematically, and outlines of presentations can be made.

Which media is better? The answer is not clear, although transparencies seem to be more versatile. Figure 7-8 itemizes the major points of comparison between the two media.

FIGURE 7-7 Making a picture from a magazine article can produce a useful overhead transparency.

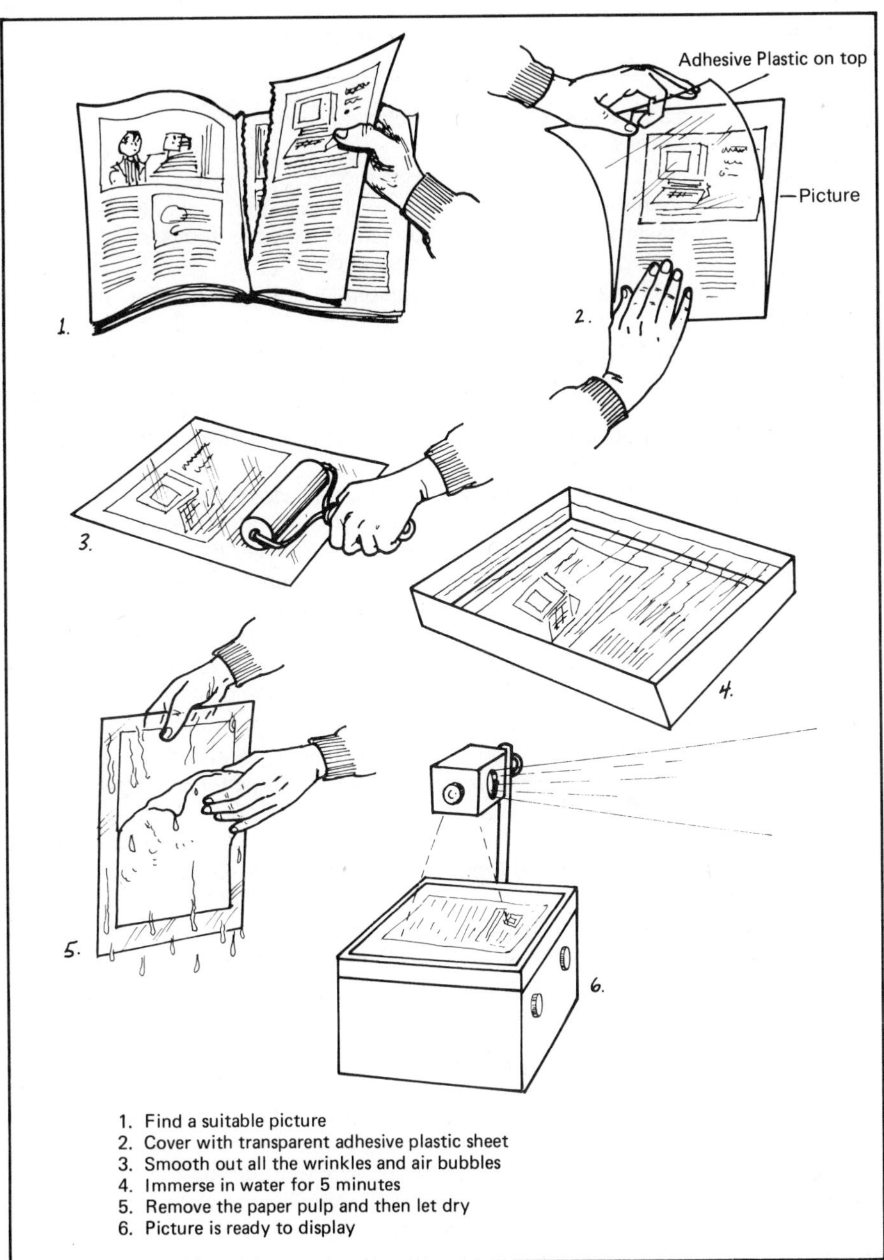

FIGURE 7-8 Comparison of Chalkboards and Transparencies

Chalkboard	Transparency
Traditional media that has been with us a long time and is widely accepted	Relatively new media
Stationary media	Has mobility
A ubiquitous technology which is found in every classroom	Unavailable in some schools because projector, screen, and special pens are needed
Chalk, even the dustless variety, can be messy	Equipment and pens are dust-free
Noiseless except for the squeak of the chalk	Motor may be noisy, masking instructor's voice
Hard to write quickly because of the size of writing required, and the angle of chalkboard	Teacher can write quickly, because the activity is just like writing on paper
Material must be erased once the board fills up; information is lost forever	Information does not have to be erased; the acetate sheets or roll can be saved or discarded
A large amount of information may be visible at all times	Only the contents of one sheet is visible at one time
Mainly used for displaying textual information; drawings are too time consuming	Illustrations, pages from books, and diagrams are easy to display; drawings may be done quickly
Chalkboard is sometimes hard to see	Easy to see, unless room is too bright
Color does not show up well	Color works well and is distinct
Teacher walks back and forth when writing on the board	Media encourages teacher to remain stationary near the projector; movement therefore must be purposeful
Hard to write on the board and face the class at the same time	Teacher naturally faces class when writing on the transparency
Teacher can send many students to write on the board simultaneously	Only one student at a time can write on the transparency

How to Make Good Transparencies

Whether the teacher makes transparencies by copying them from originals or by drawing them, a number of factors distinguish good ones from bad ones. If the transparency displays a picture or figure, be sure that the content of the transparency is *simple;* restrict the transparency to the single concept to be conveyed.

If the transparency contains textual information, limit the amount of information to several lines at the most. Use points or phrases rather than full sentences, and make the characters big enough to be seen by everybody in the room. Figure 7-9 shows recommended minimum sizes for letters that are visible when displayed on the screen.

FIGURE 7-9 A template for determining the size of the lettering on a transparency.

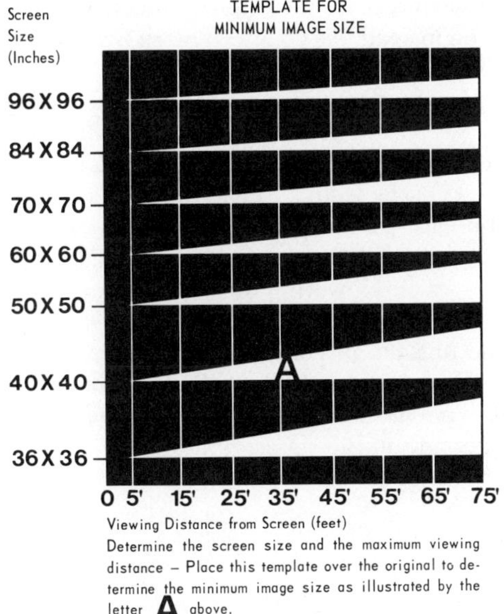

From *Secretary's Guide to Preparing Visuals* (London, Ontario: 3 M Canada, Inc.), p. 4. Used with permission of 3M Canada, Inc.

If drawing transparencies by hand, be sure that the *lettering is legible.* If you have difficulty writing in straight lines and find that the lines angle either upwards or downwards, tape a lined transparency guide onto the stage of the projector.

Use *color* to advantage, but restrict the selection to no more than three hues; if more than three are used, the color coding loses its meaning. The bulk of the text should be written in a dark shade such as black, dark blue, or dark green.

Using Transparencies Effectively

There are a number of points which, if followed, assist in giving a more polished delivery. First, *do not be too ambitious.* A common fault is to deliver a lecture with more transparencies than can be assimilated by the students. A fixed number per hour cannot be recommended, but the teacher should allow enough time for each transparency to be thoroughly read, discussed, and—where necessary—copied for notetaking before removing it.

Make sure the transparency *completely fills the screen.* Common errors are to have the overhead projector too close to the screen so that the image looks like a postage stamp on an envelope, or too far away so that the image overlaps the edges of the screen. Check the first transparency to be sure it is well positioned.

Use a *pen or plastic arrow* to highlight details on the image. When pointing, place the pen or arrow directly on the transparency so that the image of the pen or arrow does not waver or accidentally cover the important point. Never turn to look at or point to the screen; this distracts the students, who then turn their attention to you rather than the screen.

When writing on prepared transparencies, you may not want to damage the original; it is advisable to write on a blank sheet of acetate placed on top of the transparency or, even better, place the original underneath the continuous plastic roll and write on the roll instead. As you need more writing room, move the transparency upward as if it were a scroll.

When lecturing from transparencies, stand beside, rather than in front of or behind the projector. Keep the original paper master copy next to the projector so that it may read from rather than the transparency. Use the transparency as an outline of the key points of the lecture. Lead the students through the points one by one, expanding on each point as the lecture progresses. So that the students don't get ahead of you, reveal the points one at a time by covering the transparency with a piece of paper and lowering the paper to reveal the information point by point.

Don't make the mistake of completely darkening the room, as would be done when showing a film or slides. Only the lights immediately above the screen should be turned off. To *reduce the glare* and protect the eyes, tape a colored transparency (blue is suggested) on the stage, right on top of the glass. It will stay in place as the acetate roll is advanced.

STILL PROJECTION

Still projection is a commonly used media in which pictures, diagrams, or textual material are projected on to a screen. The carousel *slide projector* is the most widely used. Slides can be made by the teacher or purchased from a supplier. Fortunately, some excellent computer science slide series are available, ranging from slides of old computing equipment to those showing the latest trends in the technology. Purchased slides usually include a larger range of materials than could be photographed locally by the teacher.

A drawback to using slides often is the procurement of a slide projector. Another problem with slides is the relative inflexibility of the media once the lecture starts. The order and content of the slides dictate the order and content of the lecture, and it is difficult to skip to another topic, introduce new material, or back up for review without disrupting the flow of the slide show.

When to Use Slides

Despite these drawbacks, slides are an excellent pedagogical medium in the computer studies classroom. They can augment the lecture by introducing both *variety* and a second modality (visual) to learning. The student can now visualize the size, complexity, or other features of the object. Slides can show the *structure and function of computing equipment* which cannot be brought into the classroom. Slides also allow discussion of diagrams and figures from the textbook, such as charts, flowcharts, programs, and components from which slides have been made.

Making Good Slides

In making your own slides, there are a number of points to remember in order to have a quality product which is both pleasing and meaningful to the student. Adhere to all the rules which were detailed for making transparencies. Use *color film* rather than black and white. Take the photographs from the *student's perspective,* as if the photographer were looking over the student's shoulder. This should minimize confusion when the student tries to interpret the information on the slide. Finally, *eliminate any extraneous details* in a photograph or diagram that might distract or confuse the student.

Using Slides Effectively

Once the slides are obtained, there are a number of hints on how to use them properly. *Position* the screen at an *angle* in the front corner of the room, so that all students can see without peering around heads. Avoid reflected light, and watch for keystoning distortion due to the screen being at the wrong angle relative to the projector.

Use only those slides that pertain to the concept being taught in the lesson. *Never show more than forty slides per hour;* usually eight to fifteen per lesson will be sufficient. Show each slide long enough to allow the students to examine the contents thoroughly.

If you have individual slides, as opposed to filmstrips, *identify the content* of the slide on each frame for easy reference (Figure 7-10).

When not in use, maintain the slides within a slide library so they can be retrieved easily. Plastic page holders with pockets for individual slides are ideal for this purpose; each slide has a reserved location on a page. The pages can be stored in binders. When the pages are held up to the light, the slides can be readily examined for selection purposes (Figure 7-11).

Before showing the slides, have them ready in the carousel; preview their contents to make sure they are in the right order and correctly oriented. Keep a written list of slides so that you can skip certain ones or back up easily, if necessary.

FIGURE 7-10 Each slide in your collection should be labeled so that it is identifiable and can be easily oriented in the projector.

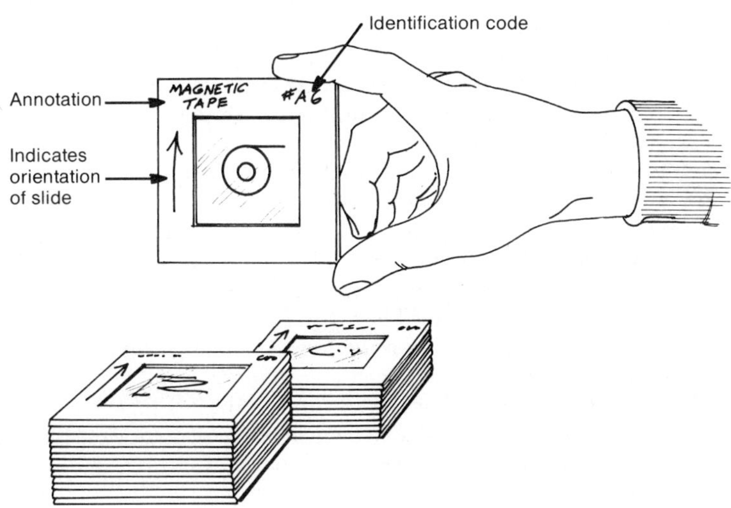

FIGURE 7-11 A slide holder may be necessary if the school has a large number of slides in its collection.

Variants of Slides

Other kinds of still projections include narrated slides, film strips—silent and sound, videotape with stills, videodisks, microfilm, and opaque projection.

The *narrated slide,* sometimes called a sound slide, involves coordinating a slide projector with an audio tape. *Filmstrips* are similar to slides. The photographic images are placed on a continuous length of film rather than in individual frames, with about twenty to fifty images or frames on each filmstrip. In this form, the cost per exposure is cheaper and the images are less susceptible to damage or loss. Filmstrips cannot get out of sequence because they have a fixed order of images. Some filmstrips, called sound filmstrips, have narrations similar to the narrated slide. Commercially prepared filmstrips are popular, and many computer science titles can be obtained.

Videotapes can be used in a manner similar to narrated slides. Still images are held on the screen for a predetermined amount of time while you discuss the image displayed on the screen. The major differences are in the equipment used—a videotape recorder and TV monitor. The order and pace of the presentation are inflexible; you must stop the recorder whenever you need to interject other techniques into the lesson presentation. There are some excellent computer science videotape presentations available, with the numbers increasing steadily.

The *videodisk* is a relatively new technology which is not yet popular in the schools. However, the versatility of the medium indicates that it will probably become a dominant audiovisual device. The disk resembles a normal phonograph record; however, it functions like a videotape, capable of storing a 30-minute television program on each side.

With the disk, a lot of control is possible on the playback. You can vary the speed of the playback, and the picture can run backwards or not at all. When used in the latter fashion, the device acts like a slide projector, and has the capacity of over 18,000 photographs per side. With a special attachment or under computer control, any of these slides can be selected within a fraction of a second. What does this mean for the teacher? All the slides for the entire computer science curricula can be stored on just one disk and distributed to every teacher in the school. Each teacher can then select the subset needed for individual lessons. As the curriculum changes, the slide collection can be easily updated and a new version of the disk distributed to the teachers.

The major disadvantage of the videodisk is that a master disk first has to be created from which copies can be made. This process, similar to the production of phonograph records, is expensive and must be done professionally. The original might cost several thousands of dollars to produce. Fortunately, the technology will become sufficiently advanced to allow users to create their own videodisks at reasonable cost.

Microfilm has been available to school systems for many years. It requires a microfilm reader, which is usually in the library or resource center. Since this machine can only be used by one student at a time and even big schools have only a few of them, their use is limited in computer studies.

The *opaque projector* allows the contents of a page from a textbook or magazine to be displayed directly onto the screen without first being transferred to a slide or transparency. In order to see the picture, the room must be very dark, making notetaking difficult. The opaque projector is excellent for classroom viewing of photographs and drawings from computer science textbooks, brochures, and manuals.

FILMS

One of the most useful media for computer science is the film. The teacher can get films on just about every aspect of computing: programming, applications of computers, effects on society, and the silicon chip industry. It is important to know what films are available and when they are available, and to validate their content in terms of grade level, jargon, interest, and value. Films should be previewed before they are shown to the class.

When showing movies, the room must be darkened in order for the images to be seen clearly, thus inhibiting note taking. However, this problem may be remedied with handouts of important notes. Many computer films are produced for the layperson and may be too simplistic for classroom use. Films quickly become outdated, and may discuss obsolete technology; some films, especially those on programming, may use content and teaching presentations that are inappropriate to the course.

Ways to Use Films

Although films have a number of drawbacks, they are fantastic additions to the computer science curriculum when used wisely. They can add *variety and excitement* to classroom activities; a good film can capture and hold the attention of the students where a lecture might not. Films bring the *real world of computing* into the classroom. Equipment and applications can be observed, and the state of the art can be portrayed.

Films and videotapes can *replace the live lecture.* In this form, known as the taped lecture, the presentation can be quite polished since its delivery can be perfected before it is recorded. Commercially available lectures are available on film for some computer studies topics.

A particularly powerful application of films is to *stimulate classroom discussions.* First the film is shown to the class; then particular items, such as controversial points, are discussed. For a long film, it is sometimes wiser to stop the projector partway through at a previously selected location, discuss the portion seen up to that point, then carry on with the next section.

Variants of Motion Pictures

Films are not the only way in which motion pictures can be shown. At least four other media are possible: videotapes, videodisks, film loops, and television programs.

There are a number of computer science *videotapes* available, and the list is expanding daily. These tapes come in three formats—VTR (VCR), VHS, and BETA—and the potential user should be aware of the equipment required to show each format. VTR units are older and more expensive; VHS and BETA are recent innovations, and the equipment and tapes are more economical than VTR. Videotapes have an advantage over films in that the room need not be darkened; students can take notes. Videotapes are cheaper than films and less susceptible to mechanical failure and damage. Also, some students might have their own videotape equipment, thus allowing them to view a copy of the tape at home.

Videodisks were discussed previously in the context of slides. Another application is for playback of films; when used this way, the videodisk functions like a videotape.

The *film loop* is a continuous strip of film joined at both ends. Its container is designed to permit repetition of the presentation until the teacher or student stops the machine. Film loops traditionally have been used for teaching repetitive skills. In the computer studies curriculum, few applications can be demonstrated in this way.

Television programs of educational films and documentaries are good ways for students to keep abreast of current events in the computing area. Ask the students to watch the program and then discuss its content in the class next day. Alternatively, if the school has a VTR, it is possible to tape the program (watch for copyright infractions) and bring it next day for presentation to the class.

Unfortunately, using TV programs in the computer studies curricula has some drawbacks. The program might be aired at an inconvenient point in the semester. A documentary on the economic impact of computers is not much use if the class is currently in the midst of learning how to program. Also, it is difficult to evaluate the content and quality of a TV program ahead of time, and you won't know if the computing content will be appropriate to the grade level and needs of the class.

AUDIO TECHNIQUES

This section deals with those media in which the student listens to someone speaking on devices such as *records, reel-to-reel tapes, audio cassettes,* and *videodisks.* It also includes live or recorded information like radio broadcast.

Ways to Use Audio

Audio technology has a number of uses in the computer studies classroom. It can be used to *replace the live lecture.* The speaker is recorded on an audio tape, which is played back to the class when required. Tapes can be used to "bring in" *outside speakers* to talk to the students. Experts, computer conference sessions, and visiting computer scientists can be recorded and played back whenever needed. A record, tape, or radio broadcast can provide the focal point for *classroom discussion.* The students listen to an audio playback or radio broadcast containing controversial statements or opinions, and then delve more deeply into the topic.

Listening to a radio broadcast can be prescribed as a homework assignment. There are numerous interesting and thought-provoking programs dealing with various aspects of computing.

Tapes can be used to deliver instruction of certain skills such as operating a disk drive or using a computer terminal. These instructions, which detail every stage in the activity being mastered, can be replayed many times as the student refines the ability to perform the task.

Making Tapes

Although numerous tapes on computing can be purchased on a commercial basis, many teachers make their own. They can tape *speakers* at a computer conference, tape *radio broadcasts,* or tape other *lecturers* in their school. Students can tape conversations or *interviews* which take place on field trips to computer installations, teachers can *record their own lectures* for use in the future. These tapes can also be used by the teacher as a mechanism for self-evaluation.

Problems with the Audio Media

Although using audio technology not supplemented by video technology can be quite useful, the media has drawbacks if not utilized properly. The visual modality is a crucial component to learning computing material, and its absence may have a detrimental effect when teaching equipment operation. Also, long radio broadcasts and recorded lectures can become boring unless performed with skill.

REAL THINGS, MODELS, AND MOCK-UPS

Computer studies students benefit from an opportunity to examine and/or manipulate, on a firsthand basis, the objects which they study. Secondhand experience is no substitute for contact with the real thing; therefore the teacher should try to provide exposure to items such as computers, disks, printouts, punched cards—the list is endless (Figure 7-12). The object can be brought into the classroom, or the students can go to the location, such as a computer store or museum, where the object can be studied.

While most examples of such objects will be actual items used in computing, some objects are too large or small to be suitable for student use (Figure 7-13); for example, the circuitry inside present-day microcomputers is too tiny to be seen by the unaided eye. As well, many items are simply too complex for the beginning student to understand, and using such objects creates confusion.

Because of this problem, it sometimes will be necessary to use a substitute rather than the real thing. These substitutes are known as *models* or *mock-ups*. A model is a representation of the actual object which has been enlarged or reduced in order to make it more suitable for human handling or observation. Thus, we might have an enlarged model of an integrated circuit or a reduced model of a mainframe computer. Some models may have part of the outer shell cut away so the student can see inside.

If the model has unimportant components left out, it is called a *mock-up*. The omission of parts is desirable when we want the student to attend to the essential details of an object, and not be distracted by other minor features.

Frequently, a model is capable of operating in a fashion similar to the real item. One useful feature of the working model is that it can be made to work faster or slower than the real thing. This is useful when demonstrating the rapid events occurring in a computer system. These events usually have durations which are

FIGURE 7-12 A sample of real objects which might be used in the computer science classroom.

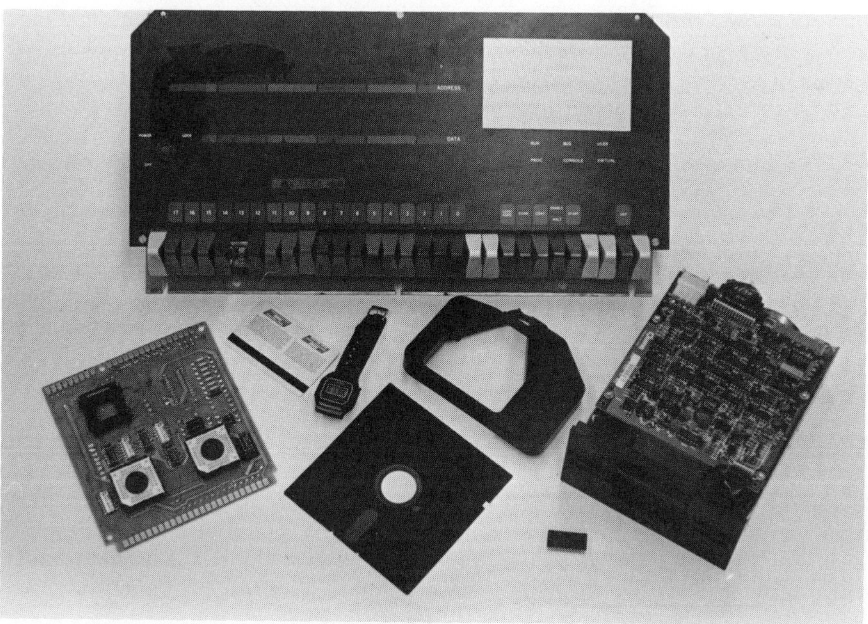

FIGURE 7-13 Some computing objects are too small to be seen by the unaided eye. This integrated circuit must be placed under a microscope in order to view its components.

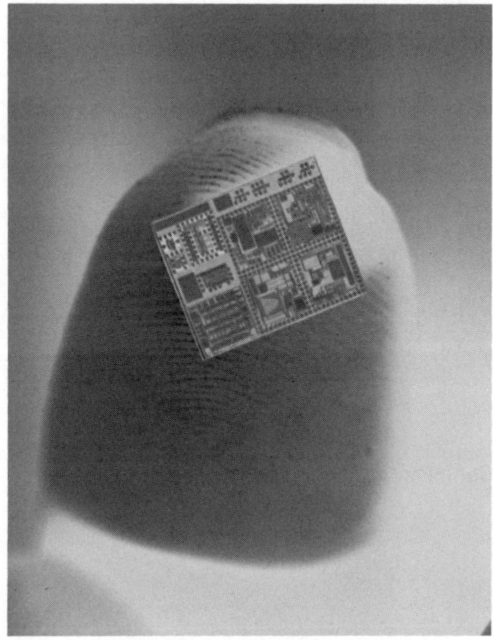

British Columbia Telephone Company

much too short to permit human observation; but if they are appropriately slowed down by using a working model, their demonstration becomes feasible.

Why Use Real Objects?

There are several important reasons for providing the computer studies students with opportunities for immediate contact with the real objects of their study. Manipulating—or even just viewing—the actual object adds a dimension of *realism* to the computer science curriculum. As a result, the student will get a better feel for the size of items; they will better appreciate the intricate nature of certain kinds of computer equipment; they will become aware of the need to handle computing equipment carefully and sensibly.

Seeing computing equipment up close is invaluable when learning about the rapid *advancements* that have been occurring in *computing technology:* plummeting costs, decreasing sizes, increasing speeds, or better reliability. These concepts are best conveyed by having available an array of equipment which spans several decades—for example, an object representing the vacuum tube era, another one characteristic of the transistor age, and a third one in use today.

Exposure to computer hardware will benefit the student outside the classroom. These objects will be *familiar* to the student, which is useful, especially when the student seeks employment.

Limitations of Using Real Objects

Although exposure to actual objects is desirable, there are drawbacks. Purchasing objects can become *expensive;* furthermore, it is distinctly possible that certain items will become *obsolete* and the school may end up with a costly collection of obsolete computing equipment. The goal is to either pick items which will not become obsolete or, wherever possible, borrow them.

Sometimes, bringing an object into the classroom adds nothing to the learning experience; *some computing equipment has no meaning* to the student in a visual sense (Figure 7-14). For example, holding up what appears to be a *black box* with cables trailing from it and stating that it is a XYZ component contributes nothing to the student's knowledge; the activity is a waste of time for both teacher and class.

Traveling to a place where computing devices can be viewed firsthand—a computer center or computer store—creates additional problems. The visit may *not* come at the *most appropriate time* in the semester. The effect is worse if the visit is

FIGURE 7-14 Some "real" objects, such as the "black box" being held by this teacher, have little meaning for the students.

conducted too soon, before the students have the background to appreciate what they are seeing. Also, the students may be exposed to *irrelevant details* which will compete with the important items and interfere with learning.

Using Real Objects

There are many ways to utilize real objects in the computer studies classroom; note some of the possibilities.

Objects shown by the teacher. A widely used technique for using objects is to show the object to the class while lecturing or demonstrating. Guest lecturers may visit the classroom and bring equipment to show the students.

Objects shown by the students. Actual objects can be incorporated into students' *show and tell* sessions or lectures (Figure 7-15). This adds interest and variety to their talk and also provides a framework for the student to work around. There are several sources students can tap when gathering computer-related objects for their talk. Items may be derived from the school's permanent collection

FIGURE 7-15 Real objects, such as the abacus, are used in Show and Tell.

or the student's own possessions, or may be borrowed from a public library or computer store.

Static displays. Computing equipment may be set out for viewing, but the students may be asked not to touch or manipulate the device. This is necessary if the equipment is borrowed or if it is delicate and susceptible to damage. Where more exposure is desired, the object should be located in an accessible area such as the resource center. If the object is too small to be seen clearly with the naked eye—optical fibers and integrated circuits fall in this category—provide a microscope or an *expanded model* of the object.

When laying out the display, the items should be *adequately labeled* and documented. Many teachers mistakenly display items without including a good explanation of what each object is and how it works. Each display should cover a single theme or concept, rather than a number of unrelated themes, such as a display of different kinds of secondary storage (disks, floppies, magnetic tapes). Other displays could be different kinds of computer systems; input media (cards, keyboards, paper tape, joysticks); or household devices containing microprocessors (digital watches, toys).

Objects manipulated by the students. Student manipulation is especially desirable if there are working models which must be handled in order to make them operate. There are a number of different possibilities for allowing manipulation of objects. *Hand around small objects,* such as diskettes, circuit boards, or printouts for each student to see at their desks (Figure 7-16). If the items are delicate, such as printed circuits, they should be placed in a protective container. To minimize the distraction, pass around objects after the lecture.

FIGURE 7-16 Some real objects can be handed around the class so students can have a closer look.

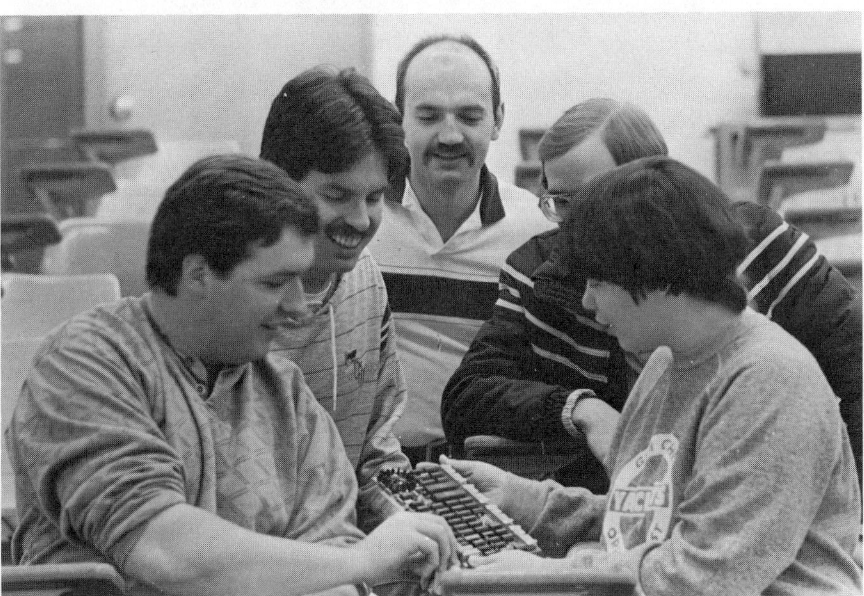

Allow the students to *assemble or disassemble computing equipment.* If the school owns a discarded computer, allow the students to open the cabinet, pull out boards and connectors, and put everything back in its original state. Keep mock-ups of different kinds of equipment—disks, tapedrives, or printers—which are made to be taken apart and put back together. Discarded digital watches, calculators, digital alarms, and other objects make excellent items for the students to examine. Always explain to the students what they are examining and why. Finally, keep a *microcomputer in the corner of the room* or in the resource center and encourage the students to use it whenever they wish.

Field trips. There are many places to see good examples of computing technology—*museums, data processing centers,* and *computing stores,* to name a few. The main problem with such visits is keeping the students from being distracted. To avoid this, *discuss* the field trip with the students *beforehand.* Point out what they will be seeing and emphasize the key points to which they should attend. For example:

> "Tomorrow we will be going to the computer center at City Hall. Inside, you will be seeing an array of equipment which is much more complex than what we have at school. However, don't be intimidated; this equipment is essentially the same but on a grander scale, and the computers are contained in several separate boxes rather than being integrated into a single box; there will be a CPU and memory and I/O equipment.
>
> "Look for the CPU; note its size. Look at the disks and note that removable hard disks are used. Examine the tape drives. Watch someone mounting a tape drive; look at the tape library; see if you can compute the overall capacity of the library. Observe the computer operator and the console where the computer system is controlled. Note the line printer—how fast does it print? Watch the paper change; what kind of paper does it use? Be aware of the security and climate controls within the computer room, and the raised floor—the wires between the terminals throughout the building are not visible because they are under the floor. Find the plotter; ask the operator to make the plotter draw a picture for you."

When visiting the site, ensure that a *knowledgeable person is on hand* to direct the students, point out items of interest, give explanations, and answer questions.

Incidental contact with computing equipment. Many opportunities will arise for the students to come in contact with computing equipment in other situations. For example, the students will have daily experiences with computing devices within their homes; they are bound to see something of interest when they go shopping (computer displays); they will probably use video games. When they go on vacation, they will have an ideal opportunity to see things which are not located in their own community, such as in museums.

Such experience is quite valuable. Take advantage of it, but make sure the student's contact is as meaningful as possible. Brief the students on what to look for when they are out on their own. Ask them to share their experiences with the rest of the class, and to acquire objects or brochures which can be brought to the class.

Using real objects for evaluation. Real computing devices can be used to get feedback on the students. The teacher might ask a student to identify a modem, describe its purpose, discuss its operation, or outline its structure.

Obtaining real objects. The biggest problem facing the teacher may be how and where to obtain real objects. While the easiest strategy is to *purchase* them, many computing devices are expensive. The school might consider alternatives, like *sharing* the equipment with other teachers; or, if practical, with other schools. Make use of equipment which is used for other purposes in the school. For example, borrow the electronic circuitry from the physics or electronic lab; or the class could visit the administrative offices and examine the word processing equipment.

Scour the *house* for devices which employ computing technology, like computerized games or digital radios. Ask the students to do the same. Look out for *hand-me-downs from computer manufacturers* and suppliers. These items are usually broken or no longer needed. A "dead" disk drive could be cut open to allow the students to see its inner parts.

Borrow equipment—it is usually available from public libraries, dealers, or other schools. Dealers frequently are willing to lend computing equipment; they recognize the market value of exposing their product to students.

What Real Objects Can Be Used?

A few commonly used objects you can utilize in the computer studies curriculum are listed in Figure 7-17.

READING AND VISUAL MATERIALS

There are many reading materials, pictures, and other textual matter that a teacher can use in the computer studies classroom. Computer studies is primarily a visual medium, so any additional material is useful.

Kinds of Materials

Books. Books are an excellent resource for teachers and students. The primary source of textual information is the *textbook.* Besides the main textbook, there are supplementary textbooks that the teacher can either keep in the classroom or in the resource center. A good computer studies library might include textbooks on various programming languages; textbooks which are similar to the primary textbook but give the student a slightly different perspective; books which emphasize the effects of computers in society (these books usually include computer applications); and textbooks which contain sample programming problems.

Student workbooks and study guides often accompany the primary computer studies textbook. These workbooks assist the student by giving overviews and objectives for each chapter, lists of terms and their definitions, and self-administered tests and answers based on the text content.

Programmed textbooks are available for teaching a number of different areas of computing. Although programmed texts are not recommended as primary reading material because they can be difficult to utilize for reference or review, they can assist the student who is having problems in specific areas of study and needs remediation.

FIGURE 7-17 Real Objects and Props for Student Use

I. Objects which can be shown by the teacher, handed around the classroom, or displayed inside the room

1. Computing equipment
   a. microcomputers
   b. terminals
   c. modems and data sets
   d. video disks
   e. disk and cassette drives
   f. joy sticks
   g. printed circuit boards
   h. vacuum tubes and relays
   i. integrated circuit chips
   j. small robots
   k. optical fibers

2. Computer supplies and materials
   a. line printer paper listings
   b. print wheels
   c. diskettes and cassettes
   d. punched cards
   e. manuals
   f. video game packages

3. Items containing computers
   a. telephones
   b. digital watches
   c. computer and chess games
   d. speak-and-spell devices
   e. toys (talking dolls, cars)
   f. calculators

4. Items using computers
   a. credit cards
   b. checks
   c. Universal Product Code
   d. social security card
   e. newspaper manufacture

5. Props to teach computing concepts
   a. abacus
   b. light switches, other memory devices

6. Objects the teacher can make

II. Oversize objects and those inaccessible to the teacher

1. Objects in the home
   a. computerized appliances—microwave ovens
   b. home computers
   c. stereo equipment

FIGURE 7-17 (continued)

2. Objects and places the student can see on field trips
   a. stores—computer, department
   b. supermarkets/drug stores
   c. computer centers
   d. museum displays
   e. university laboratories
   f. other schools
   g. conferences/exhibitions
   h. malls
   i. public libraries
   j. bibliographic retrieval systems
   k. air traffic control
   l. airline reservation systems
   m. hotel reservation systems
   n. automated tellers
   o. bank terminals
   p. chip manufacturers
   q. computer industries
   r. automated warehouses
   s. automated offices

3. Items students can see on their own
   a. arcade games
   b. point-of-sales terminals
   c. electronic scoreboards
   d. videotex terminals
   e. satellite disks
   f. computerized cars
   g. automated phone sets
   h. computing in movies
   i. computing on television
   j. automated traffic control systems

Periodicals. *Newspapers* contain many items of current interest and trends in computing, along with discussions of controversial issues pertaining to computers in society. Newspaper articles are usually well written and easy to read; aimed at the layperson, they are ideal for the beginning computing student. While the local paper can be counted on to contain several articles a week pertaining to computers, the student should also be encouraged to read similar articles in national and international papers, such as *The New York Times* or the *Financial Post. Magazines* such as *Time* and *Newsweek* regularly print excellent articles on a variety of computer topics.

In addition to popular magazines, articles are found in periodicals which specialize in computing material. These magazines are *popular computer journals,* and *professional journals.*

Popular computer journals are aimed at the person who has a definite interest in computing but may not be a professional computer scientist or researcher. The periodicals are ideal for the person who has a computer and likes to use it as a hobby. They also contain articles of interest to the beginning student, and can be assigned as supplementary reading. However, they should be previewed first because articles may be poorly written or contain information that is too technical for the neophyte. The popular computing journals subdivide into two distinct groups: general computing magazines and company magazines.

The *general computing magazines* (*BYTE, Information Age,* or *Creative Computing,* for example) feature articles on all aspects of computing. These articles cover a wide range of equipment and manufacturers. On the other hand, *company computer magazines* restrict their material to discussions of their own brand of computer.

Professional journals have a very different audience than the popular computing magazine, and many of the articles are much too difficult for the beginner. A majority of these periodicals specialize in one facet of computing (such as computers in education, database management, networking, or computer architecture), and a strong computing background is necessary to understand them. However, certain articles may be useful, especially those which survey a topic; these can be used by the student as background material for a research project or essay.

Encyclopedias. Encyclopedias can be excellent sources of reading and resource material for the student. There are two categories of encyclopedias: the general encyclopedia and the computer science encyclopedia.

The *general encyclopedia,* such as *Encyclopedia Britannica* or *Encyclopedia Americana,* covers many subjects in addition to computing. Computer studies articles found in general encyclopedias are recommended reading, since they usually deal with the topics in a cursory manner—an ideal approach for the beginning student.

The *computer science encyclopedia,* such as *The Encyclopedia of Computer Science Technology* or the *Encyclopedia of Computer Science,* specializes in computer articles. Computer science encyclopedias provide more in-depth coverage than the general encyclopedias since they are dedicated solely to computer science information.

Computer science dictionaries. Related to the computer science encyclopedia is the *computer science dictionary.* The dictionary contains many more items than an encyclopedia, and the coverage of each subject is much shorter since it only defines the terms. Every resource center should have at least one computer dictionary and one computer encyclopedia; preferably the students should have a personal copy of the dictionary. However, note that both reference sources can quickly become dated because of the rapid progress which is occurring in computing. Consequently, some entries deal with obsolete ideas, while information on the most current technology is missing. Also, a poorly designed dictionary can be a spider's web of cross references for the unwary reader; a well designed dictionary will minimize this problem somewhat.

Comic books. Comic books are sometimes used in the lower grades. The reference is not to "Donald Duck" or "Mickey Mouse," but to those comics which are designed to have educational value in the computing area. A number of these are available, and often generate student interest.

Company brochures. A useful source of reading material are brochures prepared by computer manufacturers and suppliers. These brochures can be obtained by writing to the company or filling out the *reader service cards* found in computing magazines. They can provide excellent descriptions of the uses, functions, and operation of different kinds of equipment. Furthermore, they are packed with quality color photographs which can be handed around the class or tacked up on the bulletin board.

Computer manuals. Mandatory reading resources for the class are computer manuals—that is, the manuals describing how to use the machine, how to run the software, and other relevant information. There are four sources of manuals: printed documentation, textbooks produced by independent publishers, microfiche documentation, and information on diskettes.

Printed documentation produced by the computer manufacturer is usually sold along with the computer, but also can be obtained separately. The school should keep a copy of the documentation with each machine. In addition, it is advisable to keep several copies in the library; if the budget permits, each student should have one. Quite often, documentation is stored in *machine-readable form* on disks or diskettes, and the students can display or make a hardcopy of it.

Textbooks published by independent publishers, describing how to use and program the machine, are more readable than the manuals produced by the manufacturer. *Microfiche documentation* is cheaper and takes up less room than the printed version. However, this requires the availability of a microfiche reader and may be less convenient to use.

Teacher handouts. The most popular source of extra reading material is the handout. The amount and kind of material that can be copied is limitless. Possibilities include copies of teacher notes; assignments, solutions to exams and homework and old tests for review; copies of overhead transparencies which have been shown in class; and copies of programs, flowcharts, or other diagrams.

Posters. There are many posters which depict various kinds of computing equipment. Many are available free of charge from computer manufacturers; others can be purchased. The best way to find them is through advertisements in computing magazines.

Photographs. Photographs can be a useful visual medium for displaying computing equipment or the applications of computers. Examples of what to photograph include school equipment, people using the equipment, computer usage in the student's home, and items seen on field trips or visits to computer stores.

Coloring books. Coloring books which depict computing material are available; however, they are appropriate only for very young children. Their pedagogical value is questionable; however, they are useful to generate initial interest or to introduce certain topics.

Flash cards. A flash card is information that the teacher holds up on a card for the class to see and react to. These include posters, photographs, illustrations, and other papers or cards. They may be commercially made, prepared by the teacher, or created by the students as a class assignment. They are suitable for any age or grade level; their content determines their applicability. An example of a set of flash cards is a set of cards depicting flowchart symbols.

Wall charts. Wall charts are large visual displays that are permanently positioned in the room so that they can be seen by everyone. Good locations are above the chalkboard or on side or back walls. They can be homemade or purchased; the quantity of commercially prepared material for computer studies is limited.

The wall chart should depict information that the student needs to consult on a continuing basis. Examples might be an illustration of a computer keyboard; a drawing of flowcharting symbols; a list of the major commands needed to run the computer; a diagram of how to insert and use diskettes; or a synopsis of the major features of the programming language used in the class.

Cartoons. Computer cartoons provide comic relief for the student and often are of pedagogical value. For example, they can be used as excellent attention-getters to begin a class period. The major source of cartoons are computing journals such as *BYTE*. Alternatively, the teacher could involve the students by asking them to create their own cartoons.

Why Use Reading/Visual Materials?

Reading materials provide the student with a *point of view other than the teacher's* or that found in the textbook. A new viewpoint can assist the student in understanding concepts which may have been difficult to grasp when reading the textbook. Difficulties in learning to program, for example, may be resolved by making available several different programming textbooks. The content of recently printed material is more *current* than that provided by the primary textbook or the teacher's background. Company brochures, newspapers, and periodicals are good sources of current developments and trends in computing.

Student *involvement and interest* are increased in several ways by the use of reading materials. The student is able to pursue individual areas of interest, for self-improvement or for researching materials for term papers, projects, or other homework. Or the students can collect materials and display them on bulletin boards or use clippings to make a scrapbook for the resource center.

The reading or visual material can become the focal point of *classroom discussion*. For instance, the students might be assigned a reading in a magazine describing the current state of robotics in industry and then be asked to discuss the question, "Will robots cause massive unemployment in the foreseeable future?"

Finally, the materials can be used as tools to assist and improve the lecturing process by asking the students to read certain materials in preparation for the lecture and showing the students the material at the appropriate points in the lesson.

Some Ideas for Using Reading Materials

When lecturing using visual illustrations, clippings, or diagrams, *do not hand the materials around* while teaching; the student is faced with either looking at the material, or listening to the lecture. To remedy this, either transfer the illustration to a medium which can be observed by all students at the same time, or hold up the material, discuss it, and then put it somewhere for the students to examine later.

Show the students *how to use the library or resource center* to research computer science topics. The students should know what headings and topics to look for in the card catalogues and where computer science textbooks are located; computer studies textbooks may be listed under engineering, business education, mathematics, and general science, to name a few. You can assist the students by keeping the materials as *current* as possible. Computer science textbooks rapidly become obsolete. *Circulate lists* of recent additions to the collection. Maintain a display of book jackets in a prominent location or in the library. Keep important textbooks on the reference shelf of the library and arrange specific topics together. This means keeping together all textbooks on programming in BASIC, computers in society, and so forth. This will help the student who wishes to browse.

Make sure that all reading materials are designed for the grade levels of the students. Many computer science textbooks are written for adults, and make difficult reading for the primary grades. Encourage students or their parents to *subscribe to one or more computer journals.* Or, subscribe to several computer magazines yourself. Try to establish a scheme whereby these materials can be shared with other members of the class.

Let students set up their own displays. Divide the class into groups and assign each group a topic for their display—for example, computer applications in sports, medicine, and business. To add excitement, you can assign an award for the best display.

CHOOSING A TEXTBOOK FOR COMPUTER STUDIES

Choosing a computer studies textbook is one of the most important decisions that a teacher or administrator has to make. The text primarily determines the content, pace, and order of the course. Once a textbook is selected, the rest of the material (lectures, audiovisual, assignments) should be structured around it. Bear in mind that no text is perfect. You will have to base your decision on those features most important for the course.

Is the textbook's content adequate? Although most introductory computer studies textbooks are similar, there is variation in the material they contain. In some cases, subject matter will be missing from the textbook; while in other cases, the textbook will have topics the teacher does not want to include. For example, many textbooks omit discussion of the effects of computers on everyday living—a topic which a majority of teachers would include in their courses. On the other hand, some textbooks include a section on systems analysis—many teachers feel that such material should not be included in the introductory course.

If *critical material* is missing, it must be provided in the form of readings, lectures, or films. *Extraneous material,* on the other hand, could be omitted if it does not disturb the continuity. If the flow will be interrupted, have students read the material, but downplay its importance.

Is the textual material geared to the right grade level? Computer science texts range from those designed for elementary school children to ones intended for young adults attending university; it is important to match the intended level of a textbook to its actual audience. The difficulty level, vocabulary range, depth and breadth of coverage, style of presentation, and examples and activities range in complexity for different grade levels.

Is the textbook used by many teachers? Generally, the degree of adoption of a textbook reflects the merit of the document. If 500 schools are using the textbook, it is probably a serious contender. If no one else uses the textbook, think twice about it, unless it is new on the market. In any event, proceed with caution. There are several reasons for not adopting a popular textbook. First, your curriculum may differ markedly from the content of the text. Second, high sales may result from the textbook being a prescribed text for a large school group. (In other words, one person selected the textbook—and that decision, right or wrong, affected many individual schools.) Third, selection of the textbook may not have been based on careful study. In many instances, for example, decisions are based on the superficial aspects of the textbook, such as glossy photos of people using computers or a neat cover design, rather than important criteria such as content, readability, and level of instruction.

Is the textbook obsolete? Computer technology is rapidly changing; textbooks must reflect these changes. Consequently, a computing textbook becomes dated in a year or two and must be replaced. Three factors may lead to a textbook's demise. It may include material which is no longer in vogue, such as a detailed description extolling the virtues of key punching. It may omit information about recent developments, such as a discussion of the latest models of microcomputer equipment. Or perhaps it includes statements and opinions which are no longer relevant—such as a discussion of the need to have privacy laws, when the laws are already in place.

You can minimize the effect of obsolescence by selecting a current textbook and constantly monitoring the state-of-the-art computing world so you can point out dated material to the students and add new information through supplementary readings. Finally, be ready to dump the textbook when the content becomes too old to be a viable reflection of computer science.

Are supplementary materials provided? Does the publisher provide extra materials to help the teacher with the presentation and to help the student use the text? Examples of teachers' aids are overhead masters, teaching manuals, and test banks; an example of a student aid is the student workbook. Before selecting a text, the teacher might ask these questions: Are these supplementary materials free if the text is adopted, or is there an extra charge to obtain them? Are the overhead masters merely reiterations of the textbook, or do they convey new information? Is the teacher's manual merely a condensed version of the textbook, or does it contain supplementary information, teaching tips, assignment answers, suggested teaching activities? Finally, if a test bank exists, are the questions valid? Are the answers provided?

Does the text contain an adequate number of examples? A computer science textbook without examples is like traveling without a map: you know where you are going, but are unaware of the interesting and important side trips you can take. A good computing text should contain lots of examples—to add interest and variety, and to consolidate, through repetition, the important concepts contained in the book. Indeed, much of the material can be difficult to understand without adequate repetition by means of examples, including expository material intended to expand on a concept and worked-out problems for the student to examine.

Expository material can help the student grasp a concept. For instance, consider the following hypothetical page from a textbook. The student reads that the speed at which a hardcopy terminal prints is about 45 characters-per-second. Such a statistic will not mean much to most students, and therefore is unlikely to be retained. However, by adding an example, the number will take on meaning. One possibility is to discuss the speeds of manual typing; a professional data entry operator, for example, can type approximately five characters per second. Compare this to the much faster rate of the computer printer.

One of the best ways of using examples is the *case study,* in which a concept is worked up in the textbook and a hypothetical or actual application is given. This helps the understanding of the concept while providing an interesting anecdote to read.

Another major use of examples found in computer texts are *worked-out, annotated solutions to flowcharting or programming problems.* Learning to flowchart or program is different from learning most of the other material in the computer studies course. Both topics require that the student learn a skill which is neither factual nor repetitive. The only way to master these skills is by practice; but it is also worthwhile to see how other people would do it. This is best accomplished by giving examples of good, working programs or accurate, well-drawn flowcharts.

Is the textbook well illustrated? Pictures and diagrams are very important. Without one, for example, the physical appearance of a disk pack would be almost incomprehensible to the reader. However, a photograph or drawing of the same equipment makes the device spring to life.

A good computer science text should be full of photographs and diagrams, but take some precautions. An author may fill the textbook with illustrations simply because an illustrated textbook sells well. Many of the illustrations may be irrelevant or redundant. (This can be demonstrated by opening almost any computer textbook and counting the number of photographs which depict a person sitting at the keyboard of a terminal or a microcomputer. What new information, if any, is being conveyed by each additional picture?)

A well illustrated computer textbook has pictures that are attractive and easy to understand without needing a lot of explanation. Each picture should convey meaningful information, but the picture itself should not be cluttered with details. Simplicity of design and content are most important, especially in diagrams and charts. If a complex idea is to be illustrated, it should be slowly built up by a succession of simpler illustrations.

Does the text have a good table of contents, index, and bibliography? Make sure that the table of contents, index, and bibliography of the textbook are clear and easy to use. The table of contents and index are the avenues for any nonsequential access and review of the textbook; if they are improperly organized, getting at the material can be a headache. The table of contents should have both meaningful headings and subheadings and be easy to scan visually. The index should be easy to scan and must be comprehensive.

The bibliography is the student's key to accessing supplementary reading materials; these are included to provide more detailed coverage of certain topics or to clear up points that the textbook does not treat clearly. In both cases, the references should be chosen to dovetail with the text in terms of similarity of jargon and reading level.

Is a glossary included? The study of computer science involves learning reams of odd jargon—*bit, byte, sector, floating point, precedence, subscripted variables;* the list is endless. The glossary is most useful to the reader both as a study aid and as a mechanism for reviewing or referencing items without having to find them in the middle of the text. Unfortunately, most computer science texts don't provide a sufficiently comprehensive glossary. If the book's glossary is not adequate, a separate dictionary of computer science terms may be necessary.

How much does the textbook cost? If all other factors are equal, *choose a lower priced textbook,* preferably a paperback one. Be aware, however, of some of the shortcomings of using paperbacks versions. Paperbacks do not last as long as hardcovers. Additionally, if the text is a programming textbook or contains programming material, hardcover will stand up to the high wear and tear to which programming manuals are subjected.

Is the textbook readily available for purchase? When selecting a computer studies textbook, be sure that the publisher can deliver the copies on time. This may seem like an obvious point, but some computer studies textbooks take a long time to make the trip from warehouse to school, especially new titles or texts shipped from other countries. Get a guaranteed delivery date from the publisher/supplier.

Are there sufficient numbers of good assignments? Assignments include problems, questions, and suggestions for classroom activities and student projects. A good text should have a lot of this material to consolidate learning. Exercises should span all levels and should be progressive in difficulty. Sample answers to *all* problems should be available, especially the difficult ones. A good text will supply many answers, providing instant feedback for the students as they work through the questions. In some cases, the answers are in the teacher's manual.

Does the textbook contain student objectives? Although a textbook may contain all the appropriate content the teacher wishes the students to learn, it may lack a set of well developed objectives for each chapter. This is unfortunate, because objectives are important. The teacher can use them to quickly determine suitability of the textbook. The student can use them to gain an overview of the chapter before reading it and as a vehicle for reviewing the text when preparing for exams.

Is the textbook readable? Many authors of computer science texts are notorious for their inability to convey their material in a readable, well organized manner. The content is adequate, but the style leaves much to be desired. Be sure the style is clear and precise, with correct vocabulary, sentence structure, and paragraph development. See if the material is developed logically. Are the chapters and sections consistent with the ordering of the course content? Does the author build upon previous sections of the textbook while moving towards the end, slowly increasing both the depth of knowledge and difficulty of the material? Does the author use repetition in order to clarify key concepts, and is this repetition handled in an interesting way for the student? Are the headings meaningful and easy to pick out?

Does the textbook contain adequate programming information? If your curriculum includes programming, a programming text is mandatory as a reference for learning the language and as a source of examples. When choosing the programming text, you can either recommend one which is *separate from the main textbook,* or use a *single textbook* which contains all the course content, including programming. The separate-text approach gives more latitude in the choice of texts, allowing you to get both the best programming textbook and the best main textbook.

QUESTIONS

1. Create the materials for teaching how to insert a diskette using:
   a. chalkboard/white board
   b. magnetic board/felt board
   c. flip chart
   d. covered chalkboard
2. Develop an overlay transparency (either on film or on paper) to show the parts of a computer and their interconnections.
3. Make a picture lift of a piece of computing equipment.
4. List the transparencies a teacher could make to augment a lecture on input devices.
5. There are many sources of pictures for slides on computer topics: schools, businesses, computer stores, museums, conferences. Visit businesses and make a list of all the possibilities you find. Take photographs and create a slide collection.
6. As a class, develop a list of commercially available slides, filmstrips, videos, and films on computing topics.
7. Suggest a computer studies topic which is applicable to the film loop.
8. Create a mock-up of a microcomputer.
9. Check a number of teachers' supply catalogs or go to a teacher supply store, and make a list of the materials that are available to help the teacher teach introductory computer studies.
10. Make a list of the computer studies textbooks which are suitable for introductory computer studies class. Select two which you think are the most suitable, and give reasons for your choices.
11. Clip newspaper articles for the next two weeks, and make a collage suitable for the computer studies bulletin board.
12. Refer to a general encyclopedia, a computer science encyclopedia, and a computer science dictionary. Comment on any differences in the information shown in each book for the following terms: (a) microcomputer, (b) program, (c) disk, (d) bug, and (e) ANSI.
13. Obtain several brochures from a computer supply company; comment on their use and applicability in the introductory computer studies course. Are they difficult to understand? Do they contain extraneous material? Do they add anything to the student's knowledge?

14. Create a wall chart for the flowchart symbols.
15. Evaluate the computer science materials in your school library or public library in terms of usefulness for introductory computer studies.
16. Pick any introductory computer studies text and evaluate it in terms of the criteria of a good textbook for student use.
17. Define the following terms: boards, brochure, flash card, flip chart, flowchart, handouts, magnetic board, mock-up, model, opaque projector, prop, picture lift, real things, resources, show and tell, still projection, static display, transparencies, video disk, wall chart.

8

Teaching about Computer Applications

The number of computer applications is increasing dramatically. Since so many areas are involved in the use of computers, a current comprehensive coverage would be difficult because of the rapid technological changes. However, every introductory computer studies class should contain some description of the applications of computing technology.

In this chapter, the teacher is alerted to these applications. No attempt was made to categorize the applications in order of importance. Instead, there are general topics like retail, education, and transportation. The information is not all-inclusive; the reader should embellish or update the textual information with supplementary readings. Major application categories are:

1. personal computing
2. entertainment and sports
3. the arts
4. transportation and travel
5. finance
6. retail
7. utilities
8. medicine
9. education

Personal Computing

Personal computing applications have mushroomed in the past few years. Home uses have expanded to include interaction between the consumer and business, government, entertainment, and education. The sale of computers for home use far exceeds those purchased for business use. Some personal uses of computing devices include ''*smart*'' *appliances and tools,* such as calculators, digital watches, stereos, micro-wave ovens, and videotex applications. (Microprocessors are attached to the television set and are used to access information such as yellow pages, stock market quotations, and weather reports.) There are also *home computer games,* which are too numerous and varied to list.

Computer devices in the *wired home* include environmental control (the furnace and air conditioner can be attached to the computer and activated by temperature sensing devices); security systems (burglar and fire sensors can be connected to a central computer); and light/appliance control.

Home and information management possible with the help of computers includes word processing, menu storage, budgeting, and banking.

Hobby computing possibilities include kits to build computers and components to build home computer systems.

Entertainment and Sports

Arcade games containing modern computer technology attract a wide audience. *Television and movies* have also been affected by computer technology. Ratings and statistics are stored and the results are printed by computer. Animated TV commercials are facilitated by computer graphics. Special-effects movies like *Tron* and *Star Wars* had part of their animation produced by computers. Television programs are stored on disks, thereby allowing editing of each frame. Community service channels—newscasts, weather reports, and sports scores—are produced by a computer program. Finally, statistics and service for pay-TV channels are controlled by computing equipment.

The *sports arena* has also been affected by computers. Timing of events—such as cycling and automobile races—requires computing technology. Manufacturers of sports equipment for skiing and swimming use computers in the design process. Professional sports are increasingly dependent on computers for collecting and analyzing statistics and trends. Many scoreboards at ballparks and stadiums are operated by computing equipment, and race tracks use computing equipment to control betting machines, collect and analyze the data, and display information on the tote board. Finally, although not exactly a sport, computer dating matches potential partners based on their preferences and interests.

The Arts

Computer art is used in television programs as well as in advertisements. Software packages for assistance in creating *poetry* are now available. In *music,* students learn to compose with the assistance of computer-controlled keyboards. The availability of multiple voice accompaniments makes the task interesting and enjoyable. Software is also available to analyze students' writing styles.

Transportation and Travel

Computerized traffic light systems regulate and optimize flow of vehicles. Many new *cars* contain computers which control the ignition system, activate dashboard displays, monitor temperatures and pressures, and sound alarms.

In the *rail industry,* freight cars are monitored, sorted, and assembled using computers located in the traffic control office. The operation and flow of traffic in *subways* and *rapid transit systems* would be hazardous without computer controls.

Computers even affect the elements of water, air, and space; *supertankers and other large ships* would be helpless without the array of computing equipment used to monitor, navigate, and regulate machinery. Off the ground, *air traffic control* is monitored by computing equipment which can warn of potential dangers. Pilots can be trained on very realistic *cockpit simulators* which allow them to practice emergency procedures without endangering lives.

In space programs, *ground control* is closely monitored and manipulated by computers. The *lunar lander modules* required sophisticated computing technology to assist in the landings; these were located on board to eliminate the time lag which is inevitable whenever control is exerted from the ground. And the *space shuttle Challenger* had five computers working in parallel to control the operation of the craft.

Finance

Financial institutions rely heavily on computer technology. Savings and checking accounts are stored in a central database in banks. The *automated teller* has often replaced the human teller. A computer receives and dispenses cash under the supervision of the centralized computer. *Electronic funds transfer* occurs almost instantaneously between computers—for example, the employer's computer transfers salary funds to the computer in the employee's bank. In the *stock market,* stocks are traded using information provided by computers which continuously revise quotations based on bids and sales.

Almost every *credit agency* has access to complete credit information stored in a computer database. Credit card billing is calculated and printed by computer. Credit card authorization is facilitated by a central office where a computerized validation of the card is performed.

Insurance policy records are maintained by computer. Actuarial tables are produced by the computer to minimize time-consuming manual work.

Retail

Point-of-sale terminals are another example of computer technology. *Universal product codes*—the bars found on packaged merchandise—present a unique identification number which can be read by computing equipment. They are also used in inventory control. Many other retail establishments have similar equipment which can produce bills for the customer, perform inventory control, and produce market analysis reports. Large companies, such as hotels, airlines, and car rental agencies have complex computer-controlled *reservation systems.*

In advertising, *automated billboards* are used to advertise news and weather reports, and are generally displayed outdoors by using flashing lights which are controlled by a computer.

Utilities

Computers are indispensable to the communications industry. *Modern telephone systems* use computers to redirect calls to another location, and permit programming numbers to require fewer digits. With *electronic mail,* letters are typed on a computer keyboard and are sent via the telephone system to another computer. This process replaces hand delivery, and minimizes delay. Computers are used extensively in modern telegraph systems for storing and forwarding messages. The *postal (zip) codes* are read and the envelopes sorted by computer.

Grid control—keeping a complex power system up and running—is especially difficult when the demand is high. Computers supply the speed necessary to adapt to changing circumstances and avoid blackouts. Some *gas and electric meters* contain tiny computers which monitor the consumption of the resource and send the data back to a central computer.

In *weather forecasting,* complex computers are used to perform the mathematical calculations required to make predictions. Even though these computers are among the most powerful in existence, such calculations can take almost a day to complete.

Medicine

In patient care, computer-assisted programs such as *CAT scans* can diagnose illnesses and speed up recovery. Intensive-care units are filled with computing equipment which is used for *patient monitoring.* Many computer devices, like heart pacemakers, are imbedded in the body to assist malfunctioning components.

Hospitals and other medical organizations collect data on *patients' medical problems* and their treatments. In hospitals, *drug control reports* are maintained and updated, and many blood and urological tests are performed by computerized lab equipment. Computers can also assist the *handicapped.* There are machines which allow the *blind* to ''read'' the written word by transforming the printed information into words created by a speech generator. *Quadraplegics* ''walk'' in computerized wheelchairs which respond to voice commands.

Education

Administrative duties allocated to the computer include monitoring *computer-managed instruction;* maintaining *student records* such as attendance information, grades, personal information, *timetabling* of classes, and facilitating *student registration.* For *evaluation purposes,* exam compilation, *computer-assisted testing,* and exam grading can be done on a computer. Also, it will generate report cards after grading is completed. In teaching, *Computer Assisted Instruction* is used to teach students by drill and practice, tutorials, and simulations.

WAYS OF TEACHING COMPUTER APPLICATIONS

Many methodologies may be used for teaching computer applications. There are good *movies* on film or videotape which show various aspects of using computers in the real world. Commonly, the application material is mixed with other computing studies topics.

Field trips are the best way to see the computer being used in an application area. Some favorites are the post office, data processing centers, and automated warehouses and factories.

The good *textbook* will contain a number of illustrated sections on computer applications. In addition, the resource center should contain supplementary textbooks which provide extra examples that differ from those in the main textbook. It is worthwhile to obtain some books specifically devoted to computer applications.

Television stations commonly run programs dealing with various aspects of computers; frequently these programs involve application areas, since these are topics of interest to the average television viewer.

Representatives of companies or agencies can talk about their computer application areas. Many companies have an individual assigned to meet with community groups and schools. Speakers are usually well prepared, coming armed with slides, films, hand-outs, objects or models to demonstrate to the students.

Ask the students to *write essays* on a computer application area. They should write these on the word processor. You will want the students to start thinking about the societal effects of the application as well. Make sure the students understand that research is required and evaluation will be made on the information submitted.

The following are some sample questions for an essay:

1. How are computers involved in the chosen application area? How dependent has this application become on computers? How has the utilization of computers changed the application area?
2. Is the use of computers in the chosen application area good or bad? Defend your position.
3. What would happen if all computers were suddenly turned off and every computer application had to be performed manually? Discuss two applications in your answer.
4. Comment on the complexity, speed, and accuracy of the computing equipment required for a chosen application.
5. What are the features of the software required to handle the application? Would it be hard to write? Debug? Revise?

Finally, ask the students to *write a program* on a favorite application area. Of course, the teacher must simplify the task so that it is at a suitable ability level. Examples of such programs include a computer game; personal recordkeeping system; program to calculate student averages and print out reports; dating program; encryption program; sports statistics program; and simple income tax calculation.

What do the students gain from this experience? First, they find it interesting, because they produce a program useful to themselves or their classmates. Second, by writing a program which is a simplified version of a real application area, they get some idea of the complexity of the actual application. Finally, the students will learn something about the application area since they will have to do research in order to write the program.

The teacher should get the students to *discuss the application area.* Do not concentrate just on the factual items, but expect in-depth discussions. When handling discussions, assign one or more students to be "experts" in the particular application area, which requires an in-depth research of the topic. Don't be surprised if the interaction turns into a debate about the societal effects of the application. For example, the discussion of word processing invariably leads to conflicting opinions about its effect on employment, whether it is replacing or eliminating jobs, and its health hazards. Take advantage of the situation. The societal effect is generally of greater interest than the application itself, and the students will be more likely to remember information on topics they introduce into the discussion themselves.

WHICH APPLICATION AREA(S) TO CHOOSE

Obviously, the teacher cannot cover all application areas. How do you choose which topics to cover and which to omit? First, pick topics which have good, readable descriptions available in the textbook or other readings.

Choose application areas which can be observed by the students on field trips. Select areas of interest to the students, both individually and as a group. Items that crop up in the students' everyday activities are always appreciated. Pick important application areas (word processing, income tax records, robotics), and include items which are timely.

Application areas which result in societal issues must be covered. For example, if you lead a discussion on the invasion of privacy, the students need background information on criminal records, medical records, and credit records.

Dovetailing the application to other topics in the course is always useful; that is, use the application area to introduce other computer studies topics. (The topic might be networking, so the teacher first brings up an application such as electronic mail.) Finally, topics dealing with applications in the school should be emphasized because of their proximity, importance, and interest to the student.

QUESTIONS

1. Pick an application which can be observed by a student. Outline for the student the points you want included in a field trip report.
2. Word processing is an important application for inclusion in the high school curriculum. Make a case for it so that your department head can make a presentation to the principal or school board.
3. Write a lesson plan for a discussion period on a specific computer application, either personal or business.
4. Make a list of application areas of computers which would be unsuitable for inclusion in the introductory computer studies course.
5. Major application areas not presented in this book include office applications, information industry, government, military, industry, and law. Select one of these topics, research it, and make a ten-minute presentation to the class.
6. Add to the list of applications discussed in Chapter 8.
7. Define the following terms: automated billboards, automated teller, cashless society, computer-assisted testing, computer field trip, computer-managed instruction, electronic funds transfer, electronic mail, hobby computing, personal computing, point-of-sale terminals, Universal Product Code, wired home, word processing.

9

Teaching about Societal Issues

A mandatory portion of the introductory computer studies course is the coverage of issues surrounding computers in society. An integral part of learning about any issue should include the formation of an *opinion* or *attitude* toward the topic. Thus, learning about computers and unemployment not only requires a basic knowledge of factual information—how unemployment is produced, how jobs get displaced—but also requires the student to grapple with questions such as: "Are the unemployment numbers exaggerated?" "Is being unemployed, for some people, necessarily terrible?" "How can we respond to the unemployment situation?" Answers to these questions are not factual, but opinions. As such, they *cannot be lectured* about or read in a book. Because of this, we recommend methods other than lecturing when covering these topics—methods in which the students become involved, start thinking, and come to their own conclusions.

Two techniques come immediately to mind—the *classroom discussion* and the *research essay or project.* Both of these approaches require posing a problem or asking a question which the student is required to resolve. This chapter, therefore, provides many sample questions the teacher could use to promote discussion.

THE EFFECT OF THE COMPUTER ON THE INDIVIDUAL

When the majority of today's teachers were born, computers were in their infancy. For today's students, computers are commonplace. The world has changed dramatically in just one generation. Individuals must learn to cope with these changes, though some people have been unable or unwilling to adapt.

Computers affect the way individuals *think about themselves,* and how they *interact with other people.* Living in a world dominated by machinery can affect people's basic self-worth and prompt them to question their function in society. Many human traits are increasingly adapted by metal, wire, and plastic. Some computers can see, hear, speak, touch, and move around. Our most cherished characteristic, intelligence, is being challenged by the computer. Future generations may have to cope with mechanical beings which are as "intelligent" or more so than they perceive themselves to be.

The computer may affect *interpersonal relationships,* because as telematics (computing by networks) becomes more widespread, the need to leave our homes to shop, go to work, play games, and get education may be reduced. Contact with other humans may be affected; personal contacts may be both reduced and distorted.

Questions on coping

1. Is the rate of change in our society really accelerating? Provide evidence to support your answer.
2. In what ways can advances in computing technology place stress on the individual? Explain.
3. In what ways have people adapted to this stress, or failed to adapt?
4. Read Toffler's *Future Shock* or *Third Wave* and discuss the author's viewpoints on the societal effects of computers.
5. Jobs are being created and destroyed by the ever-accelerating pace of change. Give some examples of computer related jobs which are being destroyed or created. How can individuals prepare for the situation where jobs might disappear virtually overnight?
6. In a paragraph, give your reactions to this statement: "Even though computers are present everywhere, they don't affect me! When I get up in the morning, I brush my teeth, cook on a gas stove, get dressed, go to school, come home, have dinner, play records, and go to bed. Computers have had no effect on my day."

Questions on the effect of computers on the individual's self-concept

1. List the ways in which the computer has affected how you feel about your abilities and potential.
2. Would you be threatened by the existence of a machine that is more "intelligent" than you are? Why?
3. What effect do you think the advent of machine intelligence will have on spiritual beliefs? Will our Western religious system be in turmoil? Why or why not?
4. Will people become bored with life as more and more of their functions are replaced by computers? Why or why not?
5. If computers match us in their capabilities, will we start to view ourselves as machines rather than humans? Explain.
6. Are we creating a generation of computer addicts who spend their lives programming or playing computer games? Justify your statement.

Questions on interpersonal relationships and the computer

1. Is our increasing dependence on machinery making it more difficult to interact with our peers? Will people develop a preference for interacting with machines rather than with human beings? Explain.
2. Is computer technology fostering the development of passive, introverted personali-

ties as the need for communicating with others decreases? When people have the opportunity to spend most of their lives inside the home and don't need to venture outside unless they want to, will we have a nation of social recluses? Explain.

3. Will human contacts become more and more depersonalized as we allow machines to take over? Will people be numbers in a database rather than individuals with specific needs? Why?

Privacy

Lack of privacy is one of the biggest issues facing our society as a result of the advances in computing and telecommunications. Large databases contain reams of personal information, and sophisticated network structures have been developed which allow this information to be accessed. Examples of information readily available through computer systems include

criminal records,
income tax records,
financial information in bank computers,
medical records,
employment information,
credit records, and
insurance files.

Such information, when used wisely and subjected to appropriate constraints, assists society and the individual to function efficiently. Most people do not object to the wise use of computer-based information; it is the illegal or distorted utilization of the information that makes people uneasy. For example, unauthorized access to a medical database might reveal information that allows a person to be blackmailed.

While most people realize the importance of maintaining security on monetary, criminal, and medical records, many do not realize that seemingly innocuous information must be protected as well. Examples include airline and hotel reservations and telephone records. Airline and hotel reservations can tell a criminal when people will be away from home; telephone records can be used for blackmail; while library records, indicating which books have been checked out, could be used by the police to keep track of people who are reading too many crime books (causing these persons to be labeled as possible crime suspects).

Questions on privacy issues

1. How can we ensure that our privacy is being maintained and that unauthorized access to information is not taking place? Explain.
2. In what computerized databases is information about you kept? List them.
3. Examine an existing computer system with respect to how well it prevents unauthorized access or tampering. What measures can be taken to make computer systems intrusion-proof?
4. Read Orwell's *1984* and comment on the possibility of having a "big brother" society similar to that described by Orwell.
5. Discuss the current laws with respect to privacy. Do they adequately ensure our rights?

6. Access to computer-stored personal information can be controlled as long as a benevolent, law-abiding government is in power; but what would happen in a police state if all that information were available at the touch of a keyboard? Discuss.
7. The combination of large databases and the use of networking to tie the databases together so that information is readily available hints of compiling detailed, personal dossiers on individuals. Comment on how this could be done and whether we should take measures to inhibit the practice.
8. Pick any existing database in your community and show how it could be used for devious or benevolent purposes.

Computer Crime

Some students have a keen interest in stories about people either stealing from a computer or using the computer to commit crimes. The teacher should get good mileage from this topic and generate much student interest.

Questions on computer crime

1. From your readings in books, magazines, and newspapers, list the ways in which computer crimes have been committed.
2. The average computer crime nets more money in comparison to the average holdup. Why would the "take" be so much higher?
3. The kinds of computer-related things that can be stolen are equipment, money, time, software, and information. Besides the first item, discuss what is meant by the other four. Cite examples of such crimes.
4. Industrial espionage refers to stealing secrets from a company. How could a computer be involved in such theft?
5. Some computer crimes involve extortion and blackmail. Explain.
6. Many people are enticed into committing computer crimes because of the high payoff, the absence of incriminating evidence, a low probability of being caught, and a low incidence of prosecution and conviction. Discuss why there is little evidence left behind after a computer crime has been committed, why it is hard to catch the criminal, and why the victims are reluctant to prosecute, even if they know who the criminal is.
7. What legislation exists to cover theft involving computers, and why is this legislation inadequate?

COMPUTERS AND EMPLOYMENT

Many people think that computers have the horrifying potential of putting millions of people out of work. Some have predicted that over *half* of the labor force will be unemployed. If these estimates are true—and some evidence points to the possibility—then the solution to the problem of computer-related unemployment represents one of the greatest challenges to western society. As such, it is extremely important that students of computer studies come to grips with the situation.

Automation has been developing for a very long time. It has its roots in the *industrial revolution,* starting with inventions such as the steam engine and cotton gin, which replaced employees with machinery. To understand the current effects of automation, it is mandatory for the student to have some background in its historical precedents and some insight into how previous generations met the challenge.

The Effects of Automation

While *unemployment* is one result of automation, another manifestation is a *shift in the job picture.* Jobs are changing and retraining programs have become a necessity.

The effects of automation are *not all bad,* as was eventually proven in the Industrial Revolution. Mundane, repetitive, or dangerous jobs can be handled by machines which do not get exhausted, never become bored, and can be replaced if they are damaged or destroyed. In addition, quality control is improved and overall productivity is increased. Furthermore, as machines take the place of workers, some of the positive effects of unemployment—such as a shortened work week accompanied by increased opportunity for leisure—can be observed.

The teacher should ensure that the student understands both the positive and negative aspects of computer automation. An even more important concept to get across is that this encroachment by computers is inevitable, there is little that can be done about it if the nation in which the student lives wishes to compete with other nations in the market place. The teacher must therefore endeavor to train people to adjust, adapt, and respond to the new situation.

Questions on computers and employment

1. Compare the Industrial Revolution to the computer revolution in terms of time span, unemployment, improved standard of living, and other societal effects.
2. What sets robots apart and makes them so special in the history of automation?
3. The Japanese have a ten-year plan in which they are developing an "intelligent" computer which will be commercially available. They are committing billions of dollars to its production. Why are they doing this? Do you think they will be successful?
4. Japan is one of the most industrialized nations in the world, dedicated to automating whenever possible. Thus, there are entire factories in Japan which contain no humans—just robots. Although one would expect labor unrest, this is not so; the workers, in general, seem happy. What factors have led to this truce between human and machine?
5. How does automation, especially with robots, eliminate mundane, repetitive tasks for people? Explain.
6. Suggest and discuss ways in which our government and society can adjust to the wholesale replacement of jobs by computer technology.
7. Some people have suggested that the total number of jobs is not being affected by the computer, but that the job market is just shifting. Unemployment results because people are displaced; but at the same time, new computer-related jobs are created. Do you agree with these people? Find evidence to substantiate or dispute their claims.
8. If unemployment will eventually become a fact of life, then we will have to alter attitudes toward the unemployed person. Suggest some ways in which this can be handled so that the unemployed have the same opportunities as the employed.
9. Why are certain sectors of the work force—such as assembly line workers, clerical workers, and secretaries—hit harder than other sectors?

10. The western nations have a dilemma: If they automate, the result will be unemployment; if they don't automate and other nations do, then they will lose their share of the market place because they are unable to compete. Thus, they are "damned if they do, and damned if they don't." What do *you* think they should do, and why?
11. What is the "Protestant Work Ethic"? Discuss its relevance in the modern world of computing.
12. One response to the employment problem is training people on how to handle the increased spare time they will have. Discuss.
13. Discuss some ways in which sectors of present-day society are avoiding the prospect of facing computers.
14. What government legislation do you think is necessary in order to respond to the effects of computerization?

THE COMPUTER AND THE ENVIRONMENT

One of the most *positive effects* that computers have is their potential to alleviate the drain on our natural resources. For example, the production of waste materials in a computerized industrial operation are minimized, and computers provide assistance in both preventing and cleaning up pollution. Furthermore, computers themselves are low consumers of resources: They use up little power, they are small, and they are made from abundant raw materials such as silicon. About the only thing they use in abundance is paper for line printers.

Questions on the computer and the environment

1. Why do computers cause little pollution in their operation?
2. The use of computers in business and industry has the side effect of reducing the consumption of resources by:
   a. increasing quality control so that fewer items are rejected or wasted.
   b. making sure that the delivery of raw materials and finished products is precisely timed so that there is no waste or spoilage.
   c. precisely monitoring energy consumption such as electricity or oil, and controlling its use.

   Discuss each of the above.
3. How can computers be used to monitor pollution and assist in preventing its occurrence?
4. In the wired city of the future, everything will be handled by computers in combination with the telecommunications system. These will allow the private citizen to do things such as bank, shop, work at home through a terminal, and send electronic mail. In what ways will such activities lead to a society which has less pollution and less consumption of resources?

MISCONCEPTIONS ABOUT COMPUTERS

There are a fair number of misconceptions about computing which students have that should be rectified. Examples of these are the following.

1. Computers are huge machines with blinking lights, funny noises, and whirring wheels.
2. Computers are very intelligent machines which are capable of human thought and emotion. In some cases, they surpass humans in this respect.
3. Computers are dumb machines which simply add numbers very quickly.
4. Computer programmers are high priests and priestesses who perform magic with their machines.
5. It is possible to write very sophisticated software with little training. All you need is a microcomputer, and you can write programs which will make you into a millionaire.
6. Robots have eyes and ears, and walk and talk like humans.
7. Computers often make mistakes.

Why do people have misconceptions about computers? Ignorance about computers is one reason. Also, everyone is exposed daily to half-truths about computers and what they do, and many people are unable to separate these from reality. Science fiction frequently contains descriptions about what computers might do in the future, but the reader has trouble distinguishing this from the present. The news media may present stories on computer-related research which has not been completed and isn't even close to the development stage. The computing profession is advancing so quickly that only computer experts can keep up with what is happening. Most people have a viewpoint which, to a greater or lesser degree, is out of date. Some people, for instance believe the old idea that all computers are physically large—occupying an entire room—rather than being small enough to fit in your hand.

Clearing up Misconceptions about Computers

The only way to rectify the situation is to make sure each student has an up-to-date and sufficiently comprehensive understanding of computers. This is achieved mainly by learning the factual material in an introductory computer studies course. However, due to the problem of obsolescence, this learning cannot stop when the student graduates; the individual should be encouraged to continue learning after finishing formal training.

Besides giving the student a solid foundation in the facts of computer studies, it is worthwhile to point out each of the major misconceptions. Show science fiction movies or other films which present a distorted image of computers. Then have the students criticize the content of the film and suggest ways that the film could be made more realistic. Ask the students to critically evaluate any stories about computers which they have read in magazines or have seen on television. Show a vintage movie on computing and ask the students to comment on how the state-of-the-art has advanced since the movie was produced. Finally, have students play roles in which one person is a computing expert and the other a layperson who has a mistaken impression of what computing is all about. The goal is to have the two converse and correct any false impressions which arise.

QUESTIONS

1. Work through the questions listed in the chapter, answering them as if you were a student in an introductory computer studies class.
2. Find a good article on societal computing in the newspaper; then find a poor one. Compare the two and state how they differ in quality.
3. Play the following game with a fellow teacher:
   a. One of you is extremely intelligent and will act as if you know nothing about computers.
   b. One of you is an expert explaining to the other what computers are and trying to rectify any misconceptions.

   Record the points of contention and how they were resolved.
4. Define the following terms: automation, computer privacy, database, dossier, industrial espionage, interactive, machine intelligence, network, state-of-the-art.

10
Teaching about Hardware

An introductory course in computer studies would be incomplete without information on hardware. This information provides a backdrop for the coverage of software, the practical details necessary to operate computing machinery, prepares students for computing and computing-related jobs, and supplies information needed before buying computer hardware.

The purpose of this chapter is to introduce hardware topics suitable for the introductory computer studies course. (See Figure 10-1.)

FIGURE 10-1 Hardware Topics for Introductory Computer Studies

1. The binary number system
2. CPU and memory
3. Input devices:
   - keyboards and key pads
   - card readers
   - key-to-disk and tape
   - touch-tone phones
   - pointing devices (joysticks)
   - voice entry
   - data capture
   - optical devices
   - magnetic input
   - transducers
4. Output devices:
   - character printers
   - line printers
   - page printers
   - COM
   - VDUs
   - graphics screens
   - plotters
   - TURTLEs
   - voice synthesis
   - device control
   - dumb terminals
   - intelligent terminals
5. Auxiliary storage:
   - hard disks
   - floppy disks
   - tapes
   - cassettes

THE BINARY NUMBER SYSTEM

The binary system is the basic mechanism for manipulating information on a computer, and is therefore fundamentally important to the computer studies student. The teaching of computer arithmetic and base conversion, on the other hand, does not seem nearly as important to an introductory class. The material is only useful to students who will be taking more advanced courses and working with computers in greater depth.

The teacher should explain that a binary number is composed of *bits* (binary digits) and that each bit can have *two states*—a one or a zero. Beginning students may have problems with this since they may be used to working with decimal numbers. Discussion of binary numbers will naturally lead into the concept of the *binary computer,* at which point the class should be familiar with the concept that all data and programs are stored in the computer in the form of binary numbers. The teacher should point out that computers are based upon the binary system in order to minimize the number of components in the equipment and thus minimize the cost of the machine.

Binary Arithmetic

Performing binary arithmetic can get tricky. The teacher should start with the easiest topic first—*counting in binary*—and show the class how to count up to ten. There is no need to go any further, since the progression beyond ten becomes obvious. When counting in this fashion, the numbers should be related to those in the decimal system, possibly by writing the decimal equivalent beside each binary value.

The next step is to teach the student how to *add* binary numbers. The simplest case comes first, one which does not involve carries, e.g. 101 + 010, followed by examples requiring carries, e.g. 101 + 01.

When simple addition has been mastered, the students should learn how addition actually takes place *within a computer;* this is more complicated than the pencil and paper approach. The difficulty stems from the computer having a fixed word size, such as eight bits, which places finite limits on the range of values that can be added. The instructor, at this point, would discuss the concept of *signed binary arithmetic* where the leftmost bit is used as the sign bit and therefore is not included in the magnitude of the number.

Binary subtraction is confusing to many students, especially when they examine the way that computers actually subtract. Hence it is easier to first show the students how to do it manually. The manual technique is similar to base ten subtraction, where one borrows from more significant digits whenever needing to subtract a 1 from a 0.

When the class has mastered the manual approach, the teacher can work on the more complex computer approach which utilizes a technique called *two's complement arithmetic.* Two's complement arithmetic treats subtraction as a special case of addition, in which the subtrahend is first converted to a negative number (the two's complement form) and then added to the minuend. The first step is to show the students what a two's complement negative number looks like, then to demonstrate how to produce one from the corresponding positive value (Figure 10-2).

FIGURE 10-2 Negative binary values are formed by taking the positive value, generating its complement, and then adding one to the result.

The students may find this difficult for a while, but should have no problem after they have learned the rules for conversion.

Multiplication and *division* of binary numbers have no place in an introductory class. If enthusiastic students wish to know how it is done, refer them to a relevant reading on computer arithmetic.

Other Number Systems

By now the students should be aware of the extremely long numbers that occur when large values need to be represented in the binary system. 1,000,000 in decimal needs twenty-two bits for its binary representation. Such large numbers pose no problems for the computer; unfortunately, human beings prefer to work with smaller numbers. Hence, there are two other number systems which are used extensively because they provide a notation for easily representing binary numbers in abbreviated form: the *octal* system and the *hexadecimal* system.

Although the *octal number system* is different from the binary system—the underlying radix for the octal system is base 8 rather than base 2—there is a convenient relationship between the two: Each octal digit has a corresponding triplet of binary digits, for example, 101 = 5, 111 = 7. The students can understand this relationship by counting up to 20 decimal in both binary and octal. The teacher should then demonstrate how to represent a long binary string by a shorter octal number, and also show the reverse conversion from octal to binary.

The *hexadecimal system* is similar to the octal system, except that there are sixteen different digits rather than eight. Because of the increased size of the base, when the students count up to 20 decimal, it will be necessary to demonstrate how the last six digits (10 through 15 decimal) have to be represented by the letters A through G, respectively.

Conversion between bases. It is both useful and interesting for the student to know how to convert between different number bases, especially between binary and decimal (Figure 10-3). The teacher starts with decimal to octal conversions, showing how to use the division method; then extends this procedure to convert from decimal to binary and possibly from decimal to hexadecimal. The reverse process, octal to decimal conversion, comes next, using the powers of eight technique. Lastly, the teacher shows how a similar process can be used to convert from binary and hexadecimal numbers.

Hints on teaching binary numbers. Teaching about binary numbers is probably the closest the introductory computer studies teacher will come to teaching mathematical concepts in a computer studies class. In fact, it is often included in mathematics courses. Besides relying on this possible background, the teacher can use some other methodologies.

The teacher should use many *examples,* and give students lots of *practice* questions. The exercises should be ordered in terms of increasing difficulty level.

FIGURE 10-3 Examples of conversions from binary numbers to decimal values, and the opposite operation, from decimal to binary.

A. BINARY TO DECIMAL CONVERSION:

RULE: 1. NUMBER THE DIGITS FROM LEFT TO RIGHT WITH THE VALUES 0, 1, 2, 3 ETC.

2. USE THIS NUMBER AS THE POWER OF THE VALUE 2, IF THE DIGIT IS A ONE.

3. ADD ALL THESE VALUES TO GET THE FINAL DECIMAL RESULT.

EXAMPLE:

$$1010_2$$

$$2^3 \quad 2^1 \quad = 8+2 = 10_{10}$$

B. DECIMAL TO BINARY CONVERSION:

RULE: 1. DIVIDE THE DECIMAL NUMBER BY 2.

2. PLACE THE RESULT ON THE LEFT-HAND SIDE OF THE DEVELOPING BINARY NUMBER.

3. IF THE REMAINDER IS NON-ZERO, GO TO STEP 1 AND APPLY THE ALGORITHM ONCE AGAIN TO THE REMAINDER.

EXAMPLE:

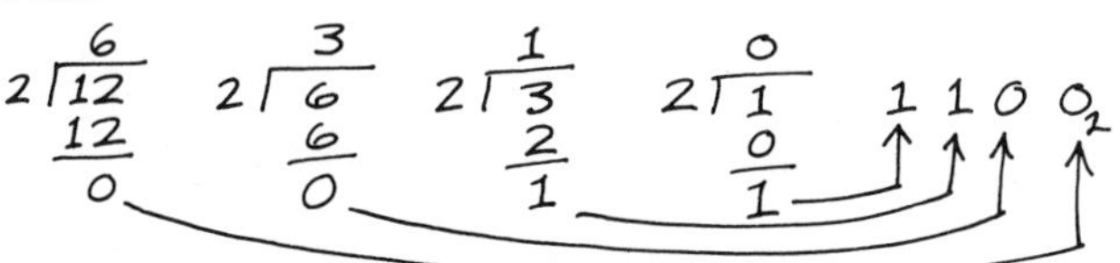

Demonstrating is usually better than lecturing in this case. Work out binary examples on the board, and demonstrate binary digits with props such as a light switch or any other familiar object which has two states (Figure 10-4). When counting in binary, use a *counting board.* Although the counting can be done on a chalkboard or table top, it is easier to see if a line drawing of a counting board is placed on an overhead transparency with opaque objects, such as poker chips, used for manipulating the numerical values. Incidentally, the counting board technique is excellent for demonstrating the efficiency of the binary system—the teacher will always use fewer poker chips when counting in binary than in decimal (Figure 10-5).

THE CPU AND MEMORY

The CPU and memory should receive only *light treatment.* It is not necessary for the beginner to understand how the CPU and memory really work or how they are constructed. Instead, the approach should be practical, concentrating on those aspects which the student needs for writing programs, operating machines, conversing with peers at a meaningful level, or purchasing a computer.

The student should know the relative roles played by the CPU and memory in the overall computer system: Memory is used to hold instructions and data, while the CPU is responsible for following the orders which reside in the memory. A simplified coverage of the parts of a CPU (control unit, logic unit and arithmetic unit) and how they interact is usually taught to the introductory-level student.

FIGURE 10-4 Various props can be used to demonstrate binary values, for example, light bulbs, light switches, and holes in computer cards.

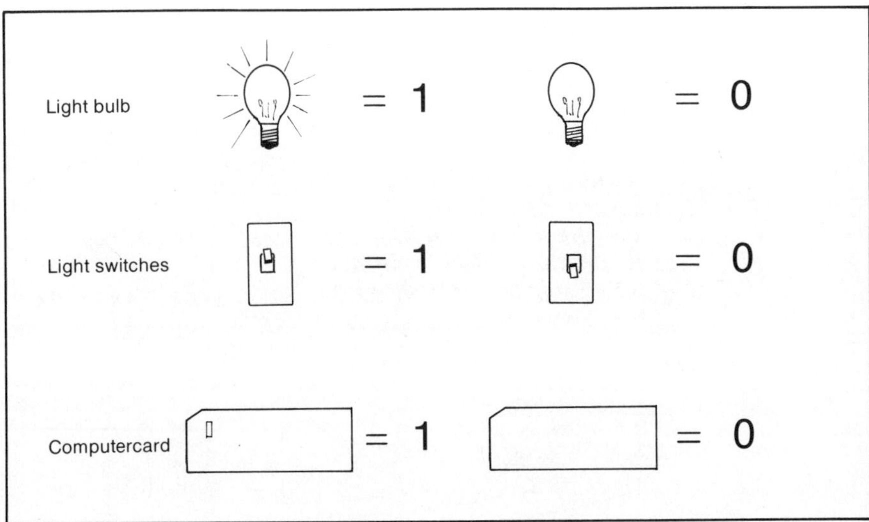

FIGURE 10-5 The counting board, which dates from Roman times, is an excellent tool for demonstrating the binary number system.

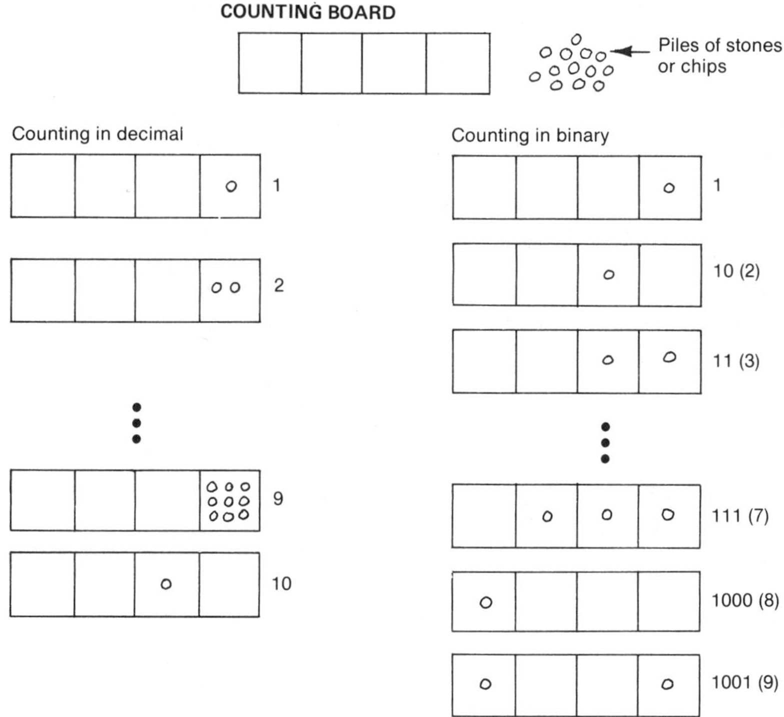

(note that counting up to 9 in decimal requires nine chips, whereas in binary only a maximum of 3 chips (or the value 7) is necessary)

Kinds of CPUs. Students should be familiar with the variety of CPUs, ranging from the tiny, limited processors found inside digital watches to the large CPUs inside expensive equipment. Many of the smaller processing units are manufactured as a single integrated circuit. These CPUs, known as *microprocessors,* are found inside every *microcomputer* that is sold, and the student should learn the names (actually, numbers) of the commonly available microprocessing units—at least the one which operates inside the microcomputer used in class.

Kinds of memory. The most important point to teach about memory is the difference between *ROM* and *RAM*. The teacher should explain the purpose and function of each, then compare them in terms of read/write capabilities, volatility of information, areas of application, and cost.

The Operation of the CPU and Memory

The student should be given highlights of the operation of the CPU memory—especially the idea of the *stored program.* Programs are stored in the RAM (or in the ROM if the program is not to be changed) as a series of instructions and, because this RAM is changeable, the programs can be altered simply by altering the contents of the memory. This is usually done by copying the new program from a file residing on disk or tape.

It might be worthwhile to show the students simple examples of *machine language instructions.* The teacher should provide examples of different machine language instructions, but should not get too ambitious—this material is difficult for the beginner. The examples should be limited to a hypothetical machine rather than a real one, eliminating much of the complexity and permitting the teacher to focus on the fundamentals.

Once the students have a feel for the rudiments of machine language, it is time to present simple examples of how the machine works when executing a machine language program. Before going through these steps, you must acquaint the students with three more concepts. First, describe how the CPU retrieves instructions from memory. Second, describe the function and operation of both the *instruction counter* and the *arithmetic register.* Third, talk about the operation of the *fetch/execute cycle.*

Once these three concepts have been discussed, the teacher can work through some examples of machine language. These examples should not be too complex. Although real machines have dozens, and sometimes hundreds, of different instructions, four or five common ones are sufficient. One might typically include examples of instructions that perform addition or subtraction, store data into memory, retrieve data from memory, and cause unconditional branches.

While going through the examples, the teacher should point out some other characteristics of the CPU and memory, like the way memory locations can be accessed randomly with no forfeiture in speed. Explain that the CPU cannot distinguish between instructions and data, because they are both stored in the same binary notation; and stress the primitiveness of the machine language instructions compared to a high level language like BASIC.

While discussing the code, it is worthwhile to put the BASIC (or PASCAL) equivalent of the machine instructions on the board. This will give the students a familiar frame of reference to help them understand how the program works.

CPU power. The *capacity* of the CPU, traditionally called the power of the machine, depends on many factors. The beginner only needs to know a few of these. The first is that the amount of computing accomplished by the computer is a direct function of its CPU speed: Some computers will do more calculations per unit of time than others. The second is that the instruction sets of CPUs are usually different. The faster computers have more versatile and powerful instructions. The third element contributing to the power of the machine is the size of the numbers which are used to perform calculations such as addition or multiplication. Many microcomputers use 8-bits for the operation; the recent ones use 16-bits; 32-bit machines are now appearing. The speed of calculation increases as the word size gets bigger because more arithmetic can be done by each individual instruction.

Memory capacity. At this point, the students should know that memory is assembled into "chunks" of contiguous bits called *bytes.* Each computer has several thousand bytes located in its memory, either in ROM or RAM, or both.

The measure of this memory size is the "kilobyte," abbreviated as "K," with values being 32K, 64K, 128K, 256K, and so on. Most computers will have a maximum memory size which cannot be surpassed—64K is typical. Many models are sold with less memory than the maximum, and the purchaser can upgrade it by adding more memory. For the interested students, a discussion of the access time of memory might be appropriate. This is the time taken to store or retrieve information from memory, usually measured in *nanoseconds* (500 nsecs is a typical value).

Tips on teaching about CPU and memory. Use *brochures and advertisements* found in magazines to expose the students to the variety of CPUs and memories that are available. Also, keep several different instruction-set *manuals* in the classroom or resource center for interested students.

Visit *computer stores,* where the students can note the great variety of CPUs and memory configurations. Bring to class some *integrated circuits* (CPUs and memories). If possible, also bring in a printed circuit board which contains CPU and memory chips and briefly discuss its operation.

Demonstrate the difference between ROM and RAM by keying in a program for the class, turning off the machine, turning it back on, and then asking the students to discover what is still in the memory and what has disappeared.

Have the students write a *BASIC program* which contains thousands or millions of iterations—for example:

```
10 FOR I = 1 TO 100000
20 X = 10
30 NEXT I
```

Such a program will take a perceptible amount of time to run, and this time lag can be utilized to study processor speeds and instruction timings. The student can determine the time required to execute the program. Once this reference time has been established, the students should add or delete an instruction from the loop and find out what effect this has on the timing. Finally, if more than one brand of computer is available in the classroom, they can compare the speeds of different machines.

Role playing can be used to teach program execution to younger students. One student can act as the arithmetic unit, another the logic unit, with the rest of the class assigned to memory locations with each location containing an instruction. The students work through the execution of a program.

Have the students note the *incredibly short time* span covered by a *nanosecond,* even by a microsecond. Some ways to make them aware of this duration is to point out that if computers add one number per microsecond, then they can add one million numbers in a second. Or, give each student a piece of wire or string and remind them that this is the distance light travels in one nanosecond (Figure 10-6). This will take on significance when it is compared to something more meaningful, such as how long it takes light to travel from the sun.

FIGURE 10-6 The instructor is holding a piece of wire showing the distance that electricity (and light) travels in one nanosecond.

INPUT DEVICES

Before teaching input devices, the teacher should have taught the basic *cycle of data processing* which takes place on a computer, that is: to take in information or data (input); manipulate this data (process); and produce results based on these calculations (output). Now it is time to provide details about each of these stages of the input-process-output cycle.

Students should learn about the *wide range* of input devices. The reason for this diversity is that there are many different kinds of data, and each device is designed to maximize the ease and efficiency of reading a particular kind of data (Figure 10-7).

In the early days of computing, when the number of input devices was limited, the only way to enter data was to flick a set of binary switches to the desired input value. The teacher can show the students an example of such a *switchboard register* and then have them try putting numbers into the switches. Once students understand how the switch register works, the teacher can discuss its suitability for entering data required in some of the applications they have studied. For ex-

FIGURE 10-7 Examples of input devices that are useful to discuss in the introductory course.

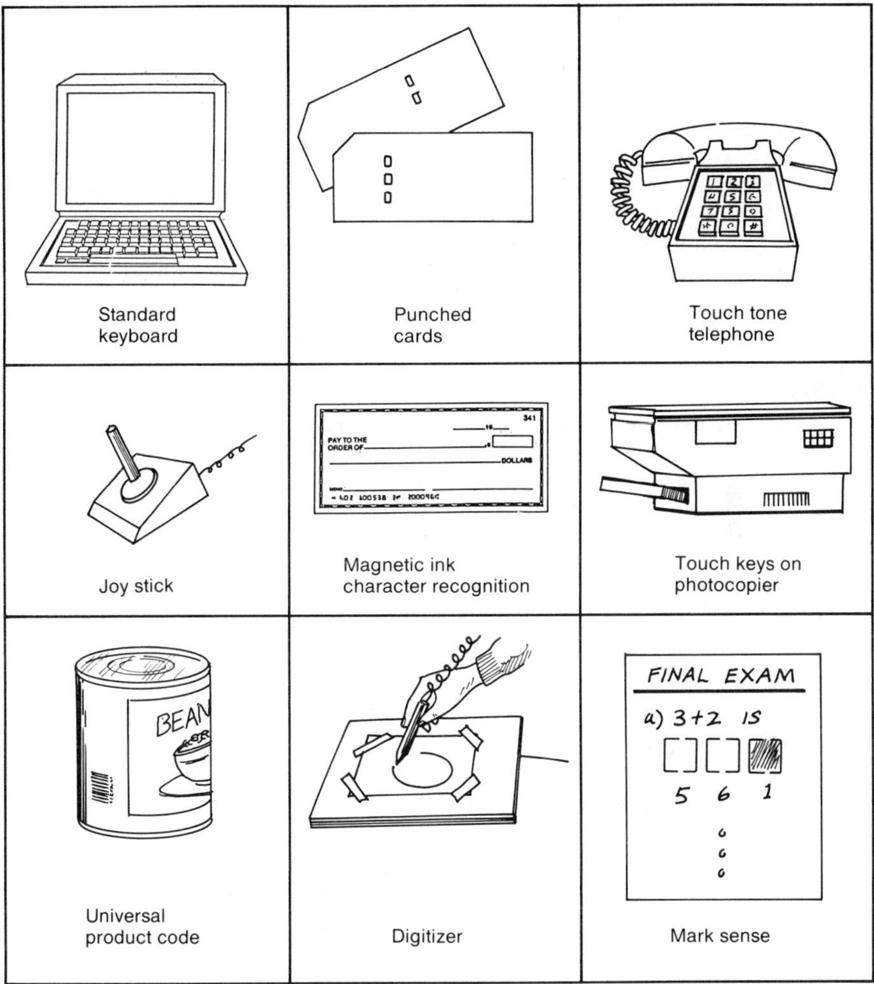

ample, would it be a good medium for entering a program? The students may be surprised to learn that it once was used this way. Could it be used for entering letters for a word processing system, or for running an airline reservation system? The student should realize why the switchboard is unsuitable and what device would be better.

Next, start working through the list of input devices. Pick those which are important or of interest to the beginning student. The important ones—namely keyboard devices, pointer devices, voice entry, optical devices, and transducers—are discussed in the following sections.

Keyboard Devices

Most students will be familiar with the computer keyboard, having used a computer terminal or microcomputer in the classroom. The first keyboard device on the agenda should be the *standard version* found on all terminals and microcomputers. Since the students will be using such a keyboard for their daily work, its operation must be learned in detail. The requisite skills include how to turn the machine on and off, knowing how to keyboard correctly, and how to use the special keys.

Another keyboard device is the one found on *punched card equipment.* Since the use of cards is almost obsolete, the discussion of punched card equipment should be from a historical perspective. The teacher could refer the class to some old magazines or textbooks to prove how extensively they were utilized.

Key-to-disk and *key-to-tape* are two of the present-day replacements to the punched card. The operator must still use a keyboard to create the data; however, the information is stored either on a magnetic disk or magnetic tape. The student should be made aware of how these approaches minimize many of the problems which were plaguing cards.

Many keyboard devices utilize *touch-sensitive keys* rather than keys that move. The students should examine the function keys on a modern photocopying machine for a good example of this input. Or, they can visit a fast-food outlet and take a peek at the cash register keys.

Another form of keyboard is the *numeric keypad*—a keyboard which just contains numeric values. They are frequently attached to the right-hand side of normal keyboards and are used for numeric input or calculations. Others come as independent units which can be held in the hand. These may be used at grocery stores for inventory.

Some students may be aware that a *touch-tone phone* can be used as an input device. When used for this purpose, anytime the user pushes one of the keys, such as "ABC" or "DEF," a combination of tones is sent down the telephone line to a computer attached to the other end. There is a unique combination of tones for each number; the computer converts these sounds into the corresponding binary value. The main advantage of this approach is that the user is able to converse with a computer without having to purchase special equipment—just a touch-tone phone.

Pointer Devices

After studying the different keyboard devices, the student should understand that different input media are used for simplicity of operation, economy, or specific applications. Next, show the class that while the keyboard is an excellent interactive device for applications such as word processing, keying in programs, and running financial spread sheet packages, it poses difficulties when entering other kinds of data. A keyboard is unsuitable for many computer games and for computer art. Young children are unable to use a keyboard properly because of their small hands; and they may not know the alphabet. Finally, many software packages allow menu selection by displaying a number of alternatives on the screen. The user can easily choose one of these by "pointing" to the desired choice rather than by using the keyboard.

The next step is to summarize the different devices used for pointing, beginning with the cursor. The *cursor* is a flashing dot or cross which can be moved around the screen by pressing special control keys on the keyboard; these keys will probably be located on the right-hand side of the classroom computer keyboards. The students should practice moving the cursor around.

An alternate device for controlling cursor movement is the *joystick.* Most students are familiar with this device, having used one when playing computer games. Compare the joystick to the cursor control keys and have the students determine which is better.

Both the cursor control and the joystick involve indirectly moving an object around on the screen; the user adjusts the controls while observing the motion of the object. Some other devices eliminate such hand-eye coordination by requiring the user to point directly at the screen. A *light pen* or *touch-sensitive screen* works this way. The light pen resembles a pen with a cord at one end. It functions by placing the end of the pen at the desired spot on the screen. The touch-sensitive screen is even simpler to use—the operator just puts a finger on the screen at the selected point.

The teacher might explain to the students how each of the pointing devices—cursor, joystick, light pen, and touch-sensitive screen—transmit the *coordinates of the screen position* back to the computer as a pair of binary values. Software within the computer then uses these values to determine appropriate actions. For instance, in a game, an airplane might be displayed at the screen location; or when drawing a picture, the points might be regarded as one end of the line.

Another device which computes coordinates but in this case does not require a screen, is the *digitizer.* A digitizer consists of a special pad which is connected to the computer. As the user traces or draws on the pad, the equipment constantly monitors the movement of the pen and sends a string of positions back to the computer.

Advantages of pointer devices. Pointing devices have certain advantages over keyboards, and as the teacher discusses each one, it is useful to point out the advantages. Joysticks are better for games. The digitizer is excellent for map drawing. A touch sensitive screen is mandatory for small children, and a light pen is good for drawing pictures. Cursor control is the best way to select items from computer-generated menus.

While working through such examples, pose the following questions: Does the user have to do less work to input information by means of a pointing device? Can the user be less skilled to use the device? How will the interaction between user and computer differ in both cases? What kind of software would be required to accommodate the device? Is the software easier to write?

Voice Entry

An interesting input media is the class of devices which can directly respond to the human voice—where the user speaks into a microphone and the device converts the sound patterns into the computer equivalent of the written word. The software can then handle this input as though it were entered in a more traditional format—as if it were keyed in on a keyboard.

Although these devices are exciting to observe, the student should be warned about their limitations. The *vocabulary* which the machine can recognize is *restricted* to no more than several hundred words; each device must be trained to recognize these words; and, finally, each one must be retrained whenever used by another person, since each individual's voice has *unique sound patterns.*

Despite these drawbacks, this device will become one of the major input media in the near future. Hence, it is a good exercise to ask for suggestions why voice entry devices will become increasingly prevalent; require the class to propose ways in which the medium will be utilized to advantage, such as for airplane pilots, who will be able to talk to a computer which is flying their plane. Thus, their hands will be free for other operations. Quadraplegics will be able to instruct a computer to do things for them. And typists will have voice-activated typewriters which will not require keyboarding.

Data Capture

The input devices covered so far are those which require human beings to interact with the machine, like keyboards, cards, and pointers. While in many cases, such as game playing, this human element is a necessary part of the interaction, there are also times when it is not necessary. Examples include traffic light systems and alarm systems. In these examples, the data must be *directly inputted* into the computer *without human intervention.*

Consider the following case study: A polling company uses a computer to determine opinions about a certain government policy. Questionnaires are sent to a randomly selected group of citizens who are asked to give their responses to a list of multiple choice questions. The completed questionnaire is sent back to the polling company, where a research assistant copies them onto punched cards. These cards are then read into the computer, the data is analyzed, and finally the results are printed. This procedure is more complicated than need be, since the data passes through an extra set of hands—the research assistant—on its journey from the person who was polled to the computer where it is processed. The assistant would be totally unnecessary if the original data could be produced in a format which was *machine readable* and did not have to be transcribed. Such machine readable copy could be obtained by asking the person to fill out mark-sense cards in response to each questionnaire. These cards can be read directly by the computer.

Magnetic Input Devices

Although magnetic devices normally are used for storing data, the student should be aware of several ways in which the media also can be used for input. The first example is reading the special characters found at the bottom of checks. These characters, which normally spell out the branch and account numbers, are printed with magnetic ink which can be read by a special reader in a process called *Magnetic Ink Character Recognition (MICR).* The amount of payment given for the check is encoded by the teller, and the check number is printed on the bank statement.

The teacher should describe why the use of these special characters is more efficient than handwritten characters. The MICR format can be read easily by both the customer and the bank employees, yet these characters can also be read directly into a computer and automatically route the check to its destination.

Another example of magnetic input is the brown or black *magnetic stripe* that is painted on many credit and charge cards. This stripe contains information in a machine-readable format—such as the person's name, account number, password, credit rating. The card is used to validate the customer's identity when purchasing merchandise or performing transactions at an automatic teller.

Optical Devices

Optical devices work by inputting visual information—characters, lines, images—in a form which can be directly manipulated by the computer.

Optical Character Recognition (OCR) is a process in which typewritten or typeset pages are scanned by a reader and converted into a machine-readable format. This facilitates the entry of data by capturing the information in its original form. The teacher should mention how technology has advanced to the point where handwritten text can be deciphered, as long as the letters are legible and clear.

Bar code readers—more commonly called Universal Product Code Readers—interpret the machine-readable lines found on grocery items or merchandise tags. In a supermarket, the bar code on the product container is moved across a table-mounted reader; in the case of merchandise tags, a hand wand is passed over the ticket. An interesting demonstration is to bring in a can of beans to show the students the product code, then ask them to see if they can figure out what the marks signify.

Mark sense readers can detect the presence or absence of pencil marks on a piece of paper. The student may have filled out a mark-sense card or sheet when taking multiple-choice exams or answering questions on certain kinds of survey forms. It is easy to find samples of such input to bring to class. If individual students are interested, they could write an exam-grading program—which uses mark-sense cards—as part of a class project.

Television cameras can be attached to a computer and used to capture still images in a machine-interpretable form by transforming the intensity of each half-tone dot of the television image into a numerical value. These values, which are stored in memory or on disk, can be analyzed by suitable software. Such TV input is used for the production of computerized photographs which can be purchased at fairs and exhibitions, and for the "eyes" of some sophisticated robotic devices.

Zip Code Readers examine the zip codes on envelopes to help route a letter to its eventual destination. If possible, arrange a visit to the post office so the class can see the device in action. If a visit is not possible, the post office might provide a movie of its operation.

Transducers

Transducers are special input devices which take some external condition—such as temperature or light intensity—and convert it into a form that can be used by a computer. There are literally dozens of varieties of this form of input, too many for the introductory computer studies class; the teacher should not go into detail about how they work or how they can be programmed. The objective is to gain an idea of the typical kinds which are available, along with an example or two of how they could be used. Accordingly, here is a list of typical transducers, along with a sample application for each.

1. *Temperature sensors* monitor the temperature in a house and pass this value on to the computer.
2. *Pressure sensors* measure the atmospheric pressure outside the house.
3. *Moisture sensors* measure the amount of water in the ground, which leads to the eventual activation of the sprinkler system.
4. *Magnetic sensors* are placed in roadways to help control the flow of traffic by means of a computerized control system.
5. *Noise sensors* result in the activation of a burglar alarm system.
6. *Light sensors* are used to count items passing through a light beam on a conveyor belt.
7. *Infrared sensors* are used to control the closing of elevator doors.
8. *Motion detectors* are used in banks to alert security personnel.
9. *Level sensors* are used in computerized automobiles to monitor the volume of gasoline.

OUTPUT DEVICES

Output devices refer to the equipment which produces the results of the computer's computations and calculations. Most output is in a form understandable to the human being: printed characters, graphic displays, synthetic speech, and so on (see Figure 10-8); but many devices communicate directly with other machines. An example is the switching circuitry operating the lights in a computer-controlled traffic system. This distinction between output meant for humans versus output destined for a machine is similar to the distinction between input entered by humans and the direct capture of data from its source.

When teaching about output devices, adopt an approach which parallels the one used to discuss input devices. Start off by going over the reasons for having such a great variety of output devices. Then work through each device, discussing its attributes and comparing it to the other available devices.

Alphanumeric Output Devices

The alphanumeric output device produces a string of characters in a form which can be read by the user. Examples are the printed copy produced by a line printer or the display created on a CRT. However, there are many more than these.

When talking about each of the character devices, it is necessary to indicate the ways in which they differ. The students therefore should be able to compare and contrast the devices along dimensions such as physical appearance of the device; speed at which the characters are produced; number of characters which can be viewed at one time; size of the characters; output; noisiness; reliability; and cost.

The most important of these attributes is whether the device produces a permanent copy of the output—such as on printed paper—or whether the output is temporary and will eventually disappear—such as the image produced on a CRT screen. The students should familiarize themselves with this distinction, especially with the terms used to discriminate between the two classes of devices—*hardcopy* and *softcopy*.

FIGURE 10-8 Examples of output devices that the teacher can discuss in the introductory course.

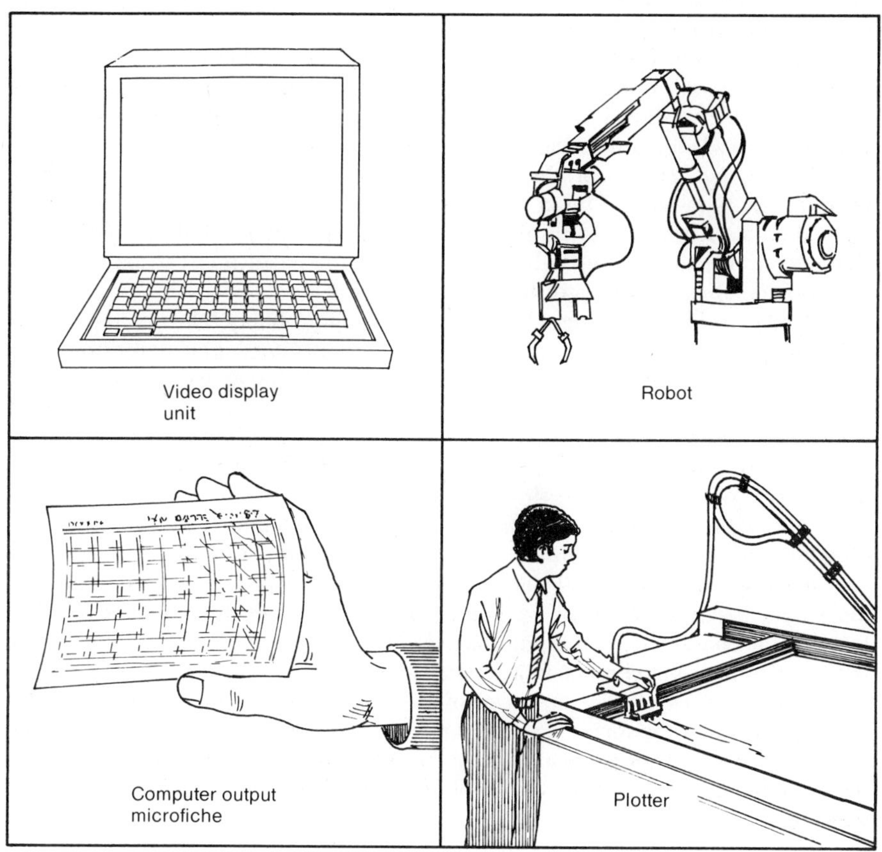

Hardcopy Devices

Hardcopy devices are collectively known as printers. They can be divided into four main groups: character, line, page, and microfiche printers. The student must become familiar with at least the first three of these.

Character printers. As the name implies, character printers produce a single character at a time. A character is printed on the page, the printing mechanism moves over, and the next character is printed a fraction of a second later. This design contrasts with the other three kinds of printers, which can produce more than one character simultaneously. There are hundreds of brands of character printers. Fortunately, the array of equipment can be categorized into a few groups: dot-matrix printers, letter-quality printers, and non-impact printers.

With a *dot-matrix printer,* each character is made up of a collection of small dots which, when seen from a normal reading distance, become legible. These printers are popular because they are among the lowest priced. Unfortunately, they tend to be slow and noisy, and produce poor quality print that is inappropriate for many application areas. They are best suited for producing interim copies of output such as program listings or debugging runs.

Although the way in which the characters are produced on a dot-matrix printer may be very fascinating, it is not necessary to delve into its inner workings unless the students show interest. Such detailed information falls into the category of useless knowledge unless the student gets a job as a technician.

Letter-quality printers produce characters equivalent to those produced by a good quality typewriter. Unlike the dot-matrix printer, the characters come fully formed on a daisy wheel or thimble. These wheels contain a full complement of characters, are available in different sizes and type faces, and can be easily removed and substituted by a different wheel.

Because of its advantages, some students will probably ask why letter-quality printers are not purchased instead of dot-matrix printers. The major drawback is relatively high cost; furthermore, the buyer also has the added expense of purchasing print wheels—a different one is needed for every typeface. Finally, print wheels and thimbles tend to wear out and the equipment is noisy. A typical application where the use of this device is justified is for the production of letters or memoranda on a word processing system.

Non-impact printers reduce noise, since there is no hammering against paper. One kind of non-impact printer, called a *thermal printer,* produces characters by moving a special print head over chemically treated paper. As the printhead moves by, it selectively heats up points on the paper which change color, thus forming the characters. Although this procedure results in very little noise, there is a price to pay: the characters are poor quality, and the paper is expensive.

Another class of non-impact printer is the *jet spray printer,* which sprays ink onto the paper in the form of a character. As a result, the device is quiet when operating. However, there is a tentative health hazard for persons who work with the equipment, so protective covers should be utilized when the machine is in operation.

Line printers. Although the printing speeds of character printers are suitable for low volume applications, they are inadequate for high volume applications. This comparison naturally leads to a discussion of line printers—devices which operate much faster because they print a full line at a time. Provide the class with some data on the printing rates of typical line printers, and compare these to the rates obtained for character printers. Obviously, the increased printing rate does not come free of charge: Line printers cost more to buy or lease; however, when they are running at full capacity, the cost per character printed will be cheaper.

The important features of line printers which should be covered include a description of the external appearance of each device; some details of how to use the printer; kinds of paper they can accommodate; and a comparative evaluation of line printers to other kinds of printers.

Page printers. Page printers are even faster than line printers, producing a page at a time rather than single lines. Page printers are expensive, and are only justified for applications requiring very high volumes of output. It is worthwhile, therefore, to discuss these applications with the students and have them decide, in each case, whether the page printer would be cost-beneficial.

It is unlikely that the average school possesses a page printer; therefore, the class will have to go on a field trip if the teacher wants the students to see one in action. If this cannot be done, the teacher can bring in a sample of page printer output so that the class can see what the product looks like. It is important to point out the difference in quality from that produced by a line printer; the characters are composed of tiny dots, similar to a dot-matrix printer. However, in this case, the resolution of the characters is much better.

Computer output microfiche (COM). When studying about high volume equipment such as line printers and page printers, the students should realize the enormous quantity of output they could produce in a single day. To illustrate this, calculate—or have the students calculate—the amount of paper, in terms of thickness of the paper stack, which would be produced by a line printer or page printer if it were running continuously for twenty-four hours. The incredible volume of paper can create a storage problem if the output is going to be kept for posterity. A room must be allocated for storage purposes, and a good filing system is mandatory because individual documents can easily get lost in the mass of paper.

Placing the output on fiche dramatically reduces the space required to store the output: A one-foot-high pile of 14″ × 11″ listings can be stored in about an inch-thick pile of microfiche cards. Furthermore, the fiche cards are easier to file and retrieve.

Microfiche can be made by photo-reducing normal listings to the required size; however, this is not necessary since equipment is available which directly copies computer output onto a fiche card. These devices are rather expensive, and the cards need special microfiche readers if the user is going to look at the output. The best place to see COM cards is to have the students visit a public facility where they are used—such as a public library, where COMs function as a replacement to the card catalog. Following the visit, discuss the pros and cons of using fiche for such an application.

Phototypesetting equipment. Phototypesetting equipment is used to produce camera-ready copy for newspapers and books. The phototypesetter draws the characters as a series of dots, but the resolution is so fine that the human eye perceives them as being like the characters printed with metal type. Bring to class a book or newspaper which has been typeset in this manner, and see if the class detects any difference from a document produced in the traditional way.

Softcopy Devices

All the output devices described so far are capable of producing a *hardcopy* or *permanent record* of the output. *Softcopy devices,* on the other hand, use a *volatile medium,* such as a CRT or a visual display, to hold the characters. With a volatile medium, the data is lost when the power is turned off. Furthermore, softcopy devices can hold only a limited amount of information on the screen before the older output must be replaced with the new data being transmitted by the computer. Despite these disadvantages, softcopy devices are an extremely popular way of producing output from a computer.

Video display unit. A video display unit (VDU) is simply a CRT which is capable of displaying computer output. Many students have been exposed to one of two kinds of VDU, namely the *normal television set* fitted with an adapter (RF modulator) which converts the digital computer signal into a form which can be displayed on the screen, and the *monitor,* which—unlike a television set—does not pick up TV broadcasts. Using a normal television set is cheaper; many people take advantage of this facility when they buy a less expensive microcomputer without a monitor and attach it to their TV set. Most business computers, and some home computers, utilize a monitor rather than a modified television set. The main reason for using a monitor is the better quality picture which is produced.

There are good reasons for using softcopy displays rather than hardcopy equipment. VDUs are usually less expensive, especially if a modified television set is used. A VDU is less likely to malfunction because it contains few moving parts. The characters are displayed on a VDU at a much higher rate, also because of the absence of moving parts. Since VDUs don't utilize paper, there is no mess involved: listings are not spread all over the place. Some VDUs have the capability for allowing random access to any position on the screen, allowing text to be selectively erased or replaced. This is most useful when correcting errors in a program or when fixing spelling errors while doing word processing.

Problems with VDUs. Despite these advantages, VDUs have several drawbacks. First, screen contents are lost when the device is turned off. This difficulty can be easily demonstrated by turning the VDU off after filling up the screen with data. When the VDU is turned on again, the screen will be empty—the data is lost. Second, when individual lines are filled up with characters beyond the right-hand side of the screen, subsequent characters are either ignored or placed on the next line—a process called *wrap-around.* As an exercise, ask the students to type characters until the line is filled up and then ask them to report what happens. Third, information can be lost when the screen is full and another line must be added. Usually the last line is inserted at the bottom of the screen; the existing lines move up one slot, and the first or top line disappears. This process is called *scrolling.*

Applications of VDUs. Before terminating the coverage of VDU devices, discuss a number of application areas where VDUs are used to advantage. The teacher should discuss editing software, printing out program listings, word processing, and airline reservations.

Visual displays. A discussion of softcopy alphanumeric devices is incomplete without addressing the visual displays used in digital watches, pocket calculators, and hand-held and lap computers. Every student has been exposed to these devices. Instead of describing what they look like, you might describe the two main technologies employed for displaying the characters—light-emitting diodes and liquid crystals; briefly describe their differences; and hand around some examples. You could refer to the low power consumption required by these displays, which allows them to be driven by batteries rather than by line voltages. The class could investigate how the characters are constructed from a matrix of short line segments. You could discuss the low cost of the displays compared to VDUs, or demonstrate the limited display capacity compared to the VDU. If there is time and the class is interested, describe the research being done in creating low power VDUs, constructed from a tightly packed matrix of light-emitting diodes.

Graphics Devices

Graphics devices are peripherals which can draw pictures as well as produce characters. They are used in numerous application areas, like computer games, computer-aided design, and television commercial production. When discussing these application areas, point out why the graphics output is preferred over mere textual printouts.

Softcopy graphics. Softcopy graphics displays are familiar to every student who has played video games in arcades or on home computers. The first item to discuss is *resolution,* which is the number of dots (or *pixels*) in the horizontal and vertical directions that affect the quality of the picture; the higher the resolution, the better the picture. The students can demonstrate this by counting the number of pixels on a high resolution arcade game and comparing it to the number of pixels on a low resolution home game.

High resolution is preferable because of the better picture which results, but these devices are costly. The picture is stored inside a memory residing within the display unit. In this memory, one bit is reserved for every pixel if the unit is a black and white display (a "zero" in the bit indicates a black dot while a "one" indicates a white dot). If the unit displays four colors (for instance, red, blue, white, and black), then each pixel requires 2 bits (00—red, 01—blue, 10—white, 11—black). Thus, as the resolution of the screen gets better and the number of colors increases, the number of bits required in the memory increases as well. As the memory size increases, so does the cost.

There are some interesting exercises which will help students learn about computer graphics. For example, ask the students to diagram what the memory contents would be for an object, such as a circle or square, placed on a simplified 10×10 screen having pixels of 4 colors (Figure 10-9). Or get the class to calculate the memory sizes required for some of the commercially available brands of graphics units. (It is best to pick ones which differ in both their resolution and number of colors.) The students can create graphics displays on the computer they are using in their classroom. The class can discuss why continuous variations in shades are not possible on a graphics display, or they might contemplate the merits of having built-in graphics symbols from which larger images are built up.

Animation. Since students are familiar with graphics screens in which the images move around, they will probably want to know how animation is produced. The underlying mechanism is easy to understand once you have described how still pictures are created. Apparent motion is simply the result of changing the contents of the memory at the appropriate rate. This can be demonstrated by showing what changes to the memory are necessary in order to move the circle shown in Figure 10-9 toward the bottom of the screen. See if anybody in the class knows how fast the picture must change in order to produce the *illusion of smooth motion.* If a graphics terminal is available, you can demonstrate the example rather than describe it; better still, ask the students to program it themselves.

The discussion of picture drawing and animation will probably prompt some questions that you should be prepared to answer at their level of understand-

FIGURE 10-9 A 10 × 10 screen requires 100 pixels. If black-and-white is utilized, 100 bits of graphics memory are required. However, if 4 colors are used, 200 bits of memory are needed, as 2 bits are allocated to each pixel.

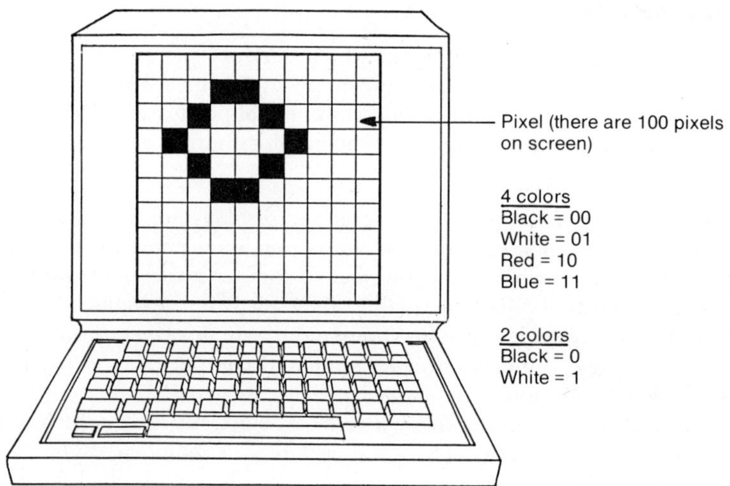

ing. Some ticklish questions might be: Can 3-D be achieved on a graphics device? What must be done when one object moves in front of another on the screen? How can the illusion of perspective be produced on a graphics display?

Programming graphics. Where possible, allow the students to begin writing programs for producing graphics displays on their computer. Students are usually fascinated by this topic; exploit this interest when assigning programming problems. The microcomputer or terminal which the students are using will probably have graphics capabilities; the students will be highly motivated when their programs run and will be able to transfer their abilities to other areas, for example, from moving figures to graphs and curves.

Hardcopy Graphics

The major drawback of softcopy devices is that a permanent copy of the picture is not possible; the picture disappears when the power is turned off or another picture is produced in its place. Because of this volatile nature, there is a need for hardcopy graphical output just as there is a need for hardcopy alphanumeric output.

The most widely used device for producing hardcopy graphics is the *plotter*—a piece of equipment which draws pictures by moving a pen in small increments across a sheet or roll of paper. Multiple colors are achieved by having more than one pen, each with a different color, or by changing the ink if there is only one pen on the plotter. Hardcopy graphics can also be produced by printing very *closely-spaced dots* on the paper—a page printer can be used in this way.

Plotters can draw a picture rapidly and accurately. They are replacing human artists in occupations like drafting and circuit layout.

Plotter output is always fascinating to examine. If a sample is available, pass it around the class or put it up on the display board. The class could also visit a computer store or data processing center which has a plotter.

The turtle. One of the best instruments to generate student interest in the details of graphical output is the *turtle*—a small machine which runs around on the floor and is controlled by a computer program. The turtle receives its commands from the computer via an attached umbilical cord or remote radio transmission. These commands—"turn left," "turn right," "move forward," "stop"—are included in a program written by the student and cause the turtle to meander around the room once the program is executed.

The turtle contains a pen which can be used to draw crude graphics; the student places a piece of paper on the floor and directs the turtle to move in the outline of the desired picture. The pen can be raised when one wishes to move the turtle to a new section of the picture.

The turtle appeals to most students, especially younger ones. Accordingly, it has been used extensively in computer science classes, particularly as a vehicle for teaching about problem solving.

Voice Synthesis

A popular item to bring into the classroom is the voice synthesizer—a device which produces words and sentences similar to human speech. If the school does not have the real thing, bring in a tape recording or have students visit a supermarket or other establishment which uses one.

As they listen to the speech produced by the synthesizer, students should be aware of its limitations—problems with inflection, speech quality, and vocabulary size. At the same time, they should consider its advantages. Application areas where voice synthesizers could be used include: in an aircraft cockpit (the spoken voice means the pilot does not have to look at the dials); for catalogue shopping by phone; and for the blind typist or computer operator.

While covering sound synthesis, it might be interesting to include a brief discussion of music synthesis. *Music synthesis* boards can be purchased for most microcomputers, and the students greatly enjoy running software packages and writing programs which play music.

Device Control

Next on the teacher's agenda are those devices which are used to *directly control other machines* rather than producing output for humans. There are a great many such devices, and their numbers are increasing constantly. It is not necessary to go into great detail about how they work; instead, discuss how they are used. A few examples of device control when using a computer are to control the lighting or other electrical devices in the home; turn on and off the valves in a pipeline; control the lights in the scoreboard at a football stadium; automatically switch long-distance phone calls to their correct destination; and turn, extend, or lift the hand and arm of a robot.

Students have so much interest in *robotics* that you will have to give it extra coverage. Indicate the different kinds of robots available—ranging from dumb mechanical arms that are only capable of repetitive tasks, to semi-intelligent machines which can see and feel in their own way, and perform some very interesting tasks.

Robots have not achieved perfection; there are still many technological problems. Discuss some of these problems, such as the difficulties involved in writing software for robots—especially the more intelligent ones.

It is exciting to bring a robot into the classroom; there are small robots which can be attached to microcomputers. The students will be fascinated watching it operate and trying out their skill at writing programs for it. An alternative is to simulate a robot on a graphics display and have the students manipulate it.

Terminals

Whenever a person interacts with a computer in such a way that both input and output are utilized on the machine, the device is called a terminal. Consequently, *point of sales units, automated tellers, remote job-entry stations, and electronic calculators* are all terminals because the user puts data in and gets results out. The term most commonly refers to those devices which have a keyboard attached to a printer or CRT; the keyboard is used for entering the data while the printer or CRT displays the results.

Most terminals are stationary, but some are portable. These terminals are usually fitted with a handle, or else fit inside a carrying case.

There are two major classifications of terminal equipment—*intelligent* or *dumb*. This will probably cause mild hysteria in the classroom, but the students will calm down after they realize that the terms are appropriate. A dumb terminal simply does what it is told. When characters are keyed on the keyboard, they are transmitted to the computer without modification; when the computer sends characters back, they are printed or displayed verbatim.

An intelligent terminal, on the other hand, processes the characters before they are sent or displayed; this is possible because the terminal contains a small CPU and a limited amount of memory. This memory holds a program which is responsible for processing the characters. On some terminals, the program is stored in ROM, so the intelligence of the machine cannot be changed. On other terminals, the program is in RAM so the capabilities of the terminal can be altered—usually by downloading the software from the main computer.

Make the students aware of some of the ways in which intelligent terminals are being used. For example, airline reservation terminals preprocess the information from the local keyboard before passing it on to the main machine, and some printers hold their output in a buffer before actually printing the characters. This feature allows the main computer to transmit characters faster than the terminal can print without data being lost.

Also, graphics terminals commonly have a lot of intelligence. For instance, a typical graphics terminal contains software for displaying individual objects on the screen, such as lines, circles, and squares. The main computer is still responsible for drawing the overall pictures, but instead of drawing each dot (of a circle, let's say) it just sends a command to draw a circle at the location x, y on the screen and the terminal takes over, displaying each individual dot.

Intelligence is necessary in the terminal because it reduces the load on the main computer, which saves time and money. Also, the terminal may be located some distance from the main machine, necessitating telephone lines to allow the two devices to communicate. This communication costs money, especially if long-distance phone calls are required. Consequently, any mechanism for reducing the flow of data back and forth results in savings.

AUXILIARY STORAGE DEVICES

Auxiliary storage devices—such as disks, diskettes, and magnetic tapes—are used for keeping programs and data on a *permanent* basis. This equipment, also called *secondary memory,* serves as an alternative to primary memory.

The student has already learned that primary memory is *volatile*—the contents are lost when the power is turned off—except for read only memory (ROM). Disks and tapes, on the other hand, utilize a different storage technology which allows the data to be preserved even when the device is switched off.

The storage media of these devices are usually *portable*—disks or tapes can be transferred from one point to another. Memory, on the other hand, is not easy to move about. Having a portable storage medium is useful—for instance, when the teacher purchases or trades software and must ship the data across country.

The *volume* of auxiliary storage is usually many times greater than primary memory. Some disks, for example, hold tens of millions of bytes; whereas on some microcomputers, the primary memory is restricted to a maximum of 64K bytes. Finally, the cost of auxiliary storage is much cheaper than primary memory.

Before the students race from the classroom extolling the virtues of secondary memory, be sure to tell them why primary memory is still necessary. The time to access data is always much faster with primary memory: usually less than a millionth of a second. With hard disks, data access takes around one-tenth of a second; with floppy disks, up to a second; with tapes, it could be several minutes. Furthermore, programs must be resident in primary memory before they can run, since software cannot be executed directly from the disk. Hence, primary memory is mandatory for two reasons: *speed of access* and a *place to execute programs.* However, although it is slower, secondary memory has a *larger capacity* and is *cheaper.* The normal configuration, therefore, is to have a main memory large enough to hold the executing program and a limited amount of data, and a much larger secondary memory for holding all the programs which are not executing plus any other needed data. When a new program or data is wanted, it is read from the auxiliary storage into main memory.

A fundamental topic to cover is the concept of *reading* information from secondary storage into memory. In addition, the students should be introduced to the idea of *writing* data, which is the movement of information from main memory into the secondary storage device.

When the class has conquered the fundamentals of data storage, it is time to look at the kinds of storage devices available. As they study each device, make sure that the students pay attention to:

1. The way the data is stored on the peripheral and how it is subsequently accessed.
2. The fundamentals of how the device operates.
3. The external appearance of the device.

4. The maximum storage capacity of the device.
5. The average time required to get at data.
6. The reliability of the equipment.
7. The purchase price of the device; this value should be equated to a cost-per-bit figure.
8. Sample applications of the equipment.
9. Some problem areas which crop up when programming the device.
10. The advantages and disadvantages of the storage medium relative to other storage techniques.

Access Methods

The first item on the preceding list—how data is stored and accessed—is a critical concept. It is necessary for understanding how to program the device properly, and it forms the basis of selection criteria if the student buys a computer. There are two basic ways of storing and accessing data: *sequentially* and *directly* (sometimes called *randomly*).

Sequential accesses start at the beginning of the medium—for instance, at the front of a tape—and the data is read (or written) item by item. If the desired information is some distance away from the starting point, the access time can be rather long; all the data in-between has to be skipped before getting to the correct location.

In direct access, on the other hand, the information is located *directly* without the device having to work through intervening data items. As a result, the access time is fast, usually a fraction of a second.

In order to understand the merits of these two modes of working with data, the student will need some background information on how data is organized and how this organization is related to the operation of the storage device. Since data organization has nothing to do with hardware—it is a software problem—it will not be discussed here. However, in the actual teaching of this material, the two topics are intertwined.

Storage Devices

When teaching this material, it is best to start with equipment that is most familiar to the students. Almost certainly this is the storage device that they are using on the classroom computer; in almost every case, it is either a *diskette* or *cassette* system—unless the students are using a timesharing system, in which case it will be a hard disk. Since most microcomputer systems use a diskette system, we will emphasize this device. The following order of topics are suggested: diskettes; hard disks; open-reel tapes; cassettes; and other storage devices. If the students are more familiar with cassette tapes, teach about cassettes and open-reel tapes first.

Diskettes

The diskette is an example of a direct access device; such devices allow any part of the storage medium to be located quickly. A disk is made up of two parts:

1. A *flexible platter* which holds the data in the form of magnetic impulses written on its surface. The data is in binary form—0's and 1's—and remains on the diskette until it is changed.

2. The *disk drive* which houses the mechanism for spinning the diskette platter. It also contains the read/write head(s) which are used for retrieving and storing data on the diskette.

Storage of data. Data is stored on the diskette in the form of concentric circles termed *tracks,* with each track being divided into fixed-size chunks—typically 128 bytes—which are called *sectors.* Each sector is treated as a unit, when storing or accessing data. An entire sector is always either read or written meaning that a subunit—for example, 5 bytes—cannot be extracted or altered.

In order for data to be stored on the diskette, a 128-byte *block* must be copied (written) from primary memory into a selected sector on the disk. Conversely, when reading back this data, a 128-byte block is copied from the sector into an area of primary memory. Since there are many sectors on a diskette, a mechanism is required for informing the disk drive which one to access. The student should know, therefore, how the individual sectors on the disk are assigned a unique identification number, called the sector address, which is used for finding the location of the sector. The process works as follows: A sector number is sent to the disk unit. The unit calculates where the sector is located on the disk. It moves the read/write head over to the correct track, and waits until the desired sector spins by. When the correct sector is under the read/write head, the data is copied or read, bit by bit, into memory until the end of the sector is reached.

At this point in the course, talk about *timings*—the speed at which disk drives operate—by itemizing each of the individual delays which sum up to form the overall timespan required to access the data. There are three distinct delays involved: The time necessary to move the head to the right track; the time spent waiting for the required sector to spin by; the time needed to read (or write) the contents of the sector. These values vary considerably; therefore, the student should obtain the specifications for a particular disk drive. Create an exercise in which the students must calculate access times based on these timings. The objective is to realize that the access time is a function of the proximity of the read/write head to the desired sector at the moment the I/O operation commences. Ask the class to determine what the largest timespan would be and, finally, what the average access time would be.

Capacity of diskettes. Another noteworthy topic is the size and capacity of diskette systems. Diskettes come in at least three sizes; the 5¼″ model is currently utilized in most microcomputer systems. In each case, diskette capacity can be increased by using two sides of the diskette *(double-sided)* and a higher density of recording *(double density);* thus capacity can be quadrupled if the user purchases a double-sided, double density drive.

Practical details about diskettes. If the students are using a diskette system in the classroom, you must teach them practical details about operating and taking care of the device. Teach, for example:

1. How to turn the machine on and off. Caution students not to do this when a diskette is in the drive: data could be lost.
2. How to handle diskettes so that they are not damaged. Inform students:
   to keep the diskette in its dust jacket when not in use.
   not to touch the surface with greasy fingers.
   not to bend, heat, or get the floppy dirty.
   to write on the diskette only with a soft felt pen.

3. What a diskette looks like and how to tell which side is which.
4. How to properly insert a diskette into the drive.
5. What the error lights and other indicators mean.
6. How to write-protect the diskette so that its contents are not inadvertently erased or changed.
7. How to create program code for reading and writing from the diskette.
8. How to use system software for manipulating the files on the diskette.
9. How to determine the amount of free space which is left on a diskette.

Hard Disks

Since the design, structure, operation, and use of hard disks are all similar to those for diskettes, the lesson material can be based on previous discussions of diskettes. Your major task, then, is to show the students how the two technologies differ. Here are the basic differences:

1. The recording medium is rigid rather than flexible.
2. There may be more than one platter placed inside a drive. The platters are stacked together on a central drive shaft.
3. Since the drive rotates much faster—at least ten times—and because the heads move in and out more rapidly, the access time of the device is much shorter.
4. Since there are more recording surfaces, a higher recording density, and more tracks, the storage capacity is much greater. Hard disks can hold millions of bytes of data.
5. Hard disks (both the drive and the platter) cost more than their floppy equivalents.

As you work through these differences, also point out how the two devices are similar. For example:

1. Both utilize read/write heads to access the information, but the hard disk might have more if there are several platters.
2. Both write in tracks and sectors, although the hard disk has more tracks.
3. Most hard disks are removable and can be placed in a disk library.
4. Both storage media are affected by dirt, dust, and grease. These problems have motivated manufacturers to develop hermetically-sealed hard disks (called Winchester disks) which resist contamination.

Before ending your coverage of disk technology, it is wise to discuss the application areas in which each one is used. Discuss several applications, such as airline reservations, word processing, and student programming. Indicate how a disk is used in each case; then get the students to discuss whether a hard disk or floppy would be better.

NETWORKING

The marriage of computers and communication facilities like the telephone system has developed rapidly since the mid-1970s. This combination—the study of which is known as *telematics*—involves hooking a number of computers together so that they can "talk" to each other and share programs and data. There are three major aspects to the study of computer networks:

1. The *technical details* of the hardware and software required to operate a network.
2. The *typical application areas* where networks are used to advantage.
3. The good and bad *effects* that telematics has on our society.

An in-depth treatment of the technical details of networking is beyond the scope of an introductory course. Only *superficial coverage* is necessary—just enough to introduce the central concepts and provide background for later discussion of application areas and societal effects. Here are some important concepts you may decide to cover:

1. The importance of networks.
2. The general layout (topology) of networks.
3. The role that the telecommunication system plays in delivering the network traffic.
4. The way modems and acoustical couplers are used to interface the computer to the telecommunication facility.
5. How digital data moves around in the network.
6. The typical speeds and volumes found in a network.
7. Measures taken to ensure accuracy, privacy, and security of the transmitted data.
8. A brief description of the notions of distributed processing and distributing databases.

Once the class has grasped the basic principles of network operation, it is time to discuss actual instances of existing networks. Select interesting examples which impact on the students' lives. Possibilities include electronic banking and electronic funds transfer, military defense networks, electronic mail, and videotext. The discussion will give the students some insight into how a network operates. The class will begin to appreciate some of the reasons for using networks. And, the students will develop a feel for how widespread the use of networks has become.

It is important to include in the discussion some of the societal issues resulting from connecting computers together and having information flowing from one machine to another. Privacy and security are good topics to pursue.

QUESTIONS

1. Using poker chips or pebbles, devise a demonstration of why the binary number system is more economical than the decimal system.
2. Create a sample drill exercise for binary addition and subtraction. Arrange the questions from easy to difficult.
3. If you are familiar with machine language programming on a particular machine, pick a subset of the instructions sufficient to demonstrate the workings of a computer at the machine language level, and indicate how you would use them.

4. Create a role-playing exercise for young students to learn about the workings of a computer system. Assign the specific roles each student will play and set out the guidelines:
   a. CPU
   b. printer
   c. user
   d. memory
   e. keyboard
   f. communications channel
   g. disk
5. Evaluate input devices in terms of suitability for student use.
6. Devise an exercise in which students look for ways in which computers could be attached to items in their homes. Do the exercise yourself.
7. If a teacher does not have a turtle, the action can be simulated using a graphics monitor on the microcomputer and creating functions in BASIC to enable commands to do this. What functions would you suggest?
8. Create a mock-up or working model of a floppy disk system. How would you demonstrate the timing?
9. Design a display case for displaying output hardware or pictures of hardware.
10. If you were taking your class on a field trip to a microcomputer store, how would you maximize their knowledge of the hardware?
11. Define the following terms: binary number, counting board, CPU, cursor, data capture, digitizer, fetch—execute cycle, hexadecimal numbers, joystick, Kbytes, microfiche, microsecond, nanosecond, network, octal numbers, RAM, role playing, ROM, touch-sensitive screen.

11

Teaching about Software

One of the major controversies in computer education is whether programming should be taught in the introductory course. Proponents of programming argue that the skill is necessary if the student is going to understand computers. Opponents argue that learning to program is unnecessary since most students will never use this skill; if programming expertise is needed, it can be taught in a subsequent course.

There is no answer to this dilemma—the school administration or teacher must make the decision. However, if programming is taught in the introductory course, it must be covered in sufficient detail to make it worthwhile for the student. Halfhearted efforts and brief overviews of the topic will not suffice.

The educator must expect to dedicate *lots of class time* to programming—fifty percent of a normal introductory computer studies course is not unreasonable—and, in addition, the students will have to spend much out-of-class time working on programming problems. The reason for this is that programming necessitates learning many different and complex skills. Often, beginning teachers mistakenly believe that learning to program primarily involves learning a programming language—such as BASIC—and once the language is mastered, the production of software will be trivial. This attitude is reflected and fostered by many publishers who produce books with titles like *BASIC Programming* or *Programming in PASCAL,* which focus almost entirely on learning the language.

Although learning the programming language is an essential component of learning to program, it is only one of several important skills that must be mastered for competent programming. These skills include problem solving using algorithms; designing software; learning a programming language; programming; debugging software; and documenting software.

PROBLEM SOLVING

A fundamental concept that students must grasp early in the course is that writing a computer program is merely the means to an end, where the end is the *solution of some problem* and the *computer is merely a tool* to help in solving the problem. Hence students first must learn how to solve problems efficiently and systematically.

Algorithms

The cornerstone of problem solving on a computer is the algorithm—a series of steps leading to the solution of a problem. The student will need to learn how to develop algorithms. The production of algorithms is not easy; therefore, a gradual buildup to the kinds of algorithms seen in everyday computer programs is necessary. It is good to start with examples from the *non-computing world,* such as a recipe for baking a cake; an income tax form; or instructions for building a model plane or swing set.

Begin by writing the complete algorithm on the board. For example, the algorithm for baking a cake as seen in a recipe book would look like this:

1. Obtain these ingredients: 1 lb. flour; 3 eggs; 1 cup sugar; 1 cup milk; 1 tbs. baking powder; 1 tbs. vanilla.
2. Mix together and pour into a greased pan.
3. Bake at 400° for 30 minutes.

This recipe is an excellent example of an algorithm in which several assumptions are made with respect to the background of the person executing the algorithm (in this case, the cook). It is assumed that the person understands the language in which the algorithm is written—English; is familiar with the terms (lb., cup, tbs.); and already knows the rudiments of cooking. You must point out, however, that if the person does not have this background, certain parts of the algorithm may be *ambiguous*—for example, 400 degrees could mean 400 degrees Celsius. Fortunately, resolving such ambiguities is straightforward since the executor of the algorithm is an intelligent human being—otherwise a recipe would be interminably long. However when the executor of an algorithm is a *computer,* the algorithm must be specified in precise, detailed terms.

Writing Algorithms

Once you have presented examples of algorithms, have the students *produce their own.* There are two ways to do this. First, ask the students to find examples of algorithms in magazines, books, their home, or the library. Require the students to comment on assumptions or ambiguities in the algorithms.

Second, ask the students to write an algorithm for some everyday problem and then test it out on their fellow students. Good examples are tying one's shoes; producing directions for getting to a room in the school; deciding whether to take an umbrella to work in the morning; or starting the car.

The results of these exercises are often amusing, especially if the suggested algorithm is not really a solution to the problem, or if the person who tests out the algorithm acts "dumb" and is unwilling to accept assumptions inherent in the algorithm.

Once students produce valid algorithms for a given problem, a worthwhile exercise is to compare them and note any differences. Some differences are to be anticipated—there are many possible solutions to the same problem. The next step is to ask the class to evaluate the different algorithms to see which they consider to be the best, most direct, most complex or poorest. The criteria for their evaluation—brevity, clarity, efficiency, understandability—should be noted.

Since the student will soon be dealing with algorithms that lead to the development of computer programs, the preceding exercise is important. When they start writing programs, students will realize that there are infinite ways to write the code to accomplish the same task, especially if the problem is complex and the resulting program is large. The objective of the programmer, in this case, is to select one of the better algorithms from the many which are available.

Heuristics

There are problems for which there are no algorithms—that is, there exists no specific set of instructions which will invariably lead to a successful solution. Examples of such problems include living a long life; getting a good grade; getting a good job; being popular; winning at chess; or picking a winner at the horse races. In these cases, the problem can only be approached by using rules of thumb to maximize the chances of success. For example, in the case of living a long life, a number of factors—eating well, avoiding stress, not smoking—all increase the probability of living longer, but do not guarantee long life.

Examples of problems requiring rules of thumb—more formally called *heuristics*—can also be found in the computing world. For example, there are chess-playing programs; software to guide a cruise missile; and software to find the fastest route for a letter through an electronic mail network. Heuristics currently play a small role in software production; the vast majority of computer programs are based on algorithms.

DESIGN TOOLS

While discussing algorithms for everyday problems like those listed earlier, you should simultaneously introduce the design tool which the students will eventually use to define algorithms for computers programs. You should select one of the two major design tools commonly used in the computing industry—namely, *flowcharts* and *pseudo-code.* While either one is applicable for the introductory computer studies class, our coverage will be limited to teaching about the production and use of flowcharts.

Flowcharts

Flowcharts are a standardized way of specifying algorithms in two-dimensional form. They consist of a combination of differently shaped *boxes* connected by *directed lines or arrows.* The boxes represent the steps of the algorithm, while the arrows indicate the order in which the steps are executed. Decisions are represented by diamond shaped figures. A sample flowchart on how to pet a cat is illustrated in Figure 11-1.

Figure 11-1 The first flowcharts should be for problems that are not computer-related, but deal with common events in the students' lives.

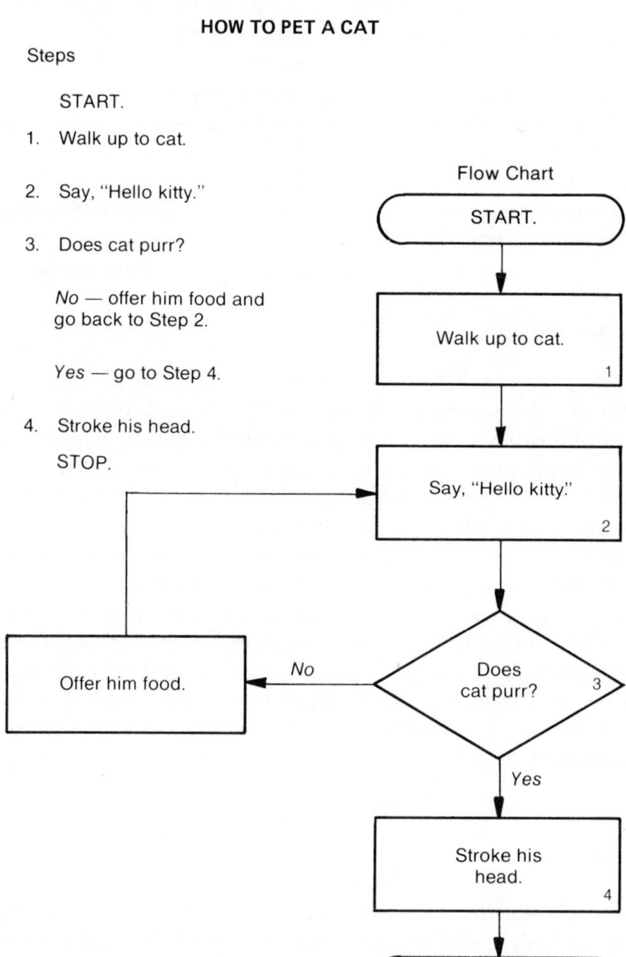

In order to draw flowcharts that are easy to understand and to modify, there are some basic rules which the student should follow.

1. Flowcharts should be written in pencil so they can be altered neatly and easily.
2. The contents of each box should be printed, rather than cursive.
3. A template should be used in drawing flowcharts (see Figure 11-2). A template is necessary to avoid the unreadable product which often results when the flowchart is drawn freehand.
4. Whenever possible, the flow of control (direction of arrows) should be from top to bottom, left to right.

Figure 11-2 An example of a flowcharting template, which is used to create neat flowcharts quickly.

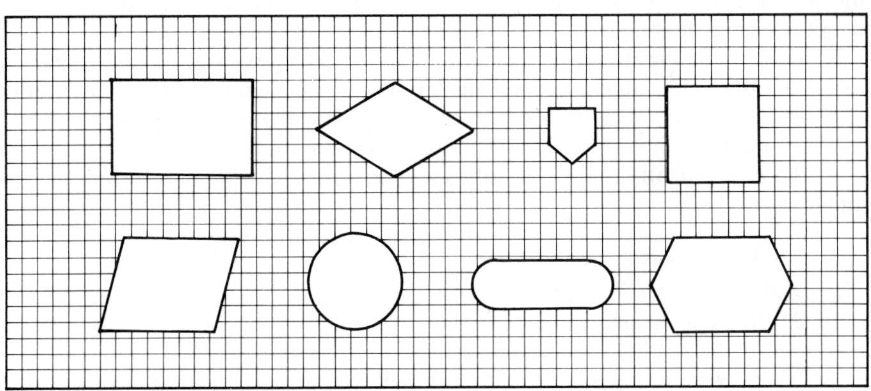

INTRODUCTION TO PROGRAM WRITING

Once the student has been introduced to problem solving, algorithms, and flowcharts in a nonprogramming environment, the next step is to start writing *real programs* for real problems. At this time, emphasize that the computer is similar to the human in that the machine is responsible for taking a series of instructions in the form of an algorithm, going through them one-by-one while solving the problem. However, the computer differs from us in several notable ways.

First, the computer *does not understand English.* Instead, a special language—the *programming language*—is necessary for communication between programmer and computer. Second, algorithms written in this programming language cannot contain *ambiguities.* There is only one meaning for each statement in the language; even if the programmer intended something else, the computer nevertheless will do what it is programmed to do.

Third, the programmer must be *precise* when writing the instructions of the algorithm in the form of a computer program. Unlike us, the computer cannot read between the lines to figure out what to do if something is left out. Finally, if a computer program does not work properly, the *computer cannot sense this failure.* Instead, it performs the wrong operation until a human stops the program and makes the necessary changes.

For the average student, learning to use a programming language is not easy. Much is to be learned—usually in a short time. Therefore, the introduction to the programming language must be carefully planned or the student will get lost. There are three ways to maximize the student's experience:

1. Start by working with a *hypothetical programming language* that is much simpler than a real programming language.
2. When dealing with the actual programming language, introduce the concepts *one by one,* waiting until each item is clearly understood before going on to the next one.
3. Ensure that the student *understands* the reason for learning each programming language construct.

Introductory example. When teaching the introductory computer studies class, first utilize an imaginary computing language which gives the students an introduction to the basic concepts of programming without getting mired in the details of a real language.

Start by telling the students that they have an *imaginary robot* which is placed inside a room. The robot is capable of stepping forward one millimeter at a time, and can turn only in a clockwise direction. The objective is to program the robot to get out of the door which is in the top left-hand corner.

To start off, the robot has only three commands in its programming language:

1. STEP—step forward 1 mm.
2. TURN(N)—turn N degrees clockwise.
3. STOP—stop the program.

Then, with the class' help, write the following program on the board, which solves the problem of the robot getting out of the room as shown in Figure 11-3.

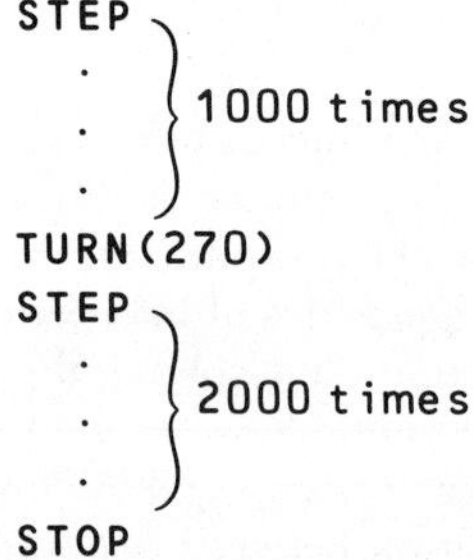

Then draw a flowchart which corresponds to this program.

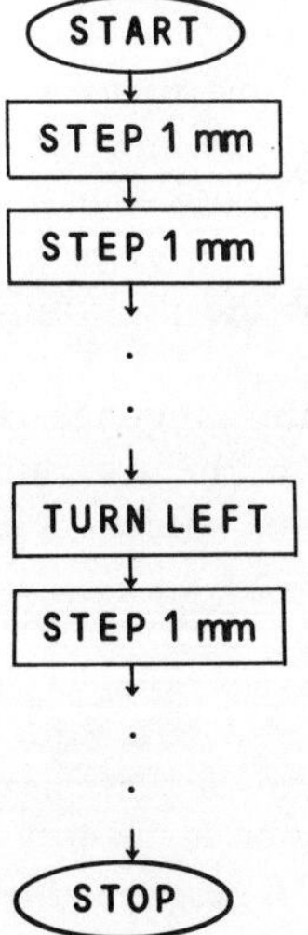

Figure 11-3 Robot placed in room 1 meter from one wall and 2 meters from the other.

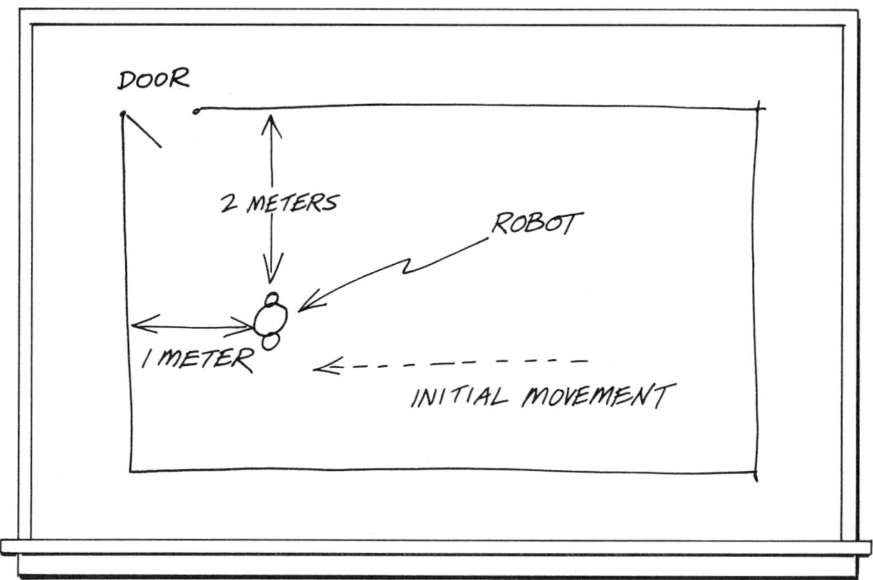

Point out that the program is an example of *linear code,* which is one of the building blocks of all programs. Also point out that the statements in the flowcharting boxes are not identical to the corresponding statements as they appear in the program. This is an essential feature of any good flowchart, since one of the purposes of the flowchart is to make a program easier to understand. (If the flowchart and program were essentially the same, then the flowchart would be redundant.)

Ask the class if the flowchart is *efficient*—obviously, it is not—and suggest changes to the flowchart as follows.

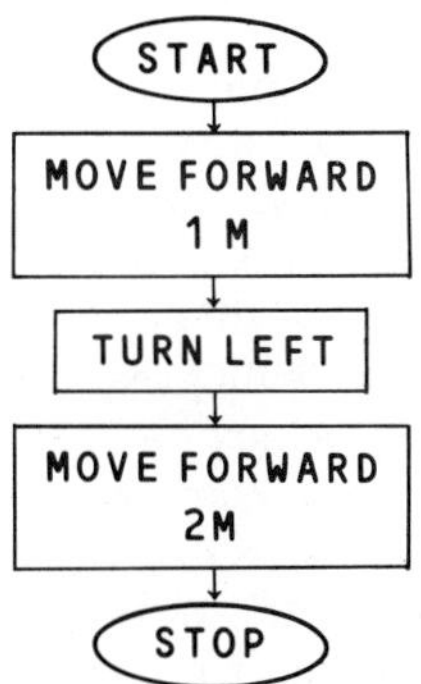

What results is an even better example of making the flowchart and program different from each other. In this case, the flowchart is *easy to understand* compared to the program. Having it understandable makes it easy to transcribe the flowchart into the program.

The decrease in the size of the flowchart thus far has produced no reduction in the size of the program which, as written on the board, contains code that occurs over and over again (STEP, STEP, STEP), making it lengthy. However, a corresponding reduction is possible if we introduce another programming construct which is capable of handling repetition. The students should realize that the phenomenon of repetition occurs in all software.

When the REPEAT command is added to the program, a greatly *shortened version* is possible:

```
REPEAT 1000 TIMES
   STEP
TURN (270)
REPEAT 2000 TIMES
   STEP
STOP
```

The algorithm can be handled another way, by adding some additional features which permit the robot to count up to 1000 while taking a step each time until the limit is reached:

```
100 COUNT = 0
200 STEP
300 COUNT = COUNT + 1
400 IF COUNT NOT EQUAL 1000 GOTO 200
```

In the second case, five new features have been included which are standard components of most programming languages:

1. The use of a variable (COUNT).
2. The use of arithmetic operations—in the present example, = and + .
3. The IF or decision statement.
4. The branching statement (GOTO).
5. The use of labels (100, 200) at the start of each program statement.

The next step is to introduce the concepts of *input* and *output*—both in terms of the required flowcharting symbols and the language statements which are used. Start discussing the concept of output by suggesting that the ROBOT speak the words "I am at the door" at the end of the program. This capability requires the symbol for output ▱ at the appropriate point in the flowchart and a corresponding statement such as `SPEAK "I AM AT THE DOOR."` in the program.

To deal with the concept of inputting information, assume that the robot understands numbers which are "whispered in its mechanical ear" and which are subsequently placed in the robot's memory, residing in one or more numeric variables. The format of the input statement is something like:

`INPUT NUMBER(N)`, where N is the name of the variable.

Before continuing, point out that the algorithm as it stands is restricted, allowing the robot to get out the door only when it is placed precisely two meters from the wall and one meter from the door. If the robot is placed anywhere else in the room, it cannot get to the door. In order to accommodate this new case, another algorithm must be developed and a different program must be written. Fortunately, real programs usually do not work this way. In most cases they provide more *generality,* being able to solve a class of problems rather than one specific problem. Hence, in the robot example, a more realistic algorithm would work no matter where the robot is placed in the room—one program would cover all cases.

Achieving this generality is easy if we tell the robot where it is in the room before it starts to move. Thus, we include two input statements to enter the x, y

Figure 11-4 Updated version of the robot flowchart and program.

FLOWCHART:

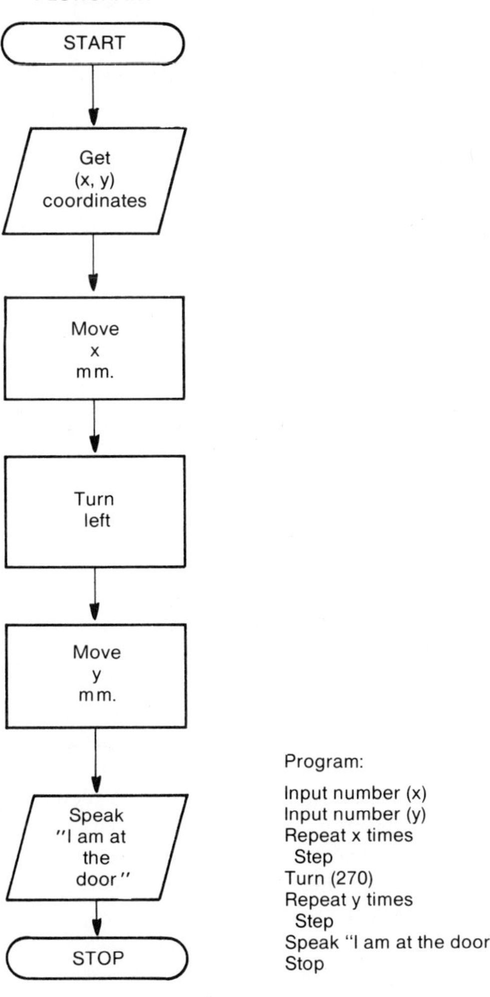

Program:

```
Input number (x)
Input number (y)
Repeat x times
  Step
Turn (270)
Repeat y times
  Step
Speak "I am at the door"
Stop
```

coordinates into variables, and the robot uses these variables as counters to control the amount of movement. Thus we insert the statements **INPUT NUMBER (X)** and **INPUT NUMBER Y** at the beginning of the program and change the REPEAT statements to **REPEAT X TIMES** and **REPEAT Y TIMES**. The updated flowchart and program is shown in Figure 11-4.

Finally, we assume that the robot is placed anywhere in the room (facing the top wall) and is required to find its own way out without first being told where it is. Doing this is impossible without some kind of sensor, so we provide the robot with three feelers—one on the left side, one in front, and one on the right side. The action of the robot is to check whether the front feeler is touching a wall. If not, it moves forward one millimeter and repeats the operation in the following manner:

```
500 IF FRONT FEELER GOTO 700
600 STEP
650 GOTO 500
```

Once the robot is touching the wall and the program branches to statement 700, it turns 270 degrees and then moves forward step by step, using an **"IF RIGHT FEELER GOTO"** command, until the right-hand sensor is *not* touching, which means it is at the door.

The preceding modification is the last one to make in the ROBOT program. By this time, the students have learned much about programming without facing the realities of an actual programming language, and are ready to tackle the real thing.

For homework assignments, ask the students to work on problems such as:

1. What happens if there is no door in the room?
2. What happens if a door exists in the top wall in line with the robot's initial movement?
3. Place the robot anywhere in the room—but not directly facing the wall—and program it to get out.

LEARNING THE BASIC LANGUAGE

There are a number of different programming languages used in the introductory computer studies class; BASIC, PASCAL, and LOGO are the most common. BASIC is the *most popular,* and is chosen by the majority of teachers. Hence, our discussion of programming languages used in the classroom is restricted to BASIC.

When the reference manual for any programming language is examined, it is evident that there is much to be learned if complete mastery of the language is desired. BASIC is simpler than most languages, but even in this case, learning all its intricacies takes a long time.

Fortunately, it is not necessary for the introductory computer studies student to learn the entire language. The primary objective of the course is not to learn the language, but to learn the basics of good programming. To achieve this goal, it is necessary to learn a *subset of the BASIC language*—a subset that is sufficient for the student to write the programs which will be assigned. The rest of the language can be taught in subsequent courses or simply left for students to learn independently.

CORE ELEMENTS OF INTRODUCTORY BASIC COURSE

Which fundamental concepts of the BASIC language should be stressed in introductory computer studies? The following lists comprise the *core* elements.

Program Statements

1. A program consists of a series of statements terminated by the END statement.
2. Each statement is preceded by a line number uniquely identifying the statement in the program. Line numbers have a specific range (for example, 0 to 99999) depending upon which version of BASIC the student is using.
3. Statements are executed in sequential order in terms of increasing line numbers, unless some form of branching statement is encountered.
4. Statements always contain reserved words (like IF and PRINT) which cannot be used by the programmer as the name of a variable.
5. Some statements are not executable, but are used for documentation. These statements, which begin with the keyword REM or !, can contain any combination of letters, numbers, and punctuation since they are not bound by the normal grammatical rules of BASIC.
6. All other BASIC statements must adhere to a specific, predefined syntax; any deviations from this syntax results in an incorrect statement.

Data

1. There are three major categories of data used in BASIC programs: integer numbers, real numbers, and strings. Each of these data types can appear in two forms: as constants or as variables.
2. The student should learn the format of integer constants, real constants, and string constants.
3. There are strict rules about what legally constitutes a variable name, both in terms of the combination of characters and the size of the name.
4. Each variable has a notation for indicating its data type: integers (X%); reals (X); and strings (X$).

Arithmetic (Numeric Manipulation)

1. The standard arithmetic operators are:
   a. addition (+)
   b. subtraction (−)
   c. multiplication (*)
   d. division (/)
   e. unary minus (−)
   f. exponentiation (↑ or **)
2. Variables, constants, and arithmetic operators can be combined to form numeric expressions (e.g., x + y − 2).
3. The arithmetic operators have a precedence relationship which defines which opera-

tion is done first. The order is unary minus, exponentiation, multiplication and division, and addition and subtraction. For example, in the equation x + y*2, the multiplication is performed before the addition.

4. The normal precedence relationship can be overridden by the use of parentheses. For example, in (x + y)*2, the addition is performed first.
5. The results of an arithmetic expression can be placed into a variable by means of the assignment statement, which has two forms:

   a. `LET X = Y + Z`

   b. `X = Y + Z`

   An arithmetic expression is also legal wherever a simple numeric value would be valid. For example:

   `PRINT X + Y` or

   `IF Y*2>Z-3 THEN GOTO 400.`

6. Integers and reals can be mixed together in the same expression. The student should understand the rules for mixing modes in this way.
7. When a real value is assigned to an integer variable, the fractional portion of the real number is truncated.
8. A subset of the numeric library functions should be learned, namely:
   a. INT
   b. SGN
   c. ABS
   d. SQR
   e. EXP
9. If the class is mathematically oriented, then the trigonometric functions can be studied, for example SIN, COS, TAN, ATN, LOG.
10. Random values can be generated by using the RND function. These values range between 0 and 1.

String Manipulations

1. Strings can be stored in string variables using the assignment statement. For example, `X$ = "BILL"` and `X$ = Y$`.
2. Two or more strings can be tacked together to form a larger string using the concatenation operator, as in `X$ = "BILL" + " " + "SMITH"`.
3. The following string functions should be covered: length of string (LEN), extract a substring from the left or right end of a string (LEFT$, RIGHT$), and extract a substring from the middle of a string (MID$).
4. Search for a substring within a string (INSTR).

Memory Manipulation

If the students are using microcomputers which provide *peek* and *poke* functions in BASIC, it is worthwhile to cover these instructions. However, you should emphasize that their usage is not an example of good programming practice.

Data Structures (Subscripted Variables)

1. Cover both one-dimensional arrays (lists) and two-dimensional arrays (tables).
2. Subscripted variables are declared by means of the DIMENSION (DIM) statement which is used to specify the number of cells in the list or table.
   a. DIM X(10) sets up an 11-element list.
   b. DIM X(20,30) sets up a 21 by 31 table.
3. If a subscripted variable is not declared with a DIM statement, then a default size is established.
4. Arrays and tables can be used to hold integers, reals, or strings. The data type is established using the same rules that apply to simple variables.
5. The individual cells of a list or table are referenced by giving the cell number: X(I) and X(I,J) where I and J can be numeric variables, constants, or numeric expressions.
6. Students should be careful to avoid writing code which generates out-of-bounds array references, in other words, the subscript is greater than the dimension size.
7. If a real, fractional value is used as a subscript, the subscript is first truncated to an integer.
8. The first subscript of a table is commonly called the *row,* while the second subscript is called the *column.*

Data Entry

1. There are two ways to enter data into a BASIC program: with the READ statement and with the INPUT statement.
2. The READ statement gets its data from values which are inserted into DATA statements elsewhere in the program.
3. The INPUT statement gets its data from values entered on the terminal keyboard.
4. INPUT's and READ's can be used to enter integer, real, or string values.
5. There are specific rules governing the format of the data values which, if broken, cause a run-time error to be generated.
6. All values are placed into variables when accessed with a READ or INPUT statement; either simple variables or subscripted variables are suitable.
7. More than one data value can be entered by a single INPUT or READ statement by including more than one variable, separated by commas.
8. Since prompted input is utilized so frequently, the INPUT statement can contain a string which is printed out before the data values are entered.

Printing the Results

1. The PRINT command is used to generate output from the user's program.
2. It can be used to print out numeric values, strings, or a combination of both.
3. If more than one value is printed, the values are separated by commas or semicolons in the PRINT statement.
4. A comma between two values causes the second one to be aligned in a print zone. The student should consult the programming manual for a precise definition of the print zone for each type of machine to be used.
5. A semicolon between two values causes the second one to be placed immediately

after the first one. (A space may be inserted in certain cases; the programming manual should be consulted to determine when this will occur.)

6. A comma or semicolon at the end of a PRINT statement (that is, with no value after it) causes the new line to be omitted. This means that a subsequent PRINT statement does not produce output on the next line of the screen, but it is tacked to the end of the previous line.
7. A PRINT statement on its own causes the output to skip one line on the screen.
8. The TAB function is used to position the output at a specific position on the screen.
9. The PRINT USING statement can be utilized for formatted output; however, we do not recommend its inclusion in the introductory computer studies course.

File Manipulation

Students normally are not required to write software which manipulates tape or disk files in the introductory computer studies course. However, if it is deemed necessary, teach just simple sequential input and output.

Graphics

Performing graphics manipulations may or may not be possible, depending upon the computer and the BASIC package that are available. If graphics functions *are* available, make use of them. Most students are highly motivated to write programs which draw pictures, partly because most of the software they have used (like video games) works this way. Most student software which does not involve graphics requires calculations to be performed on numbers—for example, converting Fahrenheit to Celsius or adding numbers and computing the mean. Programs which generate graphics output provide a welcome change. Also, since programs which produce graphics images are output-oriented, debugging the software is easier.

Since the technique for creating pictures and the commands available in BASIC vary from machine to machine, it is impossible to specify exactly which BASIC statements should be taught. But we can make the following suggestions:

1. Students should understand the concept of screen resolution and how it varies from machine to machine, and should be aware of the relationship between the resolution of the screen and the amount of memory necessary to hold the picture.
2. All graphics systems have a coordinate system which is used to specify a particular point (pixel) on the screen.
3. The programmer can randomly select a particular point—a cursor—on the screen from which to start drawing a subpicture.
4. Some computers have special keys which display images instead of the traditional alphanumeric letters. These images are usually the same size as a normal letter. The programmer creates a picture by piecing the small images together.
5. Other computers have a plotting package wherein specified BASIC statements are used to perform graphical functions such as "draw a line," "draw a box," "print characters on an angle," or "draw a circle." There is no restriction on the size of the image.
6. If available on the computer, the teacher should include features which allow clearing the screen, erasing specific parts of the screen, and "homing" the cursor (placing it in the top left-hand corner).

7. If color graphics are possible, the commands necessary to utilize color manipulation should be covered.

Simple Control Structures

The GOTO command is used to unconditionally branch to another statement in the program. The STOP command is used to terminate execution anywhere within a program.

Relational Expressions

1. Relational expressions are conditional statements normally utilized in the IF statement.
2. Relational expressions evaluate to either TRUE or FALSE.
3. A relational expression consists of data values combined with relational operators and possibly Boolean operators.
4. Relational operators compare two values to see if they are the same, less than, greater than, and so on. They can be used with either numeric values or strings.
5. The relational operators are:
   a. < less than
   b. < = less than or equal to
   c. > greater than
   d. > = greater than or equal to
   e. = equal to
   f. < > not equal to
   Examples are: A>B, J< >I + 2, S$<Y$.
6. When comparing string values, the meanings of = and < > are obvious. The other relational operators produce a truth value according to the position in the alphabet assigned to the letters of the string (called the collating sequence). Thus, "ABD" is less than "EFG" but greater than "ABC."
7. If the version of BASIC supports Boolean operators, you should cover at least the following: NOT, AND, and OR. An example of an expression containing a Boolean operator is "A>B AND C>D," which is true only if both relational expressions are true.

Conditional Transfer

The relational expression can be used to conditionally branch to another statement in the program. There are two ways to do this:

1. IF relational expression THEN line
2. IF relational expression THEN GOTO line

A branch occurs to "line" if the relational expression is true; otherwise, execution continues sequentially. Some examples are:

```
IF A>B THEN 300
IF X<B and X<C THEN GOTO 400.
```

Multi-way Branch

1. A commonly occurring construct in programs is when the algorithm requires a branch to two or more places, depending upon some condition. An example is the input to a menu request where the user keys in a number indicating which option is wanted:

```
TYPE IN THE NUMBER OF THE OPTION YOU WANT:
   1. Delete a record.
   2. Add a record.
   3. Change a record.
   4. Print a record.
```

In this case, the programmer would provide four segments of code which handle each of the options respectively. The number which the user keys in would be stored in a variable, and the programmer could handle the subsequent transfers with a multi-way branch such as:

```
ON NUM GOTO 200, 300, 400, 500
```

where NUM is the option, and the line numbers represent the beginning statements of the four code segments.

2. The student should be aware of what happens if a number (in this case, NUM) is out-of-range (that is, <1 or >number of options).

Conditional Execution

1. Most versions of BASIC provide the option of conditionally executing a statement or statements depending upon the value of a relational expression.
2. These constructs allow the student to produce code which is more "structured" than the code which would be created if conditional transfers were used, and their utilization should be encouraged.
3. There are three major forms of statement provided: Single statement IF; Multiple statement (Block) IF; and IF-THEN-ELSE.
4. The "single statement IF" causes the command that follows on the rest of the line to be executed if the condition is true; for example, `100 IF X>0 PRINT X`.
5. The "multiple statement IF" will cause two or more lines of code to be executed if the condition is true. Example:

```
100 IF A>B THEN
200     PRINT Y
300     Z = 0
400 END IF
```

6. The IF-THEN-ELSE is used to select one of two blocks of code to execute depending upon the value of the condition. Example:

```
100 IF A>B THEN
200     PRINT Y
300     Z = 0
400 ELSE
500     PRINT K
600     Z = 1
700 END IF
```

Iteration

1. There are many constructs available in BASIC to simplify the construction of iterative code. One of these, the FOR loop, is available in all versions of BASIC. The rest may not be provided; even if they are, teaching them is not necessary.
2. The FOR loop is used to repeat a section of code one or more times. An example of such an iteration is:

```
100 FOR I = 1 TO 6
200     PRINT I, I↑2
300 NEXT I
```

   which will print out the first six integers and their squares.
3. The students should understand the three main components of the FOR statement, namely the controlling variable ("I" in the example); its initial value; and its final value.
4. The initial and final values can be any valid numeric expression. The controlling variable can contain a real number and thus take on fractional values.
5. Normally, the controlling variable increases by unity for each iteration. This convention can be overridden by including the STEP keyword to force increments other than unity. Examples:

```
FOR I = 1 TO N STEP 2
FOR I = 6 TO N STEP -1
```

   Note that in the second case, the program counts backwards (I equals 6, 5, 4, 3, 2, 1).
6. The concept of nested loops (one inside the other) should be stressed.
7. Show the students several examples of how FOR loops are used to manipulate the cells in a list or table.

Subprograms

1. There are two main subprogram mechanisms available in BASIC: the subroutine and the function.
2. Subroutines use the GOSUB statement to call the subroutine and the RETURN statement to go back to the main program.
3. The students should understand the nature of parameter passing between a program and a subroutine and realize that BASIC subroutines provide no mechanism for passing parameters, but this must be done explicitly in the code of the program.

4. They should understand the dangers of branching either into or out of a subroutine without using the GOSUB and RETURN statements, respectively.
5. Functions are created using the DEF statement, and are used in the main program by simply giving the name.
6. In most versions of BASIC, there is a restricted convention for the name of the function.
7. Functions come in two forms: the single line function and the multiline function. The teaching of single line functions in the introductory computer studies course is questionable due to the restricted utility of the feature.
8. Functions provide an explicit parameter passing mechanism which makes their usage preferable to subroutines.
9. Functions are easier to understand if the teacher relates their structure and utilization to the examples of library functions which the student has encountered previously in the course.
10. The relationship between subprograms and modular design should be stressed.

TESTING AND DEBUGGING

Experienced programmers will concede that any program they write—no matter how carefully they design the algorithm and write the code—will not work properly right away. It will contain errors which must be eradicated before the program functions correctly. Beginning programmers are especially prone to these errors; hence, a substantial portion of the study of programming must be devoted to training the student in the best way to create error-free programs. Four major topics must be covered in this respect:

1. The kinds of errors that can occur and how they can be spotted.
2. Techniques for testing a program to see whether it functions as specified.
3. Methods for systematically working through a program and removing any errors which might exist.
4. Ways of writing programs to avoid errors.

Errors

The term most computer scientists use to indicate an error in a program is *bug*. The process of removing bugs is called *debugging*. There are three kinds of bugs that can occur; these include syntax, run-time, and logic errors. The first two are relatively easy to fix, while the third one can be much more difficult.

Syntax errors. Syntax errors are caused by incorrect usage of the programming language. Examples of syntax errors in BASIC are:

```
100 LAT A = 2
200 FOR I EQUAL 1 to 3
300 PRINT X.Y.Z
```

which should be correctly written as:

```
100 LET A = 2
200 FOR I = 1 TO 3
300 PRINT X, Y, Z
```

Other than ensuring that they have a sound foundation in keyboarding techniques, you cannot prevent the students from making *typographical errors* in their programs. Unfortunately, no matter how well the students keyboard and how well they have mastered the language, syntax errors still arise. Since syntax errors always cause *error diagnostics* to be printed out, a basic objective is to familiarize students with the meaning of such diagnostics and the conditions under which they occur. Consider the following exercises in order to achieve this goal.

1. Require students to study the list of error messages (diagnostics) provided in the programming manual.
2. Ask students to type in incorrect code (you provide this code), examine the errors diagnostics which are produced, and make corrections.
3. Assign homework problems which require the student to examine listings of incorrect programs. Their task is to identify the syntax errors and then rewrite the code in its correct form.

Run-time errors. With run-time errors, a program is syntactically correct; but when it runs, an illegal condition is encountered, which causes the program to abort. Examples of illegal conditions include attempts to divide a number by zero; running out of data on READs; and referencing array elements which are out-of-bounds. As in the case of syntax errors, BASIC prints out an error diagnostic. If the student is familiar with these diagnostics, a run-time error is not hard to rectify. Learning to identify and correct run-time errors is basically the same as the procedure outlined for syntax errors.

Logic errors. Logic errors are the hardest category of errors to handle. A logic error is an error which causes the program to *work differently from how it was intended to work.* Here is a simple example of a logic error in a program which is supposed to find the average of three numbers:

`LET AVE = (X + Y + Z)/2` divide by 3, not by 2!

Of course, most logic errors are not as simple and straightforward as the one shown, primarily because the error is hidden in many lines of code. Unfortunately, compared to syntax and run-time errors, logic errors do not generate error diagnostics; therefore, the onus is entirely upon the student to determine whether the program works correctly or if it contains one or more logic errors; and which statements are in error and what adjustments are necessary to correct them. Most of the work of testing and debugging which will be discussed next entails this kind of error.

TESTING THE SOFTWARE ON THE COMPUTER

Once syntax errors have been eliminated from a program, the student must perform tests to see if it works properly. This is done by *running the program, supplying appropriate input data* wherever necessary, and *examining the output* of the program to see if it is the same as what was expected. If it is not, the bugs which are causing the discrepancy are tracked down and eliminated; then the program is rerun. For example, if a student has written a program to calculate the average of three numbers as follows,

```
100 INPUT X,Y,Z
200 PRINT (X + Y + Z)/2
```

and runs the program with input values 3, 4, 5, the program will produce 6 as the result. Since the student is expecting 4 as the final answer, a bug is lurking somewhere and must be fixed.

Since most programs are written to accommodate some generality—by processing more than one set of data values—it follows that a program should be thoroughly tested with different input values to show that it works properly. Suppose we have a program which is designed to add up "n" positive numbers and compute their average:

```
100 SUM = 0
200 N = 0
300 INPUT NUMBER
400 IF NUMBER = -1 THEN GOTO 800
500 SUM = SUM + NUMBER
600 N = N + 1
700 GOTO 300
800 PRINT "AVERAGE IS "; SUM/N
900 END
```

The student would begin by showing that the program works for any 2 values (that is, 7, 13), 3 values (4, 7, 9), and so on. Unfortunately the program cannot be tested for all possible values; this would take forever. At some point the student must conclude that if the program works for several test cases (in other words, if it works for 2 and 3 values), it works for 1 value, 4 values, and 5 values, etc. Making this conclusion would be almost valid in the present example; however, there are two other conditions which must be examined in order to be absolutely sure.

First, the student should test to see if the program works for *zero values* (that is, the first input value is – 1). If such a check were done a run-time error would be obtained because of the attempt to divide by zero. Consequently, the program should be altered to accommodate this situation by adding the following statements:

```
800 IF N<>0 GOTO 850
810 PRINT "YOU MUST TYPE IN AT LEAST ONE DATA VALUE."
820 GOTO 100
```

and by changing the line number of the original statement at 800 to 850.

Second, the student should test to see what happens if *non-numeric values* are entered; for example: `one, six, end, bill`. Once again, a run-time error will be produced, and the code should be altered so that the program works properly.

Most beginning programmers fail to test their programs properly. Often they try out the code on a few restricted cases and, if the program seems to be working, they assume that everything is all right. Hence, it is necessary to stress the importance of thorough testing. It is also wise to give the students ample opportunity to practice this skill by examining prewritten programs, testing out the code, and correcting any errors as they proceed. The habit of testing thoroughly also can be ingrained by giving it particular emphasis (in terms of mark deductions) when grading student programming assignments.

Often, the omission of adequate test runs is the result of cumulative fatigue on the student's part. After working on a program for many hours, there is great temptation to simply quit when it finally seems to be working. The best way to avoid these shortcuts is to have the students indicate, before they write the program, how it will be tested. Examine these documents and make suggestions and improvements. This "testing itinerary" is then used as a guideline during the final stage of programming. Assign marks based upon how closely the original plan is followed.

DEBUGGING OF PROGRAMS

The conscientious teacher will ensure that the students know the techniques to discover and correct bugs in a program. The students should be thoroughly familiar with the common logic errors committed by the beginner. A partial list includes:

1. *Omission* of *one or more lines of code* from the program when it is keyed into the computer.
2. *Branches to the wrong locations* in the program.
3. *Accidental use of a variable name* which is different from the one which was intended, but which is identical to a variable name which has been used for other purposes.
4. *Repetition of a loop* for one iteration too many, or one iteration too few.
5. Inadvertent *alterations to the index variable* which is used to access the cells of a list or table.
6. *Mixing up the rows and columns* of a table.

You should stress the importance of using a systematic debugging procedure which gradually eliminates the bugs one by one. To illustrate how this works, briefly examine the *nonsystematic* approach used by the majority of beginners. Suppose a student-written program contains ten bugs, and the manifestation of these errors is that the program seems to do absolutely nothing when it runs. To get the program working, the student stares at the listing, guesses at the cause of the error, changes the code, and reruns the program. The almost inevitable result of this procedure is that once again nothing happens—the bug may have been fixed, but the nine remaining bugs are still causing problems. Or the student might have made things worse by the haphazard approach. Incorrect code may have been changed to a different (but still incorrect) code. Or previously correct code may have been changed, thereby introducing another bug.

A student using the preceding approach to debugging can wander aimlessly and never get the program to run. The systematic approach to debugging, on the other hand, is designed to converge upon a solution—the elimination of all the bugs in the program.

In this method, the student starts at the beginning of the code and slowly works through to the last line, methodically eliminating each error as it is encountered. This task is accomplished by inserting PRINT statements at *strategic locations* in the program which will allow the student to check both where the program is going as it branches around, and what is happening to its variables.

The first set of PRINT statements is placed *near the start* of the code, the program is run, and the output from the PRINT statement is examined to see if it corresponds to what is expected. If the output differs from what is anticipated, a bug (or bugs) is assumed to be the culprit. Fortunately, finding and correcting the bug(s) should not be difficult, since the programmer is almost certain that they reside somewhere between the beginning of the program and the location of the PRINT statement—a restricted subset of the program. Once this section of the code has been corrected, the programmer inserts additional PRINT statements a little further along in the program (the previous PRINT statement(s) are usually removed) and the entire process is repeated. If a bug is detected in the new situation, it is remedied as before. Once again, finding the bug is relatively straightforward since it almost certainly resides between the location of the previous PRINT statement and the current one. The student continues the procedure until the entire program has been perused and debugged.

While this procedure is regarded as being very effective, it is frequently shunned by beginning programmers since they are unwilling to spend the additional time required to do a thorough job. Unfortunately, the time spent making haphazard changes and randomly chasing after bugs can completely eclipse the extra time needed to accommodate the systematic approach.

Some versions of BASIC provide special tools to assist in the debugging process. One of these—the *trace package*—functions by printing out the sequence in which the statements are executed as the program runs. On completion, the programmer examines the trace output to determine whether it worked in the expected manner. To facilitate interpretation of the results, the values of selected variables can also be displayed as the trace is taking place.

Another debugging tool, the *breakpoint package,* allows the student to specify locations where it is desirable to temporarily stop the program (called the breakpoint). The program is then executed normally until the breakpoint is reached. When this happens, the program stops running, allowing the student to examine various data values, insert another breakpoint(s), and request the program to continue.

You should stress the relationship between the proper utilization of *structured programming* technique and the ease of debugging a program. One aspect of structured programming is the *absence of uncontrolled branching* within the code. Uncontrolled branching can make a program difficult to debug, since it becomes hard for the programmer to keep track of what the program is doing as it bounces around.

Avoiding Programming Errors

Most beginning programmers spend too little time on the original design of the program and rush hastily into writing the code. The inevitable result is a program which is full of bugs that take a long time to remove. Obviously, avoidance of these unnecessary errors is extremely important if the student wishes to create a working program within a reasonable amount of time. How does the student write a program so that errors will be avoided? Here are some suggestions.

Emphasize the importance of thoroughly *understanding a programming problem* before working on its solution. By doing this, the student will minimize the chances of misinterpreting the problem and writing a program which, although it works, is not a solution to the original problem.

Emphasize the use of *proper design techniques*—that is, the careful production of a comprehensive flowchart (or pseudo-code). It is particularly important that the flowchart or pseudo-code be completed before coding is even started. It is much easier to spot and fix bugs in the flowcharting stage than it is later.

The student should adhere to the tenets of *structured programming* whenever possible. In particular, special effort should be made to produce code in which the flow of control is managed and understandable. Furthermore, student programs should be divided up into small modules rather than consisting of one giant piece of code. Small modules each represent a less complicated component of the overall problem, and the ensuing algorithm and program will contain proportionately fewer bugs.

The students must *write out their program code by hand* (preferably in pencil) before keying it in to the computer. This helps eliminate unnecessary bugs which crop up as the algorithm is transcribed from the flowcharted version to the actual program statements.

Once the program has been completely written out, care must be taken to ensure that the code *corresponds exactly* to the algorithm as expressed in the flowchart. If a discrepancy exists but goes unnoticed, it can cause problems later on in trying to track down the resulting bug.

A recommended practice at this point in the program development process is to *walk through* the program code statement by statement, pretending to execute the code just as the computer would do it. This technique can quickly isolate discrepancies that would not be noticed just by rereading the code.

After the program finally has been keyed into the computer, *compare the program listing* with the handwritten version on a statement-by-statement basis. When keyboarding, the student frequently will make minor errors or even leave out lines of a program. These errors are easy to spot if a checking procedure is immediately used; however, if the discrepancies are left unknowingly in the program, they will cause needless problems later.

DOCUMENTATION

One of the most neglected topics in many introductory computer studies classes is the ways and means of producing adequate documentation for the students' programs. Documentation refers to the set of auxiliary materials supplied with the program code to make it more understandable. In industrial programming, this documentation typically consists of a *description of the program algorithm* in the form of a flowchart, pseudo-code, or another design tool; non-executable statements, *comments* interspersed in the program code which describe what the program is doing; and one or more *manuals* which specify how to use the software.

If the student is to learn how to program properly, a good foundation in the methods of proper documentation is necessary. There are a number of reasons for doing this which apply to both actual programming as an occupation and programming in the classroom.

Documentation—particularly flowcharts or pseudo-code—functions as an *aid to the programmer* when developing software. The programmer first creates a flowchart as a solution to the programming problem; then, using the flowchart as a guide, writes the actual code for the program. This procedure is faster and less error-prone than creating the program code directly.

Documentation facilitates the *readability of the program* while it is undergoing development so that changes or corrections to the code are easier to make. It also *expedites the alteration of programs* at some point in the future if the user's needs change. These alterations, which are often termed maintenance, are particularly difficult if a person other than the original program developer has to make them. When this happens, there must be a clear understanding of the program's intent, structure, and operation—goals that are best fulfilled by providing clear, understandable documentation.

Most large computer projects are usually undertaken by a team, since the task is too great for one person. When *team programming* is utilized, each person works on a section of the code; at the same time, each must be aware of the overall product and, hence, of what their colleagues are doing. In-depth documentation of their work is the best vehicle for enabling effective communication between team members.

In most large commercial data processing departments, the methods for creating program documentation are *standardized.* Standardization implies that a specified set of procedures are laid out for documenting programs so that it is done in the same way for all software developed by the company. These rules, called *standards,* make program maintenance much easier since all the programmers in the organization are working within the same framework.

Good Documentation

Well-documented examples of student-produced software should consist of a *neatly drawn flowchart* or clear pseudo-code and program code liberally interspersed with comments (REMARKS in BASIC) which explain, in clear English, what the statements are supposed to do.

In student software, the *variable names should be meaningful,* clearly mirroring the underlying use of the variable. For instance, a suitable name for a variable representing the average set of numbers would be AVE; on the other hand, a name like X would not be adequate since the name is not related to the variable's meaning.

At the *beginning* of each program, the student should include a *list of comments* which include the following:

1. Name of the student and any other identification.
2. Teacher's name.
3. Name of the program.
4. Date when the program was completed.
5. Purpose of the program.
6. Brief summary of the algorithm, if it is not included separately as a flowchart or pseudo-code.
7. Instructions on how to use the program.
8. List of the variables and their meaning.

The programmer should make liberal use of the following features to ensure that the code is visually appealing:

1. A full line of dashes (---) or asterisks (***) to separate logical sections of the code.
2. *Vertical white spacing* to separate the logical units of the program. (The good programmer will use a combination of both dashes or stars along with the white space.)
3. *Indentation* (to the right) of certain programming statements such as the body of a loop or the alternatives of an IF statement.

Long programs should be divided into *modules*. Each module should begin on a new page (or screen), and the name and purpose of each module should be included as comments before the code. The students should be discouraged from writing "fancy" code which may be efficient but difficult to understand.

Tips for Facilitating Good Documentation Techniques

1. Make available a complete set of programming standards for the classroom, so that the students know precisely what is required for documentation.
2. Separate the class into two groups and hand out two versions of the same program, one to each group. One version should be fully documented, while the other version should contain no documentation at all. Ask both groups to figure out what the program is doing and see which group takes less time.
3. Hand out examples of poorly documented programs and ask the students to make suitable alterations to improve them.
4. Require the students to make changes to the algorithm of an existing piece of software. Use a program that has been well documented, and ask the students to comment on how the documentation assisted in the alteration process.
5. Assign marks on programming assignments for the use of proper documentation.
6. Ask the students to exchange their programs with other students and have their colleagues comment on the clarity of the programs.

QUESTIONS

1. Using a BASIC programming manual, list the features of the language that differ from those described in this chapter.
2. Find a description of pseudocode in a textbook; compare and contrast it

to flowcharts as a design tool for use in the introductory computer classroom.

3. Create a program which can accept, as input, the ROBOT commands described in the case study, and run them as a program, displaying the robot on the screen of a CRT.
4. Why is the use of "peek" and "poke" not a good example of programming practice?
5. What kinds of errors would you expect to be dominant early in a student's programming career? How would you get the student to overcome them?
6. Write an assignment which has errors in it, and require your students to correct them and run the program. The assignment must have: 5 syntax errors, 5 logic errors, and 2 run-time errors.
7. Define the following terms: algorithm, array, command, collating sequence, concatenation, constant, data, data entry, debugging, design tool, diagnostics, documentation, error diagnostics, file, flowchart, function, heuristic, iteration, logic error, nested loop, precedence, print zone, problem solving, program testing, programming, pseudocode, relational expression, run-time error, screen resolution, software, string, subprogram, subroutine, substring, syntax error, template, variable.

12

Evaluation in the Computing Course

Student evaluation means making judgments about the students' growth and development with respect to the objectives of the computer studies course. It is based on measuring student achievement by using a variety of tools such as tests, assignments, student projects, and teacher observation.

WHY EVALUATE?

Evaluation can be used to make decisions about mastery of the course content, and as a diagnostic and prognostic tool.

Evaluating mastery of the course. At the end of the computer studies course, the teacher must examine how well each student mastered the material. This mastery is usually reflected as a letter grade or percentile. The measure of achievement will either be *norm-referenced* or *criterion-referenced.* A norm-referenced mark means that the student's performance is measured in relation to the performance of other students. In such an approach, the best student will get a high mark while the poorest will probably fail. Criterion-referenced evaluation does not involve comparison to other students; instead, the grade reflects how well the student has mastered the specified objectives.

Whether the teacher opts for criterion- or norm-referenced evaluation, any overall mastery statistic must cover all aspects of a computing course rather than concentrating on a few points. Furthermore, the resulting grade must reflect a weighted average of all the topics covered in the course relative to their degree of importance.

Using evaluation as a predictor. The grade obtained in the course can be used as a predictor of success in future endeavors involving computers. The grade can be used to determine whether the student should *proceed into more advanced com-*

puting courses. Since a low grade in the introductory course almost guarantees problems in more advanced courses, the student getting such a grade would be advised not to try a more complex course.

The grade can be used by the student to determine the *chances of success in a career in computing;* once again, the higher the grade, the higher the probability of success on the job. However, many times the student who has done well on the school aspects of computing buckles under in the practical job environment. Conversely, many students who did poorly in computer studies courses have turned out to be excellent computer scientists.

In many cases, predicting success using *overall grades* is reasonably valid. However, the grade obtained in a *portion* of the course might sometimes be better especially when predicting job success. If a job stressed programming ability, a better predictor would be the mark obtained for the programming section rather than the overall course grade. Because introductory computer studies is a survey course, it typically covers more than just programming. A student may do extremely well in programming, poorly in the rest of the course, and yet be a successful programmer.

Student/parent feedback. Evaluation provides the student with continuous feedback on daily (or weekly) progress in the course. Such feedback indicates weaknesses to parent and student while there is still time to do something about them. This is particularly important when learning to program, where the results of one's endeavors must be seen in order for learning to take place. Fortunately, with programming, the feedback mechanism is somewhat automatic since the student has immediate knowledge about how well a program works.

Diagnosis and prescription. A relevant but somewhat under-utilized variety of evaluation is identification by the teacher of areas in which students are having difficulty. These difficulties are examined to diagnose their causes; usually the teacher will prescribe assistance in the form of remediation, extra work, tutorials, and assignment to student groups.

Diagnosis and prescription work best in the early stages of any problem encountered in the computing course, so it is best to provide such evaluation regularly. Daily evaluation or feedback is recommended.

Providing teacher feedback. Most computer studies teachers try to be sensitive as to how well their course is progressing, making sure the class has understood the material. If difficulties are perceived, the teacher responds by reviewing, reteaching, slowing down, or speeding up. This kind of evaluation, sometimes called *formative evaluation,* must be done regularly if the teacher wishes to detect weaknesses in teaching methods and adjust accordingly.

Generating student motivation. The threat of being tested, accompanied by the desire to get positive feedback, can be powerful student motivators. For some students, it is the only mechanism for getting them to work; for others, it is an efficient stimulus for producing regular study habits.

One of the authors recently conducted a computing course in which this kind of testing was most useful. Most of the students were reluctant to read the textbook regularly, preferring instead to cram just before exams. This behavior created problems whenever the students were expected to have read the relevant sections of the book before they were discussed in class. When the policy of giving weekly quizzes based on the contents of each chapter was instituted, the preparedness of the class increased significantly, with the added bonus of producing excellent results on the final exam.

MEASURING DEVICES USED IN THE COMPUTER STUDIES CLASS

In order to effectively evaluate the computer studies class, the teacher must utilize a valid and reliable measuring tool. A variety of commonly used measurement devices are listed in Figure 12-1. The good teacher will use as many of these tools as possible.

Creating a testing environment which uses a variety of procedures is important for a number of reasons. Some forms of tests are better suited for evaluating certain content areas. For example, the essay test is not ideal for examining programming expertise; the practical programming test is better. Nor is the pencil and paper test an effective format for measuring the formation of attitudes such as "computers are worthwhile"; student observation is better.

Students usually have a favorite form of examination—multiple choice questions, essay questions, or oral tests. The wise teacher will try to be fair and use a wide range of testing techniques.

If the purpose of evaluating is to obtain continuous feedback, then certain measuring tools are unsuitable because of the time lapse between answering the questions and getting the results to the students; for example, essay questions are unsuitable because they take a long time to grade. Thus, techniques in which the answer-feedback time is short are much better; verbal questioning by the teacher, and self-administered and self-marked objective tests fall into this category.

Variety in format, accompanied by a regular testing program, adds validity to the test results. A single kind of test given only once or twice in the semester is

FIGURE 12-1 Evaluation Tools

Tests and Assignments

Pencil and paper tests	Oral exams
Programming tests	Performance tests
Written assignments	Essays/term papers
Programming assignments	

Classroom Activities

Question/answer sessions	Discussion
Demonstrations (show and tell)	Student observation

Other Measures

Parental feedback	Student interaction

inadequate. A sequence of tests, given as often as possible and using many different testing tools and formats, provides a fairer profile of student success or failure.

Pencil and Paper Tests

The pencil and paper test—or the written test—is used heavily in computer studies evaluation. Questions on written tests fall into two major categories: objective test items and essay test items.

Objective test items are those in which the student selects or generates a response from a limited range of possible answers. *True/false, multiple choice, matching* questions; and *fill-in-the-blank* items fall into this category. Here is an example of each.

1. Circle the correct response.

   Multiprogramming is the concurrent execution of two or more computer programs on one computer system. (T or F)

2. Insert the number of the correct response.

   The most expensive computer is: (_______)

   a. the microcomputer.
   b. the minicomputer.
   c. the maxicomputer.
   d. the mainframe.

3. Insert the letter of the item which matches in the space provided.

   Match the person to the discovery or event for which he is famous:

_ 1.	Babbage	a.	Punched card code
_ 2.	Hollerith	b.	Stored program
_ 3.	Von Neumann	c.	ENIAC
_ 4.	Eckert	d.	Difference engine
		e.	FORTRAN

4. Fill in the blank(s).

   A ______ channel allows data to be transmitted in only one direction.

Essay test items ask students to *construct* a medium-to-long answer to the question. As such, the number of answers in a single question is essentially limitless in contrast to the objective test items. Here are some examples.

1. Explain how programs written in high-level languages are translated into machine-readable form.
2. Discuss the several types of primary storage. What are the advantages and disadvantages of each?

Comparison of objective and essay tests. Both categories of test items have their place in computer studies, and are valid evaluation devices if used properly. *Essay questions are easier to create* since they take little time to prepare. However, the grading may become subjective and difficult since there may be many ways to answer the question.

On the other hand, developing a good objective test is much more time-consuming than an essay test since more questions are necessary; each question requires the construction of four or five alternate answers (in the case of multiple choice); and each question must be carefully worded to avoid ambiguities or clues to the answer.

Objective tests are easier to grade. The teacher usually needs just an answer key to follow while marking. The tests can also be graded by the computer. Fill-in-the-blank questions might require a little more time to grade. In contrast, essay questions are difficult to grade because there are many possible answers; student handwriting and grammar may make the paper difficult to read; the answers are longer; and the teacher must make subjective judgments about the degree of correctness of the response.

Objective tests are easier for the student to answer because the correct answer is included in the possible responses. Essay questions, on the other hand, are usually open-ended. Hence, the student often agonizes over what the teacher really wants in the answer. Misinterpretation of what is required may occur. But essay questions allow the student to demonstrate knowledge.

Objective tests encourage the examination of trivial detail. The questions on an objective test often become picayune, such as:

1. There are ________ bytes are on an IBM 3330 disk.
2. In the following question, match the different CPU models with their average execution speeds.

Such questions require knowledge one usually would not expect the student to possess. Although essay questions are generally less specific, they too can sometimes become too detailed. For example:

> Discuss in detail the chronological evolution of computers. Include in your answer the names of specific machines, the dates of important events, and the names of persons who were instrumental in the development of the technology.

Objective tests encourage guessing. On a *true/false* test, there is a fifty percent chance of getting the item correct by just guessing. On a five-part multiple choice test, the chances are twenty percent. However, guessing on an essay test is impossible.

Objective tests may cover a wider content sample. Any test represents a restricted sample of the content which the student is required to know. Thus, a test with one question is not a representative sampling of the student's knowledge; the more questions, the better. Since objective tests usually contain many more items than an essay test, the mark obtained may represent a more reliable measure of course material mastery.

True/False Test Questions

In its basic form, the *true/false* test item consists of a statement which the student must judge to be either true or false. For example:

1. Algorithms always lead to the solution of a problem.
2. The access time of a tape cassette is significantly faster than that of a floppy disk.

True/false questions are ideal for examining the retention of *factual knowledge*. However, they should not be discounted as tools for measuring *higher-level behaviors* such as problem solving and evaluation. Here are some examples:

1. Examine the following program code:
```
LET X$ = '2'
LET Y$ = '3'
LET Z$ = X$ + Y$
PRINT Z$
```
The program will produce 5 as the answer. T F

2. Bubble memory is a form of secondary memory. It would, therefore, be suitable for storing programs during their execution. (*Authors' note:* The student has never heard of bubble memory before.) T F

Tips on writing true/false items for computing tests.

Beware of Concentrating on Trivial Details. If you are unsure about what is trivial, determine whether the question examines a stated objective of the course. If it does not, it should be discarded.

TRIVIAL	Pascal was the father of computing.	T F
NOT TRIVIAL	John Von Neunan introduced the concept of the stored program.	T F

Make Sure That Each Item is Definitely Either True or False, Rather Than Having Elements of Both. Here is a question which could be either true or false:

If a program does not work properly, it has a bug in it. T F

This question would be *true* if the student realizes bugs cause malfunctions, but *false* if the student is thinking about hardware problems causing the malfunction. Here is a better alternative:

One of the reasons for program malfunction is bugs in the code. T F

Careful Thought Should be Given to the Construction of False Items. The teacher should not insert negatives into true statements to convert them into the false form. This often makes them confusing to read. Instead, a plausible statement, phrased positively, should be provided.

BAD	An interrecord gap is not an interval between the records on the tape.	T F
BETTER	An interrecord gap is a hole residing on the circumference of a floppy disk which is used to indicate where each record starts.	T F

True and False Items Should be the Same Length. The tester must avoid the tendency to create *true* items which are long and qualified in order to be sure that they are really true.

Program malfunction is usually a result of bugs in the programming; however, other factors, such as hardware problems and bugs in the system software, can also be a cause. T F

To Deter Guessing, Use the Following Variation of the Question.

Answer *true* or *false* to the following items. If you think an answer is false, fill in the blank with a word which can be substituted for the underlined word to make it correct.

An example of a memory device is the *CPU*. _____ T F

Avoid the Use of Qualifiers such as "usually," "generally," "frequently," and "sometimes," since they could indicate to the student that the item is true. For example:

1. Line printers are usually slower than page printers. T F
2. A user can frequently purchase software which is built into the hardware and is called firmware. T F

Likewise, words such as "all" and "never" provide clues that the item is false, and should also be avoided.

1. All computers are built in the United States. T F
2. In the present day, programmers never write software in assembly language. T F

Use words which have precise meaning, and avoid vague adjectives and adverbs such as "many," "similar," "much," and "very." Such words are open to student interpretation and might be construed differently from what was intended.

BAD	Many companies own microcomputers.	T F
BETTER	The sales of microcomputers in our offices is increasing faster than any other product.	T F

Multiple Choice Questions

The multiple choice question consists of two parts: a stem in the form of a question or incomplete statement followed by a list of possible responses, one of which is correct or clearly better than the others. The correct alternative is called the *keyed response,* while the rest are called *distractors*. The student has to choose from the options as shown here.

1. Which of the following might be a record in a direct-access environment:
   a. A-24.
   b. 013604.
   c. 814 High St.
   d. Disk 7 Track 25.
   e. None of the above.
2. A characteristic of third-generation computers was the use of:
   a. integrated circuits.
   b. transistors.
   c. magnetic drums.
   d. vacuum tubes.
   e. microprocessors.

Although multiple choice questions are used most frequently for measuring the retention of *factual information,* they are easily adapted to examine *higher-level behaviors.* The student must perform the correct decimal-to-binary conversion in order to answer this question.

1. Which of the following binary numbers is equivalent to 17 decimal?
   a. 11011
   b. 111
   c. 1111
   d. 10000
   e. 11100

In this question, the student must be able to determine that computerized weather prediction requires plotter output, even if this relationship was never specifically taught in the course.

1. Which of the following computer applications would you expect to utilize a plotter?
   a. Word processing.
   b. Computerized weather prediction.
   c. Computer Aided Instruction.
   d. Supermarket checkouts.
   e. Automated tellers.

Multiple choice questions can be used to measure *skill in programming.*

1. Which of the following BASIC statements is correct?
   a. LET X = Y$
   b. LET X + Y = Y + Z
   c. LET ABC = DEFK − 1
   d. LAT X = 3
   e. LET X > 3

2. What is printed by the following program?

```
10 READ A, B
20 LET A = A + 3
30 LET B = B + A
40 LET C = A + B
50 PRINT C
60 DATA 2, 3, 6, 5
70 END
```

   a. 13
   b. 14
   c. 9
   d. 11
   e. 3

3. Which statement needs be inserted in order to make the following program segment correctly print out the first 10 elements in an array with the name XY.

```
10 FOR I = 1 to 10
20
30 NEXT I
```

   a. PRINT XY
   b. PRINT I
   c. PRINT I(XY)
   d. PRINT XY(I)
   e. PRINT XY + I

Tips for making good multiple choice questions. Good multiple choice questions require attention to details. *Avoid giving clues* such as:

1. *Nonsensical alternatives:*
   The speed of a typical computer is
   a. about 1000 instructions per second.
   b. about 1,000,000 instructions per second.
   c. faster than a speeding bullet.
   d. about 100,000,000 instructions per second.

2. *Grammatical hints:*
   A series of steps leading to the solution of a problem is *an*
   a. problem attack.
   b. stepwise refinement.
   c. algorithm.
   d. solution reduction.

3. *Obviously unacceptable alternatives:*
   The storage capacity of a typical disk is
   a. 20 bytes.
   b. 40 bytes.
   c. 200 Kbytes.
   d. 60 bytes.

Avoid using generalities such as "usually," "generally," "all," "never," "many," "much," as described in the *True/false* questions.

Avoid putting negatives in the stems; they make the question harder to understand. Thus,

1. Which of the following is *not* an example of a microprocessor?
   a. 6502 c. Z80
   b. IBM 370 d. 6800

would be better written as

2. An example of a mainframe computer is:
   a. 6502 c. Z80
   b. IBM 370 d. 6800

Put as much information into the stem as possible and avoid redundancies in the answer alternatives. Thus, instead of:

1. The function of the control unit of a CPU
   a. is to store data. c. is to direct the sequence of operation.
   b. is to process data. d. is to control the peripheral devices.

write instead:

2. The function of the control unit of the CPU is to
   a. store data.
   b. process data.
   c. direct the sequence of operations.
   d. control the peripheral devices.

Avoid quoting or paraphrasing the textbook or other instructional materials. This procedure encourages rote memorization rather than thoughtful analysis of the materials. Relying on the textbook can yield questions which have more than one correct answer—the one derived from the text, plus one or more which are still correct but are not in the text; for example:

1. One of the largest problems in the programming field is
   a. the communication gap.
   b. costs.
   c. lack of speed.
   d. none of the above.

Suppose this question was derived from a statement in the book which reads: "One of the largest problems in the programming field is the communication gap. . . ." The unwary teacher lifting this as a question for an exam would designate "a" as the keyed response. However both "b" and "c" are also considerable problems facing the programming field and thus are viable alternatives.

Avoid placing a definition in the stem and asking the student to match the items to the terms. Instead, use the definitions as answer alternatives.

BAD 1. Each digit position in a binary number is called a
   a. bit.
   b. byte.
   c. character.
   d. BCD digit.

BETTER 2. What statement best describes the term byte?
   a. A code to store characters.
   b. A digit position in a binary number.
   c. Eight adjacent bits.
   d. The unit of measure for memory.

Make the distractors plausible and consistent with the correct answer. A question like:

1. The second computer ever made was the
   a. UNIVAC.
   b. PASCAL.
   c. EDSAC.
   d. ABC.

is unsuitable because the second alternative, PASCAL, can be eliminated on criteria other than that desired for the question. We want the student to think about the chronological sequence of computers; however, PASCAL is not a computer but a programming language, so it can be easily eliminated.

Keep the stem as brief as possible. However, it must always contain a complete idea so that the student is aware of the question *before* reading the answer alternatives.

1. The CPU:
   a. stands for Central Peripheral Unit.
   b. contains primary memory.
   c. executes the user's program.
   d. is slower than the disk.

is unsuitable because the stem is virtually meaningless to the student. The following question is better.

2. Which of the following responsibilities are in the domain of the CPU?
   a. Executing programs.
   b. Storing programs.
   c. Monitoring I/O devices.
   d. Correcting hardware malfunctions.

Make sure the alternatives are approximately the same length and parallel in construction. Having answers of varying length distracts the student. It also may give clues to the correct answer. Thus,

1. Information which is placed into EPROM
   a. was built in during manufacturing.
   b. can be erased anytime.
   c. can be erased, but only by placing the chip under an ultra-violet light for several minutes.
   d. is easier to change than that in RAM.

is almost a giveaway, due to the inordinate size of ''c''.

Completion Test Questions

Completion items are those in which the student is required to complete a sentence having a word or phrase omitted. For example:

Two examples of non-print output are _____ and _____.
A byte consists of _____ bits.

The number of possible answers is unknown in such a test item. Hence, it is not a pure objective test item—some subjectivity is involved when judging the student's answer. However, it is less subjective than the typical essay and is easier to grade.

Tips for making good completion questions. Unless phrased properly, completion items can be ambiguous, leaving the student confused about what the teacher expects for an answer. This problem is especially prevalent when the question is lifted from the book and the teacher is looking for a memorized statement. Here are some examples:

Flowcharts are read ____.

Although the teacher is expecting "from top to bottom," the question is ambiguous. Answers such as "carefully," "before writing the code," and "as algorithms" are equally correct.

> Hardcopy printers are used when ________________________________.

The anticipated answer is "Permanent output is needed." But "Power is turned on" and "You don't have anything else" are other acceptable answers.

Each of these examples should be rephrased so that the question focuses the student's attention toward the desired response. For example:

1. The preferred direction, when reading flowcharts, is from ________ to ________.
2. Hardcopy printers are used for the production of ________.

Because unanticipated answers may be equally correct as those the teacher is expecting, the grading system must be geared to whether the item is correct or not, regardless of whether it matches the teacher's expectation.

Place the answer blank near the end of the sentence. In this format, the questions are easier to understand. For example:

BAD The ________ performs the logical operations required for the processing of data.

BETTER The logical operations required for the processing of data are performed by the ________.

Avoid unwanted clues to the answer, such as:

Grammatical

1. A machine language instruction is composed of an operation code and an ________.

The size of the blank

1. The first commercially available electronic computer was the ________.
2. The concept of stored programs was introduced by a man whose name was ________________________________.

Make sure the deleted word or term is important. Thus in the question, "The ________ <= means "less than or equal to" in BASIC," the response "symbol" is not important to the task of determining whether the student understands the concept of arithmetic comparison in BASIC. It is thus better to omit "<=" or "less than or equal to." Hence, "Less than or equal to" is represented, in BASIC, by the symbol ________," is much better.

Avoid using too many blanks in the same question. If a completion item contains nearly as many blanks as words, it almost certainly measures rote memorization. Compare these two examples:

BAD _______ is faster than a(n) _______ but slower than a(n) _______.

BETTER One device which is faster than a card reader but slower than a disk is a(n) _______.

Completion items can be used to test programming expertise. Here are some examples:

1. The BASIC statement, DIMENSION X(_____), will create an array having 3 elements by 4 elements.
2. Add statements to the following code so that it computes the average of all the numbers in the DATA statements:

```
10 LET SUM _______
20 FOR I = 1 TO _______
30 _______
40 LET SUM = SUM + N
50 NEXT _______
60 _______
70 PRINT "AVERAGE = "; AVE
80 DATA 1, 2, 3
90 DATA 6, 7
100 _______
```

Matching Test Questions

Matching items are most easily used to measure low-level skills by asking the student to make associations between items in one list—called the *stimuli*—and items in a second list—called the *responses.* A typical matching item might ask students to link a programming language keyword to its description:

1. Match the BASIC keyword with its description by placing the letter corresponding to its description beside the keyword.

___ 1. LET	a. used for arithmetic assignment.
___ 2. FOR	b. not a BASIC keyword.
___ 3. CONTINUE	c. used for iterating.
___ 4. DATA	d. will stop a program.
	e. used with READ statement.

The stimuli don't have to be words; a test item using pictures could have students match the flowcharting symbols with their usage. By using matching items, the instructor provides a compact means for testing a number of related concepts simultaneously.

Writing matching items. The *items in the question should be closely related* to each other; otherwise, certain pairings will stand out from the rest, giving the student little difficulty. For example, the item "microsecond" is easy to answer in this question:

Match the following terms with their definitions.

Term	**Definition**
___ 1. Byte	a. Numbers are stored there.
___ 2. Microsecond	b. The basic unit of storage.
___ 3. Bit	c. Consists of more than one data element.
___ 4. Word	d. One millionth of a second.
	e. Used for storing a character.

Avoid obvious hints such as responses which are similar to the stimulus:

Stimuli	**Responses**
CPU	processors
floppy disk	disk
microsecond	millionth of a second

Keep the lists short—ten items or less—or the student will waste valuable time searching the items repeatedly.

Provide more responses than stimuli, making it difficult for the students to get a "free" answer by the method of elimination. Avoid establishing more than one match between a stimulus and several responses; this is confusing. For example:

Match the peripheral device to the computing function.

Device	**Function**
___ 1. CPU	a. Input of data.
___ 2. Intelligent terminal	b. Processing of data.
___ 3. Primary memory	c. Longterm storage of data.
	d. Shortterm storage of data.

Unfortunately for the student, "intelligent terminal" matches both *a* and *b*, conflicting with the answer for CPU.

Arrange the stimuli—not the responses—in some logical order to aid student comprehension. Some possibilities are:

Alphabetical	**Chronological**
Key words	Generation
___ 1. DATA	___ 1. First
___ 2. FOR	___ 2. Second
___ 3. LET	___ 3. Third
___ 4. PRINT	___ 4. Fourth

Essay Test Questions

The essay test is perhaps the most widely used form of testing in the computer science classroom. Its greatest single advantage is that it requires the student to synthesize a response and, by doing so, to *demonstrate understanding* of the material. Since the essay test allows a great deal of latitude in the student's response, it should be reserved for evaluating higher-level behaviors.

Writing good essay questions. *The student's task should be clearly described.* Avoid questions that are too broad and openended; for instance, "Discuss the effects of computers on our society," leaves the student in a quandary. Which points, out of dozens, should be discussed? On the other hand, a question such as: "Discuss the effects of word processing on the role of the secretary," sharpens the focus of the answer and directs the student's thinking. Because there is a restricted set of correct answers, the question is also easier to mark.

Include many different brief-answer essay questions on a test, rather than one or two long ones. A test containing many short essay questions has the potential to cover more aspects of the course and thus provide a more valid indicator of student achievement. The long essay question is a potential disaster. Too much is riding on it; the students who miss the question are in trouble. This approach would be acceptable if a single question adequately sampled the objectives of the course; unfortunately, in most cases, one question is not representative of the student's mastery of the subject matter. If you feel a long essay question is necessary, it might be better to provide it as an out-of-class assignment where it can be researched, edited, and polished to produce a suitable answer.

Avoid giving multi-part essay questions in which the student is allowed an option about which question to answer. For example:

Answer one of the following questions:

1. List the three generations of computing hardware, and briefly discuss the important events which occurred in each generation.
2. Compare disks and tapes in terms of their ability to handle sequential and indexed files.
3. Describe the steps that a systems programmer follows when developing a software package.

By giving students optional questions, the test measures different objectives for different students. Unless the goals of the individual students in the class are different, a common test should be given to everyone. In addition, it is usually difficult to equate the options in terms of difficulty level. One further disadvantage of questions with optional answers is that they take longer to grade—you must work with three different answers rather than with just one.

If you must give questions which have options, *strive for parallelism.* Examine the following questions:

1. Discuss the effects of computers on one of the following application areas:
   a. medicine.
   b. business.
   c. education.
   d. industry.
   e. government.
2. Discuss the merits of using a high-level programming language. Your answer should include specific references to one of the following languages:
   a. PASCAL.
   b. FORTRAN.
   c. BASIC.
   d. COBOL.

Allow sufficient time to answer the question. The students need to collect their thoughts, organize the answer, and then write. Try taking the test yourself, then multiply your time by three to five to get an approximation of the time required by the student. Or determine approximately how many words will be needed for the answer and then provide at least one hour for every 1000 words.

If beautiful style and flowing prose are not essential ingredients for a good answer, consider allowing *point-form answers* instead. These are easier for the students to write and usually easier to mark. For example:

1. List, in point form, the steps a person would follow when trying to find out why a computer is not working.
2. Indicate at least two advantages and two disadvantages of using a joystick rather than a keyboard for computer input. Point form is permissible in your answer.

OTHER KINDS OF TESTS

Open-Book Tests

The open-book test allows students to consult the text, other reference books, and their notes during the test period; the students are required to pick out pertinent information from this reference material and use it in their answers. As such, open-book tests are unsuitable for the examination of factual information; the student could just look up the answer and regurgitate it verbatim. This kind of test is better suited for the examination of higher-level behaviors such as the student's ability to make decisions, make judgments, and conduct research. The open-book exam discourages memorization of facts and encourages understanding. The test should never contain items examining factual knowledge such as: "List the generations of computing equipment and describe each in turn," but must be directed to higher-level thinking which the student cannot copy from a book, such as:

> You have studied in some detail the evolution of computer hardware. List, in chronological order, this evolution and then, for each stage in the progression, discuss what were the effects of each hardware change on the evolution of software.

Correctly formulated, open-book examinations are highly recommended in the computer studies class. Practicing computer scientists do not memorize reams of information; they depend upon a broad overall knowledge coupled with the ability to seek out specific facts whenever needed. In this context, the good programmer usually has a language reference manual to use when necessary.

When taking an open-book test in computer studies, there are a number of resource materials the students could bring in. Some examples include the textbook; supplementary books; programming language manuals; reference cards; operating system manual; hardware manuals; class notes. Sometimes you may want to restrict the materials which the students access. You might permit a programming language reference manual, but deny access to the textbook.

Hints for giving open-book tests. Tell the students—several times—to bring the relevant materials to the exam room unless you will be providing them.

Make sure the questions are sufficiently complex to prevent the answer from being looked up in the resource materials—unless, of course, the main purpose of the test is to examine the ability to research information. If only certain materials are permitted, monitor for crib notes which might be smuggled in.

Take-Home Tests

In the take-home test, the student receives the examination questions and is given a day or two to generate the answers. This testing procedure is similar to the open-book test, since the student has access to resource materials when answering the questions.

A basic premise behind the take-home test is that the student will give a better answer than on an in-class test, being able to think out the problem, do the necessary research, organize the answer, and produce a neat, readable result. Despite these advantages, there are some obvious problems with this testing procedure. Cheating, copying, or collaborating are impossible to control. The student answer may be lengthy compared to an in-class test, and takes longer to grade. Or, students may have difficulty accessing research materials, especially if materials are limited in availability.

Oral Tests

The oral test is used infrequently in computer studies because it has several drawbacks. It is time consuming, unreliable, and hard to grade objectively. However, certain situations warrant its use. It is frequently used as an evaluation procedure in a reading course where most of the student-teacher interaction is verbal.

The oral test is an effective *diagnostic tool.* For example, imagine that a student is having trouble writing a program. The teacher walks over to the student's terminal and asks, "Are you having difficulty?" The student says, "I don't know how to write the program." The teacher realizes that the problem is probably some specific area of weakness rather than an overall inability. The teacher must track down this weakness by verbal questioning and then provide assistance.

The oral test has the advantages of being administered immediately (in our example, at the student's terminal) and being an efficient, flexible tool for narrowing in on the problem without asking a lot of irrelevant questions.

CREATING PENCIL AND PAPER TEST

A pencil and paper test is a collection of test items which, when taken together, measure the students' proficiency in the topic(s) covered by the test. The creation of such a test should not be taken lightly; good planning is mandatory. The planning of a test includes attention to content and form.

Determining the Content of the Computer Studies Test

A well-planned computer studies test must be *valid.* It must fairly and accurately measure the degree of mastery of the course content. Many tests do not meet this condition because they are hastily prepared. Often, the teacher may start planning the test an hour or two before it is to be administered, piecing together a question on history, something on disks, and a programming problem. Unfortunately, such a test has a low probability of measuring the mastery of the individual topics of the course.

A good testing procedure must be much more systematic. Begin by going back to the list of *objectives* which define the content of the course. Items on a test should measure the level of mastery of these objectives.[1]

Since there may be too many objectives to fit into a one- or two-hour test period, the next step is to decide which ones to actually include. To tackle this problem, take the original list of objectives and randomly select the topics for the exam. Make sure that the chances of picking a given topic are directly proportional to its importance in the course and/or the class time taken to teach the topic. Strive to cover all the different levels of behavior rather than sticking to factual topics.

Examine an example of the test-item selection process which might be used for the final examination in a computer studies course. For simplicity, assume all the questions will be multiple choice. Presume that the course has taken fifty days (ten weeks) to teach, and the major units of the course have each taken up the following times:

History	2 days, or 4%
Hardware	10 days, or 20%
Algorithms	5 days, or 10%
Programming	20 days, or 40%
Society	10 days, or 20%
Other topics	3 days, or 6%

Based on these proportions, the relative emphasis on the final exam should be about the same. Thus, in a 100-question exam, there should be about 4 questions on history, 20 on hardware, 10 on algorithms, 40 on programming, and 26 on social applications and other topics.

The next step is to construct the questions. What are these questions? Look at the case of programming and see what those 40 questions would be. The approach involves subdividing the questions in the same way the entire course was subdivided—according to the relative emphasis of the subtopics. Suppose, therefore, that the 20 days of programming was really divided into three parts:

Syntax of BASIC = 6 days, or 12% of the course
Running programs = 2 days, or 4% of the course
Writing programs = 12 days, or 24% of the course

Thus about twelve questions should deal with BASIC syntax, four with running programs, and twenty-four with writing programs.

Continue this process until you run out of either questions or objectives. At some point, it is time to actually assign the questions. For example, consider the 12 questions to be assigned were on BASIC syntax. Since more than 12 qualita-

[1]The major outcomes of objective-setting was to determine if the students, upon evaluation, fulfilled the objectives.

tively different questions can be asked on this topic, random sampling must be used to select them. Thus you would look at the list of objectives listed under BASIC syntax—let's assume there are 50—and pick 12 of these such as the LET statement, FOR-NEXT loops, and arithmetic precedence. Unfortunately, some topics (objectives) will be omitted—38 in the example—but this is the nature of sampling techniques. For the 12 that were included, 12 exam questions subsequently will be developed.

When doing the final selection, keep the following two points in mind. First, avoid assigning more than one question to an objective unless all the other objectives have had a question assigned. Second, if certain concepts or topics are extremely important, force their inclusion on the test. A test question on finding bugs in a BASIC program is a good example.

Creating Test Items

Once you have determined the content of the exam, the next step is to create the questions. First determine the format of the items, whether multiple choice, true/false, or essay. The normal test will be a mixture of these types. Strive for *variety* in the test format. Include both objective and subjective questions in the test, and have a mixture of objective test formats rather than just one category, such as multiple choice. There are several reasons for this. Since the course objectives vary, especially in terms of the level of behavior required, it is important to use question formats which are best suited for a particular objective. Also, some students find one test format preferable to others.

Have test items from *different difficulty levels.* It is best to make some questions easy to answer and others difficult, and there should be a number of test items with difficulty ranging between the extremes. Here are some examples of possible questions of varying difficulty.

Easy What is the name of the concentric circle formed by the data on a disk?

Moderately hard Describe how a disk reads and writes data.

Hard Suppose you were given the job of selecting and purchasing disk storage for a microcomputer in which the disk would be used for saving student report cards at your school. Indicate, with supporting arguments, the specifications of the disk storage necessary to handle such a job.

A wide spectrum of difficulty levels increases the *validity* of the test, thereby giving the teacher a clearer picture of the students' actual level of ability. The validity of a test is compromised if all the items have the same level of difficulty, that is, moderate. On such a test, the below average student could conceivably get a zero—all the questions are too hard; while the above average student could get 100%—all the questions are too easy.

Assigning a value to the difficulty level—commonly called the *difficulty index*—can be hard, especially with essay questions. With objective questions, scientific criteria are possible. By having previously administered the test items to other classes, the teacher can calculate difficulty indexes based on the proportion of the number of correct answers to each question.

Ask many questions. A test's *reliability* improves as the number of questions increases; one or two long essay questions will lead to an exam of dubious reliability.

Make use of existing questions, if they are suitable. Much time can be saved by using prewritten questions found in previously administered examinations; in textbooks; in the instructor's guides; or in test banks provided by textbook publishers. The teacher should use discretion with these sources, especially those which are available in a test bank. Quite often, test bank questions for computer studies contain items which have not been validated; are too picky, measuring irrelevant facts and details; are not pertinent to the course; and are not comprehensive.

Grouping and Ordering

After the teacher has created the test items, they must be placed together to form the overall test. Usually the teacher groups the items in a systematic way. He or she can *group by difficulty level* or by the *time required to answer.* Place all the simple, quickly answered questions at the start of the test, and the harder items later. On such a test, the objective questions are at the beginning; then short-answer questions; then essay questions; and at the end, programming questions. By grouping questions in this way, the students first encounter questions they can easily answer; this generates motivation and alleviates anxiety, thereby producing incentive to complete the exam.

A suggested practice is to make the first few questions so easy that every student will get them right and thus be off to a good start. For example: "What is the name of the programming language used in this class?" or "The first electronic computer was built in the sixteenth century, T/F."

Group by the format of the test items, that is, place together all the multiple choice, all the true/false, all the essay and all the programming questions. Students prefer to work through one type of question format and then proceed to the next type. This allows them to enter the frame of mind necessary to respond to each question type.

Group by subject matter content. For example, suppose your exam contains three essay questions on software, four on hardware, and two on societal issues; you would group them by topic and by level of difficulty. A similar grouping is advised for the objective questions.

Place the *programming questions at the end of the exam.* There are several reasons for adopting this practice. First, since harder questions should appear near the end of the exam, and programming questions are typically the hardest ones, it is better to defer these questions until the end. Second, if the students work on the programming questions early in the examination period, they easily lose track of time and do not leave enough for the rest of the test. Many beginners will persevere on a programming question until they are certain that it is correct. For this inordinate effort, they may gain one or two more points; but this is at the expense of many more points lost because they are unable to finish the test.

Deciding upon Time Allotments

A basic decision facing every introductory computer studies teacher is whether to include time as a factor on a test—in other words, whether to allow *everyone* to finish with time to spare, or to enforce time constraints.

In the introductory computer studies course, students should *not be burdened by excessive time constraints* when taking a test. Professional computer scientists give themselves extra time to do their work; they value proper technique and accuracy more than speed; so why treat students differently? Putting a deadline on the test creates unnecessary pressure, especially when programs are being written. It is difficult to predict how long it will take to write a program; furthermore, since students vary so greatly in their programming speed,[2] it is impossible to predict how long each one will take.

If the teacher decides to create a timed test, the big problem is estimating the time required. Some questions take a few seconds, while others take over an hour. Here are some suggestions for calculating reasonable time estimates.

For each True/false question, allow thirty seconds to a minute.

For each multiple choice question, allow about 1½ minutes.

For short essay questions—those requiring a few sentences to answer—allocate three or four minutes each.

For long essay questions and programming problems, accurate time estimates are impossible. The only way to come up with a reasonable value is for you to do the question—or have a colleague do it. To get the final estimate, multiply the observed time by a factor of three to five (the factor depends on how fast the teacher answers the questions). Doing the questions yourself gives you the chance to check for questions that are badly worded or which contain typographical errors.

When setting up the test paper, include these time estimates beside the question (along with the mark allotment), to assist students in budgeting their time. A particularly useful way of proceeding is to tie the marks to the time estimates in the following manner:

If the exam takes fifty minutes to complete, make the total grade into fifty marks.

If the exam is three hours (180 minutes) long, make the total grade into 180 marks.

By using the above technique, the teacher allocates one minute for every mark on the paper. This simple correspondence between marks and time makes it easy for the students to allot their time accordingly.

Allocating Marks to Exam Questions

Each test item must be given a weight relative to the overall grade. The weight, which is the individual mark assigned to that question, is usually proportionate to the time allocated for the answer. Hence, a question which takes one-tenth of the total time is usually assigned approximately one-tenth of the overall grade. However, this should not be an inflexible rule. Consider the importance of the question, since relatively unimportant ones can sometimes take longer to answer. For instance, a programming question might require fifty percent of the overall time of an exam, yet in terms of importance, programming may represent only about one-third of the course content. Consequently, the weight of the questions should not always be tied directly to the time allocation; consideration should be given to the importance of the topic.

[2]Professional programmers vary considerably as well. Fast programmers can write a program up to ten times faster than their slower counterparts.

ADMINISTERING THE TEST

On the day of the test, keep several points in mind. Establish a *suitable testing environment.* Each student must have enough desk space for writing the test; writing programs and flowcharts will require more room than the average test area. Noise and interruptions should be avoided, so the test should not be given where computing equipment is housed and in operation.

Announce, before the day of the test, whether the students should bring to the examination room any *special materials:* computer manuals, diskettes, paper for programming, or flowcharting templates.

Try to *relax the students* just before the test starts. Sometimes students get needlessly nervous taking tests that have little bearing on their final grade. At this time allow the students to *ask questions.* This reduces the possibility of ambiguities and the chance that students will be asking questions later on. Here is a typical briefing which the class might get for an introductory computer studies examination:

> Write your name on the top of every page. (pause) OK. Look at question 1. Notice it is multiple choice. Circle only one of the answer alternatives. If you circle more than one, your answer will be marked "Wrong." There are 40 questions. Each one should take no more than 1½ minutes, so you should be done by the end of an hour. Any questions? (pause) OK. Question 2 has three parts. You only need to answer two of them. If you do all three, only the first two will be marked. Question (3) asks you to list the advantages of using disk over a tape. Four distinct points are required. Question? [Student: Is point form okay?] Yes, point form is preferred.

Obviously such a procedure will take time—five to fifteen minutes—so the exam time should be extended accordingly.

Even after the teacher has gone through the exam as described, students may still ask questions. When they do, it is unwise for them to interrupt the rest of the class, so set some ground rules: "If you have any questions after the test begins, raise your hand and I will come to your desk." If someone asks a question which is applicable to the entire class, the teacher should write the corrected version or a list of addendums on the board.

Accommodating the Student Response

A test should be easy for the student to answer and easy for the teacher to mark. The teacher has many options when setting up the test in order to assist the students. Establish whether the student will *respond on the exam paper or in a separate examination booklet.* The former approach is favored, since it gives the students more structure and is easier to mark. Therefore, assuming that the students will provide their answers on the exam paper itself, here are some suggestions for setting a test paper which accommodates the students' responses.

Encourage students to answer the questions in *pencil* rather than in ink. This makes answers much more readable if changes are made on multiple choice and true/false questions. Using pencil is almost imperative when the student is making alterations on flowcharts or programming questions.

Each question should provide *ample space* for the student to respond. For a short answer question—requiring 3 or 4 minutes—at least 2 inches of paper are necessary. For a programming question, allow at least three full pages—one for rough work, another for the answer, and the third in reserve. For completion items, the blanks should be large enough for the longest answer, and all spaces provided for answers should be of uniform length.

Questions should *not be split over two pages* of the examination paper, where the question is on one page and the student's answer goes on the next page. If questions are unnecessarily split over two pages, the student will waste time flipping back to the question while trying to formulate the response.

If a question has alternatives—"Answer six of the following seven questions"—ensure that the directions make these alternatives obvious to the student. Students should be directed to circle the questions which they choose to answer and cross out the others. For long essay questions, consider requiring the students to prepare an *outline* before they write the final answer. This procedure forces the student to think about the answer without first getting involved with grammar and style. The outline will also assist you in marking the question.

MARKING TESTS

Marking exam papers is the bane of most teachers. Yet since so much rides on the results of test evaluation—from the student's perspective—it is important that marking be done as well as possible.

The difficulty of marking a question depends primarily on its question type. *Objective test items* are *easy* to mark. A multiple choice question only has one right answer. To make the marking go as quickly as possible, use mark-sense answer sheets or marking templates.

Marking *subjective items*—short answer, essay, programs, even completion items—is *more difficult.* Since more than one answer is possible, judgments must be made about the "correctness" of the student's answer. Making such decisions is time consuming, and introduces the possibility of a student getting a score different from what is actually deserved.

Although a certain degree of *test error* is unavoidable, try to keep it to a minimum. Unfortunately, some teachers promulgate testing error. For example, the teacher often has one thing in mind for an answer, and when the student gives a different but reasonable answer, the appropriate credit is not given. For example, consider the following question: "What is an algorithm?" The teacher expects an answer along the lines of, "An algorithm is a series of instructions leading to the solution of a problem." However, another perfectly adequate answer is, "An algorithm is a program written in BASIC which works as specified."

The most useful rule of thumb to follow when marking exams is to be *fair.* Here are some tips:

1. Provide adequate instructions for each question so that the student knows precisely what the teacher expects for the answer. Here is an example:

   BAD Discuss the history of computers.

   BETTER Discuss the four generations of computing history in terms of:
   a. reliability of the hardware.
   b. speed of the hardware.

c. cost of the hardware.
d. size of the hardware.

2. Make sure that the students are aware of the *criteria* that are used for marking questions; for instance, if spelling and style are important, they should know this. If efficiency is important in a programming solution, it should be emphasized in the exam question.
3. The students' names should always be concealed when the teacher marks questions so that the teacher does not know whether the exam paper is that of a good student or a poor one.
4. If the students did well on a previous exam, they should be given the benefit of the doubt; the teacher should forego the temptation to make the next test extremely difficult. A teacher might regard the average grade in the class' first midterm as being too high and, therefore, try to compensate by being "tough" when marking the next one so that the grades will equalize.
5. Mark *one question at a time* for all students—especially programming and flowcharting questions—if consistency in marking is valued.
6. Once a question has been marked for all the students, *shuffle* the exams before starting on the next question. This changes the order of marking, and any biases which may have crept into the previous question will tend to be compensated on the next one.
7. Lastly, the teacher should avoid *fatigue,* especially when marking programming questions. Mark a subset of the answers and then do something else for a while before continuing with the next stack.

Grading Essay Questions

If neatness, spelling, and/or style are important and will cause grades to be deducted, let the students know. Some people argue that such requirements are not relevant to the computer studies class. However, good writing is mandatory for the professional computer scientist who must write proposals, reports, documentation, manuals, and letters to users, among other things.

To decide on the student's mark for the essay question—disregarding style—pay heed to the following:

1. *List the points beforehand* which are required for a complete answer; the student's mark will be based on the number of these points which are included in the answer. For example, if the question is "Discuss the kinds of errors found in BASIC programs," you may allocate marks in the following way:
   Value of question = 6 marks
   1 mark for each error: syntax, logic, run-time
   1 mark for a reasonable discussion of each error
2. Many times, questions on computer studies exams have too many possible answers to list beforehand—for instance, "Discuss the ways in which computers are used in business." Such a question has literally hundreds of distinct points, and the student is not expected to list all of them. Thus the teacher should look for a *subset* of these—for instance, 6 distinct points—and mark the answers proportionately.
3. You should prepare a *template of the correct answer* for each question. Quite often, however, some students come up with unanticipated but correct responses. Such responses should be added to the list rather than stubbornly rejected. This practice encourages creativity in the answer rather than regurgitation of memorized facts.

4. *Never adjust the response* to a question using student answers. Commonly, you may start marking a question and soon realize that the answers are not as good as expected, and so change the criteria. If a lot of students answer a question poorly—especially if good students are involved—inspect the question to see if it is badly worded. If it isn't, assume that the material covered by the question has not been taught well and should be reviewed immediately after the examination.

QUESTIONS

1. For each of the following topics, create one or two questions in all of the formats discussed in the chapter.
   a. understanding the PRINT statement in BASIC.
   b. the history of computing.
   c. using a disk drive.
   d. societal effects of computers.
2. Get a test data bank from a textbook publisher; find five examples of good questions and five examples of poor questions. Give the reasons for your choices.
3. Look at the end-of-chapter questions of an introductory computer studies textbook. In general, are these suitable test questions? Why or why not?
4. How can you ensure that a test measures the mastery of the general objectives of the introductory computer studies course?
5. Some people argue that it is impossible to adequately test for programming skills on an examination, suggesting instead that the teacher use the programming assignment as a source of evaluation. Comment on this statement.
6. Obtain a copy of a school system's final examination, and comment on its good and bad points. Give your reasons.
7. Suppose you were giving the following question on an examination and wanted it to have a time limit. Determine, to the best of your ability, a suitable time limit.

   Write a program which computes the average height of the students in the class in terms of sex (male or female). Input in pairs of values—height, sex. The program is terminated when input is Sex="end".

8. Define the following terms: criterion-referenced, difficulty level, distractors, essay test, evaluation, feedback, keyed response, matching item, multiple choice, norm-referenced, objective test, open book test, oral exam, paraphrasing, pencil and paper test, qualifier, stem, subjective test, take-home test.

13

Equipping the Computer Studies Classroom

There are hundreds of computer brands and thousands of peripheral devices to attach to them. If the computer classroom has already been set up, examine the facility for equipment availability, ease of movement, noise eliminators, and seating arrangement to facilitate teaching. If the classroom is not yet equipped, the teacher must decide what kinds of computing equipment are needed. To assist in making a choice, we provide a listing of the types of machinery available and some of their characteristics. The list is neither exhaustive nor evaluative. Some general criteria for selecting what is needed from the large number of available machines are also provided.

Timesharing Versus Microcomputers

Computers can be subdivided into three major categories: mainframes, minicomputers, and microcomputers. *Mainframes* are large and costly computers; normally they are found in the big business environment. *Minicomputers* are smaller computers with a price tag to match their power. *Microcomputers* are the smallest category of computer and have the lowest price tag. All three categories are used in an educational setting, although the mode of usage can be quite different in each case. Mainframes and minicomputers are used mainly for *batch processing* or *timesharing,* in which one machine's resources are shared among a number of users simultaneously. On the other hand, microcomputers are primarily *stand-alone machines* which are used by only one person at a time.

There is some controversy about which strategy is best for educational computing. Many educators opt for the microcomputer setup because of the *safety factor* resulting from *multiple copies* of the same equipment. If one machine malfunctions, the rest are unaffected; students can still use the system, but in a slightly degraded mode. On the other hand, if the computer breaks down in a timesharing system, all the work stations are out of order until the main machine is fixed. There is, therefore, an overwhelming trend in schools toward using microcomputers.

However, there are some *advantages to timesharing.* The overall *cost per unit is smaller* for timesharing, because of the allotment of the computing facilities over a large number of work stations. Furthermore, the user gets a *superior assemblage of software* since the costs are spread over the whole school population. Changes to this software are easily accommodated: one change to the program on the main disk and the program is altered for everyone, whereas on a microcomputer system it means altering the contents of every diskette. Lastly, to keep an eye on students' progress, it is easier to *monitor* their work through the centralized facilities provided by timesharing.

MICROCOMPUTER EQUIPMENT

Each brand of microcomputer is essentially the same—consisting of a CPU, memory, keyboards, monitors, printers, joysticks, storage devices, networking hardware, manuals and documentation, and supplies.

CPU and Memory

The key component is the *Central Processing Unit* (CPU), or microprocessor, which resides on a single silicon chip—hence the name microcomputer. This CPU is accompanied by *memory* for holding the programs and data. Some of the memory, known as *Read Only Memory* (ROM), cannot be changed and is used for storing programs—such as the BASIC interpreter—that are used over and over again. The rest of memory, known as *Random Access Memory* (RAM), is alterable and can hold programs, data, or both. The contents of RAM memory change from one moment to the next. Since RAM memory disappears when the computer is powered down whereas ROM memory is unaffected, every microcomputer normally has a small program in ROM which is automatically executed when the power is turned on.

The capacity of memory is usually a function of the number of bytes (or characters) of storage; the unit of measure is the Kilobyte (K), where K really means 1028. Thus a computer might contain 16K of ROM and 32K of RAM in its memory. Each model of a microcomputer has a standard memory size (ROM plus RAM) with which it comes from the manufacturer, but this can be increased to some fixed maximum by buying extra memory chips or boards.

The Keyboard, Monitor and Printer

Every microcomputer system has a *keyboard* device for inputting information from the user, and a *CRT monitor* (and possibly a *printer*) to allow the user to see the results of the computations.

The keyboard, monitor, and printer may be sold separately from the CPU/memory, or may be an integral part of the machine. In the former case, the devices are purchased as individual units and then attached to the computer. In the latter case, the user buys the keyboard and monitor when purchasing the computer.

Keyboards are fairly standard as far as the normal characters, letters, digits, and punctuation marks are concerned; however, each brand usually has some additional special keys which have meaning only for the machine on which they are found. Examples of these special keys are the RUN STOP key on the COMMODORE keyboard. These idiosyncracies are mentioned simply to warn educators about buying a keyboard which may not be suitable for their equipment.

Monitors are television sets capable of displaying characters and/or diagrams on their screens. A number of different kinds can be purchased; they vary in the number of lines that can be displayed vertically, the number of characters that can be displayed horizontally, and the capability to display color as well as black, white, green, or amber.

If diagrams or pictures can be displayed on the screen, the monitor is known as a *graphics monitor.* In some cases, these can be used for real-time animation. If you are shopping for a graphics monitor, pay attention to the *resolution* of the screen. The resolution, which is measured in a unit called pixels, is the number of dots that can be displayed in the horizontal and vertical directions. The higher the resolution, the better the picture quality; however, the degree of resolution also affects the price.

The major disadvantage of monitors is their *inability to provide a long-term record* of the user's transactions at the keyboard. The screen can only hold a limited number of lines; when these are used up, the lines which were input first will disappear over the top of the screen to make room for new ones. Furthermore, when the power on the monitor is turned off, all the information is lost. Unfortunately, in the educational setting, there is often a need for a more permanent record of the student's work. For example, when students hand in a copy of a programming assignment, it must be in the form of a printed listing on paper.

Printers are devices which produce hardcopy. They come in many shapes and sizes, a few of which are not suitable for classroom use. Factors to look for in the selection of printers include:

1. *Speed.* The slowest printers print around ten characters per second, whereas very fast machines can produce many lines per second. The slowest printers print a character at a time; the fastest ones print a page at a time. In-between, there are printers that print a line at a time.
2. *Quality.* The quality of the print varies from low-quality characters made up of a combination of dots to high-quality typeface which is equivalent to that produced by a good typewriter.
3. *Font change.* Some printers provide the option of changing the character set by removing the print wheel and replacing it with a different font. Many typefaces are available (see Figure 13-1).
4. *Width of page.* Most printers can print a 132-column page; however, some of the smaller models have a narrower width.
5. *Noise.* Some printers, especially the impact printers, are particularly noisy, and a sound attenuating cabinet may be necessary (see Figure 13.1). Others, namely thermal printers and jet spray printers, are relatively quiet.
6. *Paper.* Some printers can use any kind of paper, whereas others require special paper. For instance, thermal printers require a chemically treated paper; printers with tractor feeds need paper with holes along the sides; platen feed printers have friction feed and can use any kind of paper.

FIGURE 13-1 A hardcopy letter-quality printer and daisy wheel. Note the plastic noise attenuator which is currently opened to allow access to the machine.

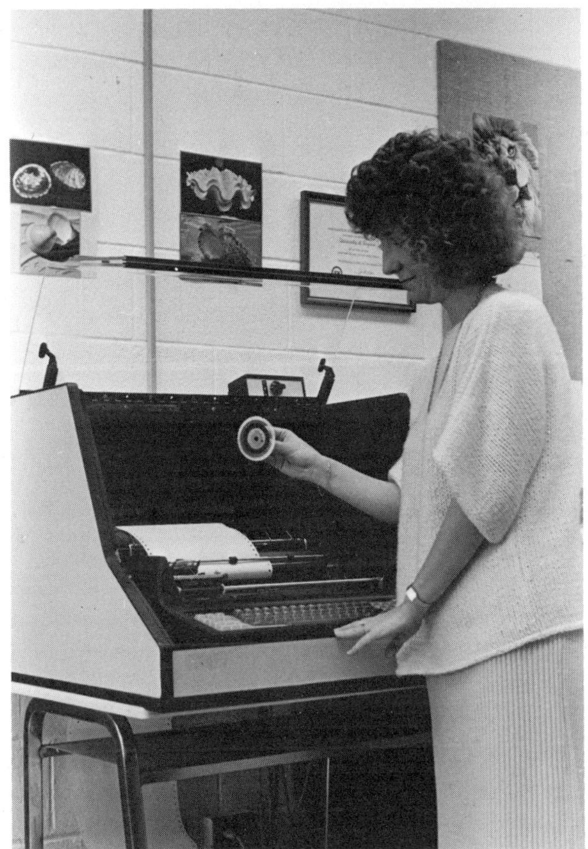

7. *Graphics.* Some printers can move in increments which are smaller than the size of a letter, and, therefore, are capable of producing hardcopy graphics of low resolution.

Joysticks are used to manipulate the position of the cursor on a graphics terminal. Their use greatly enhances the utilization of software that requires the ability to point or draw on the screen. Joysticks are indispensable if the students are going to use or write games on the computer.

Storage Devices

In order to permanently store programs and data, some kind of *storage device* is needed. In the past, keypunched cards served this purpose. However, the key punch has been superseded by three other kinds of storage devices: floppy disks, cassette tapes, and hard disks. (See Figure 13-2.)

Floppy disks are flexible platters of plastic housed in a cardstock cover. On the surface of each disk (or diskette) is a magnetic layer which is used to store data

FIGURE 13-2 A variety of storage devices used with computing equipment.

in binary form. To use a diskette, one inserts it into a disk drive. In this drive, the data is recorded and subsequently played back by a read/write head which can move back and forth over the surface of the diskette. The diskette spins at about six revolutions per second. Using these two dimensions of movement—rotary and in/out—any data on the disk can be accessed in a fraction of a second.

Diskettes come in *three sizes*. Different drives are required for each size, and therefore the diskettes are not interchangeable. The number of characters a diskette can hold depends upon the size of the diskette, the recording density, and whether one or both surfaces are utilized. However, the effective capacity of this storage medium is limitless, since the diskette can be removed and replaced by another diskette from the user's library.

Cassette tapes serve the same purpose as diskettes in that the data is recorded magnetically and the tapes can be replaced. The major distinction is that the data is recorded in only one dimension—along the length of the tape. Characters are placed magnetically side by side, until the end of the tape is reached. Reading the information back from the tape means beginning the tape and working through until the desired data is found. In some cases, this can take several minutes to accomplish.

Cassettes come in *two major forms:* those that use audio recording techniques and those that use digital recording techniques. The audio version utilizes a normal audio tape recorder, whereas the digital version requires a specially made recorder designed only for computer usage. The digital variety is more reliable, having a lower error rate on playback. The audio recorder uses the normal audio tape sold in stereo shops; the digital recorder must have a special digital tape. The user should be careful not to mix up the two, or the cassettes may not perform as expected.

Hard disks are like diskettes, except that the platter is inflexible and the capacity is much larger. Some disks are replaceable; they can be removed from the drive and replaced by a similar disk. However, because the disks must be handled carefully, this is not suggested for a student environment. *Winchester disks* are permanently sealed within a protective envelope in order to keep out dust and dirt.

Networking Facilities

Since printers and disks are expensive and are used relatively infrequently by individual students, sharing is usually warranted. Sharing a device means that a mechanism is required to monitor and control its use. On a microcomputer system, there might be twenty work stations and only one hardcopy printer and one disk drive. If a student wishes to print out a copy of a program, the printer must be temporarily dedicated to that student and other students must be prevented from using it. One way to accomplish this is by physically disconnecting the printer from one microcomputer and reconnecting it to the student's microcomputer; however, this tactic, which requires frequent mechanical intervention, invariably leads to equipment problems. To facilitate the reconnection, some companies provide networking facilities which allow the *interconnection* of a number of computers to a single device, such as a printer or disk. The network functions as an *arbitrator,* allocating the use of the device to individual students on a demand basis.

In certain applications, it may be necessary for two or more computers to talk to each other, a situation which requires that they be connected somehow. The standard for this interconnection is known as the *RS232-C interface.* Check to see if such an interface is available on your machine if you wish to attach it to another computer.

If the two computers are some distance from each other rather than in the same room, more than the RS232-C interface and a wire between the two machines will be needed; the telephone system will be required to act as a transmission medium. Unfortunately, the binary signals coming out of the RS232-C interface are incompatible with telephone signals, and an adapter called a *modem* or *data set* is required at each end. Modems convert binary data into telephone signals and vice versa.

Books and Supplies

All the hardware and software the school purchases should be accompanied by *manuals and documentation* in the form of printed materials or files stored on a diskette or cassette. The files are useful because they can be printed out whenever needed; whereas printed materials must be purchased in multiple copies if more than one document is needed. The major categories of documentation are:

1. *System documentation* describing how to use the computer system.
2. *Software documentation* describing how to use the software.
3. *Programming manuals* detailing how to write programs in each language.
4. A printed copy of the *source code* in case the user wishes to make changes.
5. *Hardware documentation* describing how each device works, how to provide maintenance, how to operate the device, and how it can be programmed.

6. *Schematics* of wiring diagrams in case the user wishes to fix or modify the hardware.
7. *Reference cards*—pocket-sized, condensed versions of other larger manuals which can be used for quick referral.

After equipment, software, and hardware has been selected, the user must acquire *other supplies* to round out the inventory. Students will be using the printer for producing listings of their programs; have a good supply of *paper* on hand. *Cassettes* may be supplied by the school, or the students may be required to purchase their own. Each student should possess at least one cassette. If *diskettes* rather than cassettes are used as storage medium, it is necessary to provide at least one per student. *Diskette holders* are needed to house and keep track of the diskettes, and *cassette holders* to house cassettes.

SELECTING COMPUTING EQUIPMENT

Selection and purchase of computing equipment for the classroom depends on many factors: area of application; number of students using the equipment; school budget; and other equipment in the school. These factors vary from school to school, and consequently the selection must be an individual school decision. No hard-and-fast recommendations for selecting specific machines can be made with confidence. However, here are some useful rules of thumb.

Match the machinery to the area of application. When selecting equipment, features such as memory size, kinds of peripherals, and software are all determined by what use will be made of the equipment. For example, the configuration for the introductory computer studies class would probably be minimal; for instance, a 32K micro with a monitor, a floppy disk or cassette tape drive, a small supply of floppy disks or cassettes, and a BASIC software package would be adequate to allow the student to write and store small programs. A printer is necessary if permanent hardcopy is required.

If the machinery is to be used for more involved applications, extra equipment and software are necessary. For example, in the business administration class where the student is studying word processing, a letter quality printer accompanied by a supply of carbon ribbons and print wheels is mandatory; a hard disk is advisable for storing the large volumes of text; and word processing software would be required.

Get enough equipment to meet the need. One computer inhabiting the corner of a resource center might be adequate if it is just used as a demonstration device in a computer awareness class. However, it would be insufficient in an intensive programming-oriented or CAI setting; the contact time per student would be too small for meaningful work. Adequate facilities to permit each student time to get the work done are required.

What is regarded as a *suitable time allotment* for student use of equipment? The answer depends largely on the kind of application you have in mind; some applications consume more computing resources than others. A resource-intensive application such as CAI requires a larger number of student contact hours per semester than a computer literacy class. In any case, you should be able to come up with an average estimate for each student. It is easy to arrive at an estimate of the amount of equipment to purchase; it just requires some manipulation of numbers. Here are the calculations necessary to determine how much equipment is needed.

1. Multiply the estimated per-student contact time by the number of students who will be using the equipment; the result is the total contact hours.
2. Divide this result by the number of days that the machines will be used, giving the total average contact time per day.
3. Divide this number into the total hours for which the machines will be available each day. The result is the number of microcomputers needed. With a timesharing system, it represents the number of terminals which will be necessary.

This is a minimal solution which assumes that an even spread of utilization will occur throughout the day and throughout the semester. In the classroom, this ideal utilization will not result. Demand for equipment will vary throughout the day. Equipment will be heavily used in the days just before an assignment is due.

You will have to *accommodate these times of high utilization.* One solution is to have extra equipment available; another solution is to develop ways to equalize the daily usage without getting extra equipment. There are several factors that dictate the acquisition of more equipment than is theoretically necessary. First, people may need access to the machines for workshops, demonstrations, or administrative purposes. Second, equipment may break down and be unusable for a period of time. Third, the assignments and projects may take longer than anticipated to program and debug, resulting in increased contact time.

Gather adequate information to make a decision. Your selection cannot be made without adequate knowledge of the kinds of hardware and software available. Sources of information include *computer magazines;* manufacturers and suppliers are always willing to supply *brochures* describing the features of their machinery. (These brochures can be obtained by writing to suppliers, by filling out the reader request cards found in journals, or by picking up brochures at a local computer store.)

Conferences and exhibits are an ideal source of information since a person can see the hardware and software first hand, get hands-on experience, and talk to the company representatives about the virtues of their wares.

Visit neighboring schools to see what is being used and how successful it has been, paying particular attention to any difficulties incurred.

A visit to a neighborhood computer store is always worthwhile. Remember to regard the dealer as a source of information and advice rather than just a salesperson. These people are usually willing to be of assistance since they recognize the market potential of educational computing.

Read computer magazines such as *BYTE* and *Interface Age.* These magazines contain much information which can be of considerable assistance when making a choice: They contain numerous advertisements, discussions, and descriptions of computing equipment and, what is most important, evaluative articles which assess hardware or software.

Select a good manufacturer. Determine if the manufacturer is a stable company. The school may even decide to buy a more expensive computer because the manufacturer is reliable.

There are several points to consider when appraising the manufacturer. *Find out how long the company has been in business.* If it is less than two years, reject the product—even if it appears ideal. There are many fly-by-night computer manufacturers who are unable to survive the fierce competition in the marketplace. The disappearance of a computer company has dire ramifications for the school; parts and service become nonexistent, and when the need arises to add more machinery, the school will be forced to have a mixture of different brands of equipment. Finally, a company's disappearance means the immediate curtailment of software development for that product, a situation which can be more disastrous than the termination of the hardware.

Find out how many machines have been sold relative to the time the company has been in business. A large sales volume usually indicates a good product. It also provides the user with bonuses. Lots of software is being developed by both the manufacturer and software houses, providing a good selection of programs from which to choose. There will be a substantial number of people owning the same product with whom you can share ideas and experiences. And there will be a good supply of used computers for resale or for spare parts.

Pay particular attention to how many machines have been sold in the educational setting. This is important because a computer might have experienced good sales in the business environment, but may be unsuitable for educational applications. Some manufacturers are not even interested in selling to the educational market.

Pick a company which has a good reputation. Talk to other users of the equipment and see if they are satisfied with the service the company provides. This is one of the best ways to evaluate a company's reputation. If you do not know any users, a request should be made to the company for a list of customers who have purchased the same equipment. Read the *product evaluations* published in computer magazines and journals; these are usually honest appraisals of the equipment's merits.

Choose a good dealer. The dealer is the intermediary between the computer manufacturer and the user, and provides hardware, software packages, journals and magazines, and possibly service. In addition, the dealer is often the customer's primary contact for information and advice. Make sure the dealer has a *good selection* of models and brands of equipment. *Working models* of the hardware and software should be available for testing. The dealer should be willing to *lend* the equipment to the educator so that the performance of the equipment can be evaluated in the intended setting. *Auxiliary supplies* should be available through the dealership (ribbons, papers, and diskettes). And the dealership should be reasonably *close to the school,* preferably in the same city. Proximity is critical when maintenance or replacement of machinery is necessary.

Getting the best deal for the money. Computing equipment ranges in cost from several hundred dollars to hundreds of thousands of dollars. Which should you, the teacher, choose? Obviously the cheapest, providing it meets all the criteria. However, if the computer does not satisfy these criteria, the school may be better off buying a more expensive one which does.

Suppose that the same brand of computer is available at two separate dealerships. The dealerships are equivalent in the service they offer, but the computer costs $1,500 at one store and $2000 at the other. All other things being equal, it is foolish to purchase the more expensive one. On the other hand, the dealerships may not be equivalent. Suppose, for instance, that one dealer offers a lower price but virtually no service (department stores are a good example), whereas the other dealer gives good service but demands a higher price. The first impulse might be to opt for the cheaper product; however, the second dealer is demanding a higher price for a reason—good service is provided.

If the brand and model of the computer has not yet been chosen, matters are more complicated. Obviously, the price must fall within the school's budget. Given this assumption, the machine must be *capable of performing all the functions* needed for the school application. For example, if it is needed for programming in BASIC, the computer must have all the power necessary to write BASIC programs. Of course, there is nothing to deter you from getting a more powerful version. Purchasing unneeded power might seem extravagant; however, it is necessary if the school is going to extend its applications later. It will be ultimately cheaper to have acquired the more expensive product in the first place, rather than going through the costly process of trading or upgrading the equipment.

When shopping for computing equipment, it is important to determine whether *price breaks* are available for the educational user. Dealers and manufacturers often provide substantial discounts to the educator. Some manufacturers have even gone to the extreme of *giving away* their product to the educational user. The action generates a favorable impression on the general public, who are more likely to buy the product if they are looking for a computer. Also, the students may buy similar equipment if and when they purchase their own machine.

Due to technological advances, computer prices are shrinking continually; what costs $1,000 today may cost $500 six months from now. This decline in prices could affect purchasers who keep waiting for further price reductions. At some point, the educator must make a decision to buy and simply ignore future possible reductions; it is better to have a more expensive machine than no machine at all.

How reliable is the equipment? The durability of the machinery is important. Computers vary in their ability to tolerate extremes of heat, humidity, vibration, static electricity, wear, and so on. The punishment inflicted by students and teachers alike surely will test the equipment to its limit.

If possible, find out the average *Mean Time Between Failures* (MTBF) under normal working conditions. The MTBF is a measure of the time that a computer runs continuously before suffering a hardware or software failure. Obviously a high MTBF is desirable; but generally this costs more.

Check to see if the computer is built to *accommodate some of the extreme conditions* that may be found in the educational setting. For instance, if the computer is to be transported from one school to another with regularity, consider a machine designed to tolerate movement and wide variations in temperature.

Get the *wiring diagram* in case the school wishes to service the equipment itself. Unfortunately these documents cannot always be obtained, since some companies regard the inner workings of their equipment as a trade secret.

Is reliable service available? Sooner or later, machinery breaks down. When this happens, there are four possibilities for getting things back to normal: (1) discard the equipment and buy a replacement, (2) trade the malfunctioning equipment for a good one, (3) fix the equipment, or (4) pay an expert to fix the equipment.

Obviously, all the approaches have their merits. The first, *replacing the equipment,* is less farfetched than it sounds. As prices continue to drop, repair charges remain constant or increase; therefore, replacement becomes a greater possibility. However, prices still may be sufficiently high to warrant replacement of the malfunctioning part of the machinery only.

Trading in the equipment is an excellent alternative. The company sells the school a new machine and makes an allowance for the malfunctioning one.

Fixing the equipment oneself is only possible if someone in the school has the technological background and time to do it.

The last alternative is to *have an expert fix the equipment.* If the school has only one or two computers, it is best to have an external agency provide the service. Dealers—and in some cases, the manufacturers—usually perform this function on a fee-per-service or contract basis. However, if the school district has many machines, it is wise to investigate the possibility of hiring someone on a full or part-time basis to fix the machinery when it malfunctions.

A maintenance contract may be better. This is an agreement with a service company to fix the malfunctioning equipment "when it's needed." The contract also usually includes preventative maintenance service, including oiling moving parts, cleaning disk heads, and testing for worn components. The customer pays a flat monthly fee for a maintenance contract and is guaranteed that the equipment will be kept working.

The actual cost of maintenance is a complex function involving the hours covered, the kind of equipment, and its value. The best, but most expensive, contracts have 24-hour coverage with a guaranteed maximum delay time. The more economical contracts have a reduced time coverage—for instance, 8 hours a day, 5 days a week, with a longer delay time. The kind of equipment is also important in determining the maintenance fee. Since some equipment is more likely to malfunction than others—for instance, printers are more temperamental than CPUs—the coverage will cost proportionately more. Finally, the value of the equipment obviously determines the value of the maintenance contract; more costly equipment costs more to service.

Does the equipment allow for compatibility with existing equipment? Can it be expanded for future applications? Educational computing equipment is normally not purchased in isolation; the school may have already bought other equipment or may intend to purchase more equipment later. Any selection must be made within this broader context; if this is not done, a hodgepodge of computers may be procured—a situation which leads to teaching and maintenance problems.

Standardization of computing equipment is ideal. Maintenance is simplified, machines can be easily interchanged, and the users learn to use only one kind of machine. Standardization also saves money when the educator purchases computing supplies such as diskettes or paper, since most suppliers provide a discount for quantity sales. Ideally, it is best to get *identical pieces of equipment.* If this cannot be done, then different models should be purchased from the *same manufacturer.* If this is impossible, the equipment purchased from different manufacturers should be *similar in function and structure.*

Is reliable, applicable software available? Many people get too concerned about the relative merits of the hardware, and often fail to critically examine the *most costly* and important aspect of computing—the *programs*. Hence, make sure the machine has a good general-purpose *operating system*. In addition, the system should have a tried and tested *language processor* (for example, BASIC or PASCAL) to meet the school's programming needs, and should have others available in case students need to work with more than one language. A good selection of *system software* such as word processors, editors, and accounting packages should also be available, even if they are not purchased right away. When acquiring software, remember that it is not necessary to purchase it at the same time as the computer, since most software is sold separately. Nor must you buy the software produced by the manufacturer of the hardware; many independent software houses produce programs which can run on a specific computer and are often superior to those supplied by the manufacturer.

Software *varies in quality and price*. Some software packages are complex, and the price tag matches this; others are simple in function and cost little. The goal is to pick reasonably priced programs which suit the student and the school needs. A word of caution is necessary, however: Cheap software packages generally have a minimum number of capabilities, are limited in documentation, and are quite often filled with undiscovered bugs. This last problem is prevalent, so give special attention to trying out the software to see if it functions properly. Insist on a guarantee which either stipulates a refund in case of malfunction, or requires the seller to fix any bugs and supply the school with an updated version of the software.

Are the hardware and software accompanied by adequate documentation? Documentation refers to the written manuals which accompany both hardware and software. In order to adequately use the machinery, this documentation should be complete and readable. Many times an inexpensive package does not even come with documentation. Remember, the best hardware and software is nearly useless without a mechanism for telling the user how to use it.

There are specific features to look for in good documentation, such as a *beginner's learning guide* which supplies sufficient information to get started on the system. Check for an *abridged reference handbook* which includes all the features on using the system. This document is useful after the user has read the complete manual and needs to refer back to certain points. A *good indexing system* is important, as is a handbook that is durable and capable of heavy usage. Ideally, pages should pull out easily so that updates can be inserted.

HOUSING THE EQUIPMENT

Once the desired computing equipment has been selected and obtained, the next stage is determining how it will be housed in the school. A number of factors must be considered, such as what room to use, the environment of the room, its security, and the characteristics of the student work stations.

Location of the Equipment

Equipment can be placed *within the classroom* where the students normally receive their instruction; within a *resource center or library;* or within a *separate computer laboratory*.

Each of these alternatives has its pros and cons. The classroom environment allows intermixing lectures with using the machinery. The equipment is also in a place familiar to the student. One major disadvantage, however, is its inaccessability to students who currently are not in the classroom. Another drawback is that the machine remains unused if the students work on other subjects in that classroom.

If better utilization of limited equipment is desired, effective means must be devised to allow *sharing* the computers. This goal can be attained by situating the computers in a central location, such as the resource center or a computer laboratory, where they can be accessed by all.

The housing of the equipment in a *resource center* involves placing the machinery and manuals in a corner of the library where they are accessible to student users, but sufficiently isolated to not disturb anyone else. Because the resource center is open to all students, the computing equipment is always available. Furthermore, the increased availability means a higher percentage of utilization of equipment. Three major problems exist, however. First, noisy equipment, such as printers and voice synthesizers, can be annoying and must be either barred from the center or placed in special sound attenuating equipment. Second, continued conversation between students or between student and teacher must be curtailed because of the disruption it causes. Third, a qualified computer studies instructor may not always be present to provide assistance to students.

Verbal interaction is a most effective learning mechanism in computer science; therefore, a resource center which permits this is ideal. Only a center dedicated solely to the housing of computers has these characteristics; such a center, often called a *laboratory,* allows students full access to machinery but also creates an environment in which noise is permissible. However, because of its dedicated role, the laboratory requires a supervisor to monitor both students and equipment.

Additional factors come into play when housing equipment. The *hours of usage* will determine whether a classroom environment is suitable. If the machinery is to be used only during school hours, then there is no problem. However, if off-hour or 24-hour access is needed, a specialized locality such as a laboratory is more practical.

Using the computer during *off hours* creates a *security problem.* During off hours, most classrooms must be locked up since it is impossible to provide supervision. On the other hand, a single locality, such as a laboratory, allows supervision without requiring excess personnel.

Proximity to people who can answer questions and help students with problems is important. If there is only one such expert in the school, a laboratory in which the resource person has a desk or office is ideal. On the other hand, if there are several such people within the school, then the advantages of centralization are lessened.

The Room's Physical Attributes

Once the decision has been made to either centralize or decentralize the computing facility, the actual room(s) must be carefully selected to find one which is most amenable to a computing environment. Since the selected room may not be perfect, bear in mind that some alterations may have to be made.

The room should contain *adequate space* for storing supplies such as paper, ribbons, and diskettes. A *variety of boards* should be available within the room for announcements, rules and regulations, and for lecturing or demonstrating. The room should have an *aesthetic atmosphere;* nothing is drearier than the standard computer room found in many schools. The use of color, pictures, posters, and suitable furnishings can liven up the room immensely while costing little. *Adequate power facilities* for running the equipment must be available. There must be a sufficient number of outlets with enough amperage to accommodate all the equipment. If these outlets are some distance from the equipment, then a mechanism for housing the cables to prevent people from tripping is mandatory. This can be achieved by placing the computing equipment on a raised floor and running the cables under it, or by fastening cableways onto the floor or ceiling and running cords inside them. If power fluctuations are a problem in the area, it may be necessary to purchase a power supply stabilizer.

Since communication between the student and the instructor is desirable in the computing environment, and noise such as that caused by printers is unavoidable, it may be necessary to provide *noise-attenuating features.* Baffles can be positioned throughout the room to absorb noise. Sound-attenuating ceiling and wall tiles, carpeting, and window curtains also help. Noisy equipment such as line printers can be placed under sound-reducing covers.

The *lighting* in the room should be adequate to allow reading of written and printed materials. However, if CRT monitors are used in the work station, take care to avoid the reflection of intense light from fixtures or windows on the screen.

The room's *temperature and humidity* must be suitably controlled. Computers vary in their capability to withstand extremes of temperature and humidity; hence, the room must be kept within the range specified by the manufacturer.

Dust is one of the greatest menaces to computing equipment, so measures should be taken to ensure a relatively *dust-free environment.* This can be accomplished by filtering the air supply, banning smoking, limiting food consumption, and avoiding the use of chalk.

The room must be *secure,* especially if it is not supervised 24 hours a day. Computing equipment presents a great temptation for the would-be thief and should be protected in some way. Locks on the door, either physical or electronic, are one line of defence. Bars on the windows are another. Chains and padlocks on the equipment are a third.

Security is enhanced if attendance is monitored. Using TV cameras is possible but expensive; another method is controlled access in which the student must identify himself or herself by punching a code on an electronic lock or by using a personalized entry card. As well as providing physical security for the equipment, it is also necessary to safeguard information and data. Sensitive information such as student programs, grade files, and copies of examinations may be stolen if adequate measures are not taken to protect them. Thus diskettes must be locked up or taken home, and care must be taken in disposing of printouts.

The Student Work Station

Once the room has been prepared in terms of environmental factors, security, and so forth, the next step is to carefully design each of the individual work stations (Figure 13-3). The work station contains all the computing equipment required for student use. In a timesharing environment, it would hold the termi-

FIGURE 13-3 A well equipped student work station.

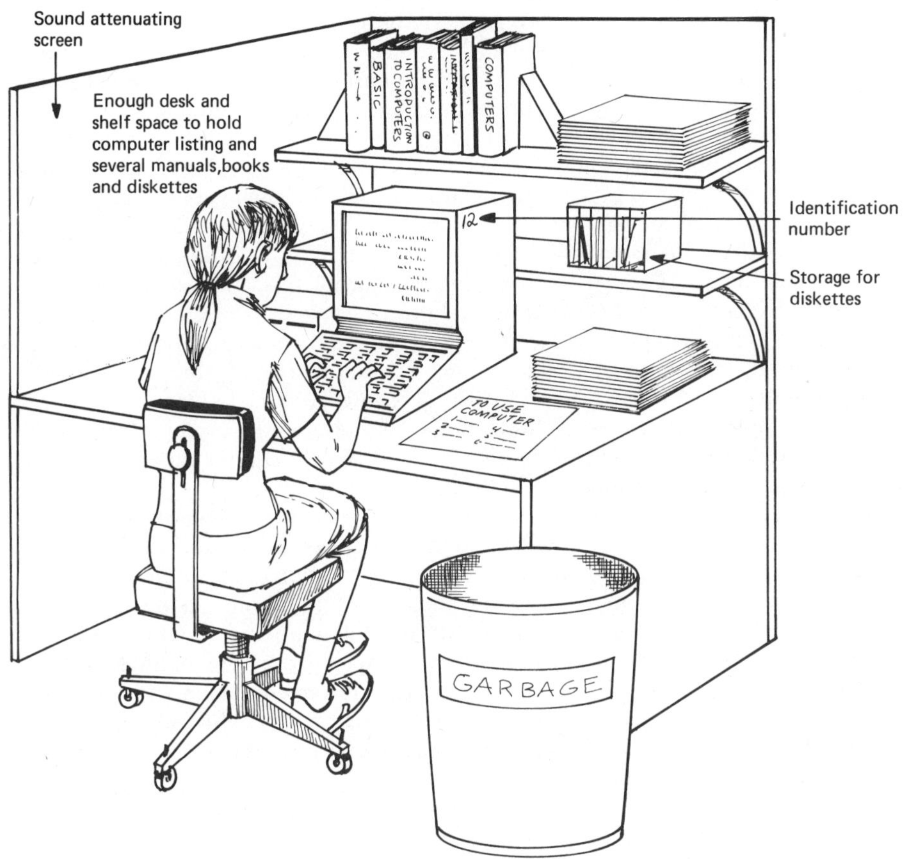

nal; in the stand-alone environment, it would have a microcomputer along with either a disk drive or a cassette tape drive. A desk or table is necessary to hold this equipment, and should provide enough additional space for the student to spread out work.

Space can be best utilized by storing the equipment vertically on shelves and placing items such as disk drives above or below the work table. The position of the keyboard and monitor within the work area is critical. The keyboard must be at the correct height to allow proper keyboarding technique without creating unnecessary fatigue. To check this, be sure that the student's lower arm is at the same slope as that of the keyboard. Since students—especially elementary school students—vary greatly in height, a mechanism for raising and lowering the keyboard is mandatory. Because adjusting the desk is difficult, the only alternative is to raise and lower the student chairs—a good reason for having swivel chairs.

Each work station should also include a large *paper disposal* system for listings and other material. *Identification numbers* on the equipment are necessary so that malfunctions can be accurately identified and reported. A *checklist* taped to the desk should detail important instructions, such as how to turn the machine on and off or what to do in case of emergencies. *Baffles* around each work station are necessary if privacy or sound attenuation is required.

CARING FOR THE EQUIPMENT

Computing equipment can break down. Some of these failures are unavoidable; however, many result from causes that are under the teacher's control. By avoiding certain situations, the failure rate of the equipment can be minimized (Figure 13-4). *Ban food and drink from the computer room.* Crumbs falling into the computer's innards create havoc; drinks spilled on a keyboard result in a sticky mess which may necessitate replacement. *Ban smoking in the area.* Not only does this habit create a fire hazard and bother other students, but it generates fine dust particles which affect sensitive equipment such as disks, tape drives and keyboards. Minimize the effects of *static electricity.* A thousand-volt spark can have a detrimental effect on digital electronic circuitry. The room should be sufficiently humidified to reduce or eliminate this hazard. Furthermore, handling of printed circuit boards and integrated circuits should be avoided unless the person is properly grounded.

FIGURE 13-4 These three activities should be banned from the computing area, since smoke, liquid, and food damage computing equipment.

Avoid jarring the machinery or letting it vibrate. Constant movement eventually results in failure by causing the junctions between electronic circuit components to break apart. Try not to drop or shake the equipment, and minimize transporting it. Turning the computer on and off a lot also produces the same problem due to the expansion and contraction of the components as they heat up and cool off. Leave equipment running, even when not in use. Although this uses up additional electricity, the expense is minimal—computers consume little power—and the procedure will extend the machine's lifetime. Never turn the power on or off with a diskette or cassette in the drive.

Do not let the equipment overheat; if the air conditioner malfunctions on a hot day, turn off the machinery. Install in the computer room a thermal overload which cuts the power if the temperature gets too high. In addition, blocking air circulation around the computer or disk drives causes overheating; therefore students should not obstruct the ventilation holes with papers or books.

Avoid taking computing equipment outside in cold weather. If this must be done, it is imperative that the machinery return to room temperature before it is turned on again.

Turn off the computer if the power supply voltage starts to fluctuate. This can occur during an electrical storm when the power is going on and off, or when voltage spikes are being produced. Shutting down may not be necessary if a regulated voltage supply is installed between the computer and the outlet. These regulators can be obtained from a dealer.

Handle diskettes with respect. Do not bend them, leave them in a hot place, or allow grease or dirt to get on the surface. When not in use, always leave them in their jackets, stored vertically, and never touch the magnetic surface. The school should obtain a diskette or cassette cleaning kit for periodically cleaning the surface of the recording medium. Diskettes eventually wear out, destroying the data. Therefore, plan to *replace* them long before they break down, or else use back-up disks in case a failure occurs.

If you must open the machinery and make adjustments such as removing boards or connectors, *turn off the equipment* until finished. Check the wiring diagram before attempting to make any adjustment or repair. Perform *preventative maintenance* on a regular basis. What is actually done depends on the equipment; examples include dusting the keyboard, cleaning the disk/cassette heads, oiling moving parts, cleaning the ink off printer heads, and making sure that boards are firmly in place.

If equipment fails intermittently, *keep track of each failure.* While a single equipment failure does not necessarily mean that anything is permanently wrong, repeated failures indicate trouble. Thus, keeping records helps determine if the failure rate is too high. Maintenance records are also useful to help the technician track down the problem.

ACCOMMODATING THE HANDICAPPED STUDENT

Most existing computing environments are not built to accommodate the physically handicapped student, with the result that handicapped students cannot use the equipment. It is unnecessary to keep these students from taking computer studies, especially when some simple measures can be taken to accommodate them.

The main difficulty facing the *paraplegic,* for example, is getting to the computing equipment. Once the equipment is reached, there is no problem, since paraplegics can use their hands. To ensure that the student has no problem with room access, the school should make sure that

1. The door to the room is *wide* enough for a wheelchair.
2. A *ramp* is installed if necessary.
3. Several work stations are large enough to accommodate a wheelchair.
4. Paraplegics have priority to use any specially designed work stations.
5. A mechanism is provided to allow the *keyboard to be adjusted* to the correct height. Detachable keyboards are ideal for this function.

The *blind person* is in a different situation. Assuming that this person can locate the work station and knows how to touch-type, the main difficulty is reading the output produced by the printer or CRT. Fortunately, a number of solutions are possible. The school could install a *braille printer;* obtain a *special reader* which, when held against the page, converts printed copy into a form which can be interpreted by touch; use a *voice synthesizer* which produces auditory output for the student; or have *student assistants* read the printout to the blind student.

PROVIDING ACCESS TO THE EQUIPMENT

When computers are introduced into a school, there are usually too many students vying to use too little equipment. Unlimited access to the machinery is not possible; mechanisms must be adopted to maximize its utilization fairly. In addition to the resource center or library, there are five other strategies to make better use of the equipment: limit access to certain people; provide 24-hour availability; introduce sharing mechanisms; move the equipment around; minimize unproductive use.

It seems that everyone wants to use the school's computers—not only the students who are taking the course and their teachers, but other students, other teachers, administrators, parents, even the public. Although highest priority should be given to students taking computer courses and their teachers, it is unfair to limit usage exclusively to them. Wise *access algorithms and sharing policies,* however, permit other people to use the equipment.

The more available the computers, the more the students can use them. Hence 24-hour access, 365 days of the year, is most desirable. However, most schools normally are closed nights and weekends, this means that the equipment is not available for about 75% of the time. If extra access is required, arrangements must be made to either schedule computer usage with other events such as PTA meetings and community courses, or have the school opened for those students needing the machines. Obviously, providing security during off hours is essential, so it is best to limit access solely to the computing area.

One way to avoid security problems is to allow students to *take the computers home* and do their programming there. Although this method extends the machine's utilization, it obviously limits machine usage to one student who may not be using the computer the entire time. The equipment also may be damaged.

The best solution is for students to have their *own personal computers.* In fact, some universities, now require students to obtain their own equipment. Unfortunately, prices have not yet dropped to the point where every student owns a computer; however, computer manufacturers may adjust their prices to make this practicable.

Sharing mechanisms. If it is necessary to share equipment, how can it be done efficiently? Three major schemes are possible. The *first-come-first-served* scheme is the simplest. Students line up for a computer and when one becomes available, they use it until they are finished. This approach works tolerably well, as long as there are adequate work stations available. However, long lines sometimes occur; particularly just before assignments are due, the waiting time for a work station may become unacceptable. As a result, some students monopolize the equipment even when they are not using it productively, in order to avoid rejoining the line.

To eliminate line-ups, a *scheduling or reservation system* is suggested. Work station access is divided into blocks of time—at least one hour is recommended—and the students either sign up or are assigned to time slots. Modifications of this approach include handing out of passes for terminal access, limiting the time-access slots per student in a given semester, and providing extra terminal access as a reward for good work. A third way of sharing the computing equipment is to have students work in groups at each station.

Another option for sharing is *moving equipment around.* If a computer is kept inside one classroom all the time, it might stand unused for a major part of the day. Better utilization of the computer can sometimes be achieved by transporting it from room to room if the times of the computer classes are staggered. Of course, a portable cart is mandatory for moving the machine.

This method can also be used for transferring the computer between schools. However, where a computer is shared by two or more schools, moving the machine back and forth every day is not feasible. Instead, one school should have it for several weeks, then the next school. This approach may require condensing the part of the course which involves using the computer.

The last tactic for increasing availability is to *minimize unproductive use* of the equipment. It is surprising how much time students waste while sitting at the keyboard engaged in computer games, figuring out the logic of their program, or trying to track down bugs. This unproductive time can be eliminated by banning game-playing except at off hours, requiring the students to have their programs designed and ready to key in before they get to the keyboard, and requiring students to debug programs at their own desks.

QUESTIONS

1. Compare and contrast timesharing versus microcomputers for the introductory computer studies class in terms of:
   a. cost per station
   b. availability
   c. processing power

   d. response time
   e. software
2. Visit a microcomputer store and report on:
   a. brands
   b. suitability to education
   c. service
   d. costs
   e. software
   f. kinds of hardware
3. Suggest what supplies, equipment, and software would be required for each student in a typical computer literacy class.
4. Pick a room in a school and describe how it can be converted into a computer laboratory. Include the following information:
   a. necessary changes
   b. problems with existing room
   c. configuration
   d. security
5. Investigate the difference between cassette tape and floppies. Include the following information:
   a. capacity
   b. ease of use
   c. error rate
   d. speed of access
   e. storability
   f. cost of storage medium
6. Using the text criteria, choose a hardware configuration suitable for a typical introductory computer studies class.
7. Prepare a list of questions which you would ask at a school you are visiting in order to help you make a wise selection of equipment.
8. Find examples of advertisements in computer journals on the following:
   a. CPUs
   b. microcomputers
   c. paper supplies
   d. printers
   e. floppy disks
   f. cassette drives
   g. diskette cleaning disks
   h. educational courseware
   i. textbooks suitable for the introductory computer studies class
   j. graphics terminals
9. Using the reader service cards in computer magazines, send for brochures on examples of each of the items in the above lists.
10. Design a work station and suggest equipment modifications for a paraplegic.
11. Define the following terms: configuration, diskette holder, floppy, font, graphics, hard disk, joystick, keyboarding, MTBF, mainframe, maintenance contract, manual, microcomputer, minicomputer, monitor, reference card, timesharing, Winchester disk, work station.

14

Preparing Students for Computing Occupations

Many students wonder what follows a course in introductory computing studies. For some students, the introductory course may be a terminal course; for others, it may be the first step in building a career in computer studies.

WHAT COURSES COME NEXT?

Many introductory computer studies courses are lean in content, typically providing a survey of the discipline. Courses which follow contain more detailed coverage, and in many cases have content which was not taught at all. Because computer studies encompasses such a wide range of topics, the variety of subsequent courses is almost limitless. Consequently, students have to be selective in developing their programs of study. What is included in the program depends on career choices, personal interest, and the level of sophistication desired. Some of the courses are offered at the public school level; however, the majority are only offered at the post-secondary level, primarily at universities.

What courses should a student choose? It is impossible to list comprehensively every course which is currently available. Some institutions offer twenty to thirty courses, with no two schools having identical offerings. The course content, therefore, will be addressed in terms of a general classification scheme similar to the one published by the American Association for Computing Machinery (ACM), which lists major topics rather than specific courses. With the ACM outline as a guide, a classification of topics to be studied follows.

1. *Programming in more than one language.* The basic syntax and semantics of one or more higher level languages, such as FORTRAN, PASCAL, or COBOL.
2. *Assembly/machine language.* The skills required to program the computer at the ma-

chine level. This programming is normally done in a symbolic language called assembly language.

3. *Computer architecture.* An in-depth examination of the internal structure and function of the computer and its peripheral equipment, such as disks, tapes and printers.
4. *Business data processing.* The use of computers in business. It includes details on setting up and using business data processing systems.
5. *Systems analysis.* Systematic methods for analyzing and implementing the solutions to computing problems, as well as methods for designing good software.
6. *Networks.* Hardware and software solutions for the interconnection of computing equipment.
7. *Theory of computing.* The mathematical foundations of computer science.
8. *Numerical methods.* Details of using computers to help solve mathematical problems.
9. *Data structures.* The ways in which data can be grouped together to form higher level conglomerates which facilitate the solution of programming problems.
10. *Algorithms.* Using algorithms in the problem solving process, including generalized algorithms for commonly occurring problems.
11. *Simulation.* The modeling of actual events by means of computer programs.
12. *Digital logic.* The basic components of digital circuitry and how circuits are developed to create working machinery.
13. *Systems software.* The usage, programming, and rationale for special software packages such as loaders, utility programs, and I/O systems.
14. *Operating systems.* The operation and construction of the operating system—the program which runs on most computers and assists the user to operate the machine.
15. *Compilers/interpreters.* The design, operation, and construction of the software required to process programs written in different computer languages.
16. *Artificial intelligence.* The use of computers to emulate various aspects of human behavior, such as vision or reasoning.
17. *Microprocessors/microcomputers.* A detailed examination of various facets of microcomputer technology.
18. *Data base management.* Mechanisms for storing and retrieving data on a computer system.

The preceding list merely surveys what is currently available; it is neither comprehensive nor detailed. If you need a more detailed description, refer to the ACM curriculum guide or the curriculum descriptions of computer studies offerings which are published in most university calendars.

Ordering Courses

Courses should not be presented in random order; there is a natural hierarchy to the material. For example, the *compiler construction* course should not be taken until the student has covered the background material found in the *assembly/machine language* course, and possibly the *systems software* course. This ordering of material is reflected in the *prerequisite structure* that the school administration prescribes on the courses a student can take. A sample prerequisite hierarchy is illustrated in Figure 14-1 (refer back to Figure 2-1 also).

FIGURE 14-1 Prerequisite structure of a computer science curriculum. This figure indicates ordering of the computer science courses in a university computer science department.

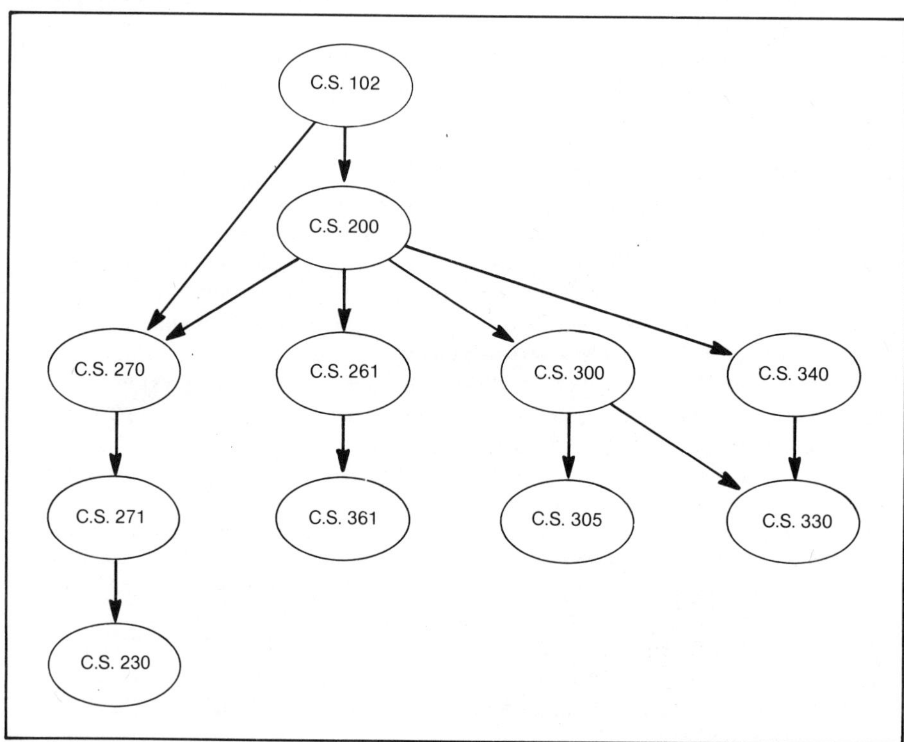

Computer Science 102	Introduction to Computers
Computer Science 200	Introduction to Computer Science and Problem Solving
Computer Science 261	Methods in Numerical Analysis
Computer Science 270	Business Information Systems
Computer Science 271	Application Program Development
Computer Science 230	Systems Software—An Application Perspective
Computer Science 300	Elements of Computer Hardware and Software
Computer Science 305	Data Communications and Networks
Computer Science 330	Introduction to Systems Programming
Computer Science 340	Programming Languages and Data Structures
Computer Science 361	Numerical Analysis I

Where Computing Courses Are Taught

Where does the student get this extra education? Obviously, the choice depends on the type of training desired—which depends on the student's goals. There are four major avenues open to the student: self-study; training in elementary and secondary schools, universities, or community/technical colleges; or on-the-job training in industry.

Self-study. Many people learn about computers through self-study; they read computing books, subscribe to magazines, and program their own computer—all without taking any formal courses. Although the approach has merit for people with a passing interest in the topic, it is not recommended for the person wishing to pursue a career. Only the discipline imposed through the formal educational system will provide the student with all the material required to create the background necessary for a position in the computing field.

Elementary/secondary school. Training at the elementary and/or secondary school is generally not sufficient to prepare students for jobs in computer science, although in many cases it is adequate for jobs requiring a working knowledge of computing. Many employers require the prospective employee for a computer-related position to have post-secondary education in computing.

University/technical colleges. Through their hiring practices, employers have demonstrated that they prefer candidates with training from the university or community/technical college. These institutions provide programs of study which are specifically designed to prepare the student for a computer science career: a bachelor's degree in computer science at the university, a certificate or diploma at the other.

The major difference between the university and the technical college is in the orientation; universities take a theoretical approach, while technical colleges usually take a practical one. Universities try to provide a broad education covering many different topics, while technical colleges strive to train for specific jobs. What this means is that the technical college graduate probably has better job-specific training; university graduates, because of the breadth of their education, have more flexibility.

Industrial training. Some companies are willing to train their new employees whether they have computer background or not. This training is job-specific, and should not be considered a substitute for computer science courses at a school. Many companies encourage university and technical college graduates to build on the education they already have, using it as a foundation for the specific training required for the job.

CAREERS IN COMPUTING

The variety of jobs available is enormous and growing; it would be impossible to list them all. Instead, we provide a categorization of the job market and give examples of particular job descriptions within each category. The job market may be subdivided into three major groupings:

Category A Jobs directly involved with *computer science.*

Category B Jobs requiring the person to *use computing equipment or software* as a part of their daily routine.

Category C Jobs requiring the person to *talk about* computers with their colleagues, the public, or computer-oriented personnel from Category A.

Category A: Computer Science Careers

The computer science career involves working in a job environment where the employee is a programmer, systems analyst, data processing manager, or one of several dozen other job descriptions. Figure 14-2 gives information on some of the job titles listed in the *Dictionary of Occupations* and includes a short description of each. These jobs can be found in all facets of industry and business which use computers in their operation. The background education necessary to qualify varies. In most cases, it is reasonable to state that the introductory computer studies course provides insufficient computing experience. In many instances, businesses require an undergraduate computer science degree and sometimes a post-graduate degree.

Category B: The Computing User

The second classification of jobs are those in which people *use computers in their jobs,* but not at the level of sophistication required in Category A. These people do not write or design programs, nor do they need detailed knowledge of the structure and function of the hardware. Generally, their only contact with programming is when they run prewritten software packages; their main contact with the hardware is when they operate the specific machinery needed in their job. Jobs which fit into this category include secretarial workers or word processor operators; accountants using financial packages; airline salespersons using the reservations terminals; factory workers using computers to maintain and update inventories; and store clerks using automated checkout systems. The list of possible jobs is endless, and new job classifications are popping up daily in almost every office, business, and industry throughout the world.

What kind of training do people in this category need? Obviously, a well rounded computing background similar to that required for Category A would be ideal; however, it may not be mandatory. Necessary, however, is specific training for the skills required to do the specific job. For instance, a store clerk using a point-of-sale terminal would need to know how to keyboard and use the special function keys; use the light pen to read the Universal Product Code; interpret the output produced by the terminal; and handle equipment problems. Another job—producing letters on a word processor, for example—requires an entirely different set of skills.

Because each job is different, it is unlikely that the requisite training could be given through the formal educational system. The major portion of a person's training thus occurs *on the job,* although—for job categories which will have a large number of employees—pretraining programs sometimes are offered by the business. For example, word processing pretraining at school is possible for the secretarial worker, although specific on-the-job training is required later to acquaint the person with the idiosyncracies of the particular system.

If schools cannot provide the unique training needed for most Category B

FIGURE 14-2 Job descriptions related to computing occupations. (From *Canadian Classifications and Dictionary of Occupations,* Department of Manpower and Immigration, Canada.)

2183-110 SYSTEM ANALYST BUSINESS, ELECTRONIC DATA-PROCESSING (prof. & tech., n.e.c.) DPT:131
GED: 5 SVP: 8 EC: I PA: S 5 6 7

Analyzes business problems, such as development of integrated production and inventory control, cost analysis, selects appropriate equipment, and develops programs for electronic data-processing systems:

Confers with department heads or project directors to ascertain specific management information requirements; such as, nature and degree of summarization, identification of items and format for presentation of results. Analyzes systems, procedures and methods used in various operations selected for conversion, determines feasibility and extent of conversion, and prepares process flow-charts and diagrams. Develops new applications and long-range plans for customer utilization of electronic-data-processing system, and analyzes capabilities and limitations of computers and peripheral equipment. Devises means of deriving input data to select a feasible and economic method for personnel operating equipment. Tests and eliminates errors in computer programs, to prepare final system of operations. Assists sales personnel of electronic-data-processing services in preparation and presentation of proposals to customer, in non-technical language. Prepares cost estimates and summary of savings resulting from proposed systems. Maintains accurate records and documentation of system analysis to facilitate follow-up action. Prepares instruction manuals covering use, operation, routine maintenance and technical specifications of key-punch machines, sorters, and other related tabulator equipment, and trains operating and supervisory personnel. Designs new forms and other documents relating to computer operations.

2183-118 PROGRAMMER, BUSINESS (prof. & tech., n.e.c.)
GED: 5 SVP: 7 EC: I PA: S 6 7 DPT:231

Writes program in computer-process language to provide required data for management and resolve business problems:

Studies business-problem work-flow chart or diagram prepared by systems analysts. Confers with systems analysts or departmental representatives concerned with program to resolve questions of intent, output requirements, input data acquisition, extent of automatic programming, coding use and modifications, and inclusion of internal checks and controls. Writes program in logical sequence, by applying knowledge of computer capabilities, subject matter and symbolic logic. Writes detailed logical flow-chart in symbolic form to represent work order of data to be processed by computer system, and to describe input, output, and arithmetic and logical operation involved. Prepares block diagrams to specify equipment lay-out. Devises sample input data to test adequacy of program. Corrects program errors by such methods as altering program steps and program sequence. Prepares written instructions to guide operating personnel during production runs. Supervises junior programmers on a project.

May analyze, review and rewrite programs to increase operating efficiency or adapt to new requirements. May compile documentation of program development and subsequent revisions. May train subordinates in programming. May plan, schedule, analyze and direct preparation of programs and be designated accordingly.

jobs, what role does the educational system play here? The answer is easy: Instead of attempting to provide job-specific skills, the educator's responsibility is to provide *general computing experiences* so that the person is familiar with hardware and software, can talk intelligently with peers about computers, has the background to make a wise job selection, and has sufficient knowledge to benefit from on-the-job training programs offered by business.

Category C: Careers Requiring Computing Background

The third class of jobs requiring a computing background are those which demand the employee's ability to converse with staff and clients intelligently about computers, without requiring the person to necessarily program or use the computer. Examples of employees filling this category include:

1. Journalists who interview people or write articles about computer science.
2. Government employees responsible for policy decisions with respect to the use of computers or their implications for society.
3. Business managers who need to talk to their data processing personnel about projects.
4. High level administrators in education who must decide on the purchasing policies of computing equipment for their school district.

The computer background required is different for each of these cases. The first two require someone with a solid foundation in computer applications and societal issues; the next group needs a person trained in business data processing; the last demands a teacher who is fluent in the uses of computers in education. In all cases, it is necessary to have at least an introductory course in computer literacy. This should be followed by several computing courses in the area of specialization related to the job. In the majority of cases, though, the person is not expected to obtain a computer science degree; the main academic degree would be journalism, business, education, or whatever; the computing courses simply augment this education.

Criteria for Choosing a Career

Suppose a student has decided to embark on a computing career. What assistance can the teacher provide to help the student make a wise choice? There are many factors the student must consider when making such an important decision. These factors include information on aptitudes and abilities, interests, job availability, salary, and job progression.

Aptitudes and abilities for computer studies. Measures of aptitude are important for students entering the computing area. Although these measures cannot be used in isolation, they do help predict how successful the students will be in computer studies and afterwards, on the job. Unfortunately there are few reliable predictors of success in computer studies. Some of the "aptitudes" suggested by educators are mathematical ability, problem-solving ability, and frustration tolerance. *Mathematical ability* appears to be important because of the mathematics background required for certain areas of computer science. *Problem solving ability* is important when the student has to come up with logical solutions in the form of computer programs. *Frustration tolerance* is necessary because the student will constantly face situations in which a program or piece of equipment does not work, and patience and perseverance are required to find the bug(s).

How do we determine whether the student has computer studies aptitudes? One approach is to simply ask students to appraise themselves; students are often astute in recognizing their own strengths and weaknesses. Or the teacher can make an evaluation of the student's abilities in several ways. In the most informal approach, this evaluation is based on daily observations of the student's performance in the classroom. A second tactic uses more objective criteria; the teacher finds out how well the student has done in other subject areas, such as mathematics, which are related to success in computer science. Another method involves giving the student standardized computer science aptitude tests. Of course, a composite of all these measures is the best way to make a sound judgment.

Ability is critical for job selection. Obviously, the student should enter a career path in which excellence has been achieved. One way to measure level of ability is to use the *student's marks.* Unfortunately, such marks are not perfect predictors of future job performance. The only way to determine whether a student has what it takes to succeed is when the student works in the real job situation. *Grades* tend to measure a person's average overall ability in computer studies. However, each job requires specific skills. For instance, a programming job requires considerable skill in writing programs, but, the ability to problem solve may not be mandatory. Both students and employers should be careful when using marks alone to assess ability; they do not tell the whole story. Fortunately, the astute employer can quickly gauge a person's abilities in the placement interview and in the first few weeks on the job.

Interest in computer studies. Enjoying one's work is one of the primary factors in choosing a career. The potential computing employee therefore should enjoy working in computer studies. Furthermore, the student should also show interest in a *specific job area.* Even a narrower perspective, such as an interest in programming, is insufficient. There are many different kinds of programming jobs available: systems programmer, application programmer, maintenance programmer, programmer in business, industry, education, and so forth. Each kind of programming has its own characteristics, and employees show inclinations for certain ones.

How can students determine where their interests lie? *Interest inventories* are useful, and there are some computer science ones on the market. Interests will also manifest themselves after the students have taken several courses in computing; by this time, students have become familiar with types of jobs and areas of application.

Job availability. Fortunately, in computer science, the job situation is excellent (Figure 14-3). There are more jobs than there are qualified applicants, and this condition is not likely to change in the near future, since the number of jobs requiring computing expertise is steadily increasing and the number of people qualified to fill them is not keeping up.

Job availability is also a function of the application area which the student wishes to pursue; some areas provide more opportunities than others. For example, business programming positions are relatively abundant, while systems programming jobs are harder to find.

FIGURE 14-3 Many different jobs are available to graduates with some computing background. These advertisements are a sample of the job opportunities listed in daily newspapers.

SENIOR TECHNICAL SUPPORT SPECIALIST

The Senior Technical Support Specialist assumes a sophisticated consulting role in design, development, modification and implementation of system software interfaces and software products.

He or she is responsible for the following:

- being a technical consultant for Project Teams
- monitoring systems software environments to ensure continuity with the WCB's Information systems service requirements
- evaluating new methodologies and procedures
- being a Project Leader on large and complex projects
- developing procedures for installation, testing and maintenance of system software
- identifying systems technology training requirements for data centre services
- teaching and tutoring study courses.

SOFTWARE SALES

YOU'VE GOT THE EXPERIENCE WE'VE GOT THE OPPORTUNITY LET'S TALK

As a top software sales producer, you want a position where the sky is the limit. That takes a forward-looking, high-growth company with a strong product line. A company that rewards innovation and solid performance. It takes a company like Software AG.

Our unique approach to providing practical business solutions had made us a leading supplier of advanced information system development software. From data base management to helping end-users, our integrated circle of products is reaching wider and wider circles of users.

Thanks to products like these, we're growing faster that ever before. All across the country, the potential for experienced salespeople is excellent. Do you have 5 or more years sales experience with mainframe software or 3 years experience in a DEC (VAX) environment?

Computer People:

Want to work overseas?

Our client in New Zealand pays for your relocation as well as providing you with permanent resident sponsorship.

The company uses the latest IBM computers, software and communications technology.

In return for your skill and commitment our client will be offering a package based on experience, training and supportive management.

The positions offered include:

— **Project Managers**
— **Analysts**
— **Analyst/Programmer**

COMPUTER SOFTWARE PROGRAMMER

A Vancouver based company is seeking a Computer Software Programmer to be part of a programming team responsible for the development and maintenance of a Nationwide Collection Management System.

Candidates should possess a recognized degree or diploma in Computer Programming and have 2 years minimum experience in RPG II using IBM System/36.

The incumbent will be responsible for problem determination, programming, testing and documentation. Excellent analytical and problem solving skills are required.

If you possess the above qualifications, please forward your resume in confidence to us.

WORD PROCESSING OPERATOR

We are looking for someone to join our growing Word Processing unit. Preference will be given to those with IBM Displaywriter experience.

If you have excellent grammar and communication skills, good dictation skills, and a typing speed of 55 to 60 wpm., **we** may be what **you** are looking for.

Duties include transcribing dictation, manual input and updates, reports and policy forms. Some switchboard relief is involved.

We offer a competitive salary and full range of Company benefits including Flextime and a Dental plan. Preference will be given to a non-smoker.

If you are interested and would like more information, please call us.

COMPUTER OPERATOR

This is an excellent opportunity for a well organized individual with approximately 1 year experience on an IBM 3081K or similar equipment. The successful candidate will have a good working knowledge of MVS/XA using JES 2 and be familiar with MVS/JCL.

Applicants must be prepared to work on rotating shifts. We offer a good starting salary and benefit package.

Finally, although there are lots of job opportunities for people entering a computer science career in Category A, the most plentiful positions are in Category B—the computer user—and the proportion of such jobs can be expected to rise.

Salary. Salaries paid for Category A computing jobs are substantial. The high salaries are the result of competition for a relatively sparse commodity: qualified and well trained people. Of course, the computing jobs which require less training, as in Category B, generally receive a lower salary. Category C users, because they are professionals, usually receive a good salary.

Location of the job. Currently, most computing jobs are available in medium to large cities. Few positions can be found in small towns and rural areas unless large industries are located there. Companies large enough to own computers are usually in big cities; head offices of corporations are found there too, as are manufacturers and suppliers of computing equipment.

Work hours. The computer scientist's work hours often differ from the norm. Computer scientists sometimes work through lunch, bring programs home, and even work into the night. Sometimes overtime is unavoidable; for instance, when there is a breakdown and employees have to get things running quickly.

Helping Students Choose a Career

How can teachers and counselors help a student choose a computing career? They should ensure that the student has as much *information* as possible before making a decision. Sources of such information include:

1. Educational material supplied by the computing industry indicating job availability, salary range, and other information.
2. Filmstrips and pamphlets from the local library depicting societal issues, computers in factories, etc.
3. A dictionary of job titles for computer science, describing job specifications in the computing industry.
4. Speakers' and counselors' bureaus, listing people in industry who are conversant with student concerns and are willing to talk about the job market.
5. Government speakers' bureaus, listing representatives of government departments who are responsible for talking about high technology jobs or who are willing to provide information on job recruitment and placement.

The counselor can advise the student how to *contact employers and arrange interviews.* In addition, the counselor can provide lists of job opportunities or names of companies where computing positions exist.

The counselor can make sure that the student is *properly prepared and academically qualified* for the job. This means that the student not only should be prepared for the specific computing job sought, but should have a sufficiently diversified education to provide adequate background for related jobs. This diversified background is important in case the student cannot get the job desired or changes career plans before graduating. The capability to exercise options when selecting a career is why most university programs provide such a wide range of topics rather than concentrating in one specific area.

The Flexible Career

The era of the twenty-year company employee is over; currently, people prefer career mobility—to work for one company for a few years and then move on to the next. This is especially true of people who work in computer science; there is an extremely *high turnover rate.* Computer scientists are in high demand and can therefore afford the luxury of switching jobs. They have little fear of unemployment.

Given the basic condition for *job mobility,* why do computer scientists change jobs rather than stay where they are? A main reason is monetary; since there is such demand for certain kinds of computer scientists, companies are willing to offer exorbitant salaries in hopes of attracting graduates or professionals who are presently working for other industries. Hand-in-hand with increased salary is the chance of being promoted; employers frequently offer promotion to more responsible positions in the hope of attracting qualified personnel.

Another reason for job movement is the rather volatile nature of the computer science job market. Since computer science is a relatively new discipline, jobs appear and disappear almost overnight. This situation also acts as a catalyst for job hopping.

Accommodating job flexibility. How can the teacher prepare the student for a career in a discipline as changeable as computer science? This is difficult because by the time the student graduates, the whole area can have changed drastically; some jobs which may have attracted the student to computer science may have disappeared, while new ones have been established. Obviously, a rigid course of studies geared toward a specific job market is not suitable. A *broad computing background* is necessary which gives the student flexibility and the capacity to move in many different directions.

A second facet of the student's training should emphasize *generalities rather than specifics.* Specifics (such as the internal details of a particular brand of microcomputer) are useless if they are no longer applicable by the time the student needs to use them. On the other hand, by learning generalities, such as the internal workings of the average microcomputer, the student can apply fundamental concepts to a new situation without undergoing a complete retraining program. What we advocate is the "transfer-of-training" methodology, in which what was learned in one situation is transferred to a new situation. This ability to apply previous knowledge to learning new material is essential to the computer scientist's survival on the job.

This ability to adapt to new situations must not end when the student gets a job. The computing world is moving so fast, it can quickly leave an employee behind. Because of this, many employers are willing to subsidize professional development and additional learning in computer studies through *in-service education.*

QUESTIONS

1. Select calendars for two universities. Look at the computer studies section (undergraduate). Which courses are the same? Which are unique to just one university?

2. In what ways would a programming class taken in a business setting differ from a similar class taken in a school setting? In what ways are they similar?
3. What additional training would a counselor need to advise students on careers in computer studies?
4. Examine a large city newspaper for computer-related positions. Categorize them into: programming, systems analyst, or management. If possible, compute an average pay range for each category. Compare the number of computer jobs to other professional jobs.
5. Go back ten years in the newspapers and randomly examine computer-related careers. Make comparisons from the information derived from the previous question.
6. As a class, gather materials to create a package which would be useful for counseling students for computer studies.
7. Conduct a survey of people from various occupational groups; find out what background they have in computing knowledge, and determine what (if any) computing knowledge is required for their jobs.
8. List the pros and cons of working in a volatile computing job market.
9. Do you think that the number of computing jobs will continue to increase at the current rate, accelerate, or slow down? Substantiate your answer.
10. Write a short essay explaining why self-study may not reap optimal results.
11. Define the following terms: abilities, aptitudes, attitudes, flexible career, industrial training, self-study.

15

Key Competencies for Computer Studies Teachers

How can an administrator determine who should teach computer studies? The most qualified instructor should be assigned to teach a specific course at a specific grade level. Criteria may be established for the qualifications of the computer studies teacher. No two administrators would use identical criteria, which vary from grade to grade and school to school. With this in mind, criteria are listed which may be the basis for making a wise selection. Each teacher should have:

An inherent interest in computer studies. The term "interest" implies knowledge in computer studies.

Some degree of competency in the area. This implies computer studies subject background, practical experience in computing, and on-going study in computer studies.

An arsenal of teaching methods and strategies related to computer studies.

Knowledge in the resources available in computer studies.

Familiarity with the computer studies curriculum for the state or province; if possible, an awareness of what is happening in the computing field, in the community, in the business, and in schools in the region.

Awareness of the prior computer studies knowledge of students entering the course.

An understanding of the principles of the psychology of learning.

How Teachers Get Their Training

Although most teachers have the basic "teacher training" program, many graduated and received their teaching certificates before computing studies was offered. Educators are beginning to recognize the need for all teachers to have some knowledge of computer studies. There are at least three types of teachers who become qualified to teach computer studies. Some are presently teaching computer studies courses, applying their training in methodology in other disciplines to the field of computing. Others are volunteering to teach the new computer studies course. These teachers may have to supplement their present understanding of computer studies content as well as acquire methodology suitable for computer studies. Some prospective teachers may be attending teacher preparation institutions. These students need sufficient content and methodologies to do an effective job in preparing students to work with the computer for business and personal use.

Training Available for Computer Studies Teachers

Teachers are trained via may routes. It must be decided if these paths fulfill the objectives and result in teacher competency in computer studies. These items must be included:

1. Professional education related to computer studies.
2. Adequate acquisition of computer studies subject matter.
3. An understanding of the psychology of learning.
4. Competency in appropriate method utilization or delivery systems for computer studies.
5. Knowledge of appropriate computer studies resources to supplement subject matter.
6. Knowledge of the computer studies curriculum and the evaluation procedures in computer studies.

In addition, the computer studies teacher must know:

1. The hierarchical structure of the content.
2. How computers developed.
3. What the computing applications are.
4. What computer language(s) need to be taught.
5. How to program.
6. What equipment should be used.
7. What computer systems should be set up.
8. How to set the order of presentation of content.
9. How to pace the presentations.
10. How to determine the delivery system.
11. How to choose the main and supplementary texts.
12. How to select computer studies resources and media.
13. How to provide for individual needs—enrichment and remedial.
14. How computers affect other subject areas—cross articulation.
15. How to take the computer studies knowledge of the student from where it is to where it should be.

HOW TEACHERS ACQUIRE THEIR COMPUTER STUDIES BACKGROUND

Most computing studies teachers or those teachers including computer applications in their classrooms are basically self-taught. They may have used programmed textbooks or distributor's machine manuals, learning basically by the trial-and-error method. Other teachers may have taken the introductory computer science course at their community college or university. Workshops and seminars are good ways to introduce new computer languages, but they provide only surface knowledge. Other teachers may have a degree in education or computer studies, but seldom both. All these are helpful, but cannot replace the formal intensive preparation program designed to prepare computer studies teachers.

Formal Preparation Programs

One of the early uses of computers in schools was CAI, or computer assisted instruction. Teachers were not expected to write the software, but were expected to administer it in their classrooms. Following this, it was accepted practice to teach an introductory computer science course in the senior year of a high school program. This was generally an exploratory program and may or may not have required the use of computing equipment. The student then went on to a community college or a university to take course(s) in computer science. Prospective teachers of computer studies, however, were not required to take such a course in a teacher preparation university program.

Teacher training in computer studies at the university. Teacher requirements in computer studies are changing because business is giving preference to high school graduates who have some familiarity with computing. As a result, universities are gradually making mandatory the inclusion of at least one computer studies course in the prospective teacher's program as well as in the programs of all university students.

No one will argue against the need for a teacher preparation program for computer science at the university *undergraduate* level. The entrance requirements of the programs, however, are frequently under debate. The desirability of work experience in computing is also controversial. There is some question as to what should be included in the program to train computer studies teachers. The need for specialized training is generally recognized.

What is desirable varies with the trainers and the institutions. Teachers should have at least three of the following courses in the computer studies area: an introductory course; one or more programming languages; a problem solving course; an applications course in education (for example, CAI, word processing, spread sheets); and specialized methodologies in computer studies.

Graduate schools generally have fairly rigid entrance requirements. Having gained entrance, there are at least three paths to take at the post graduate level. First may be to acquire a second undergraduate degree. An individual may receive a baccalaureate degree in computer studies, then re-enter the university to obtain a teacher education degree. Or, individuals who already have a baccalaureate in education may decide to get additional expertise in the field of computer studies by entering the faculty of computer science.

A post-graduate degree may be sought by a teacher with a specialty in computer studies. Or teachers may decide to enroll in a doctoral program.

Informal Training

Individuals with work experience in computing or other related experience may decide to enter the teaching field, or a practicing teacher may obtain summer employment in business for the opportunity to work with computers.

Many teachers enrich their backgrounds through supplementary materials such as textbooks, programmed texts, and other professional books. The limitations of using these materials in isolation cannot be overemphasized. Publisher's catalogs give a comprehensive listing of books like computer science, an introduction to computers, computers as used in educational institutions, an introduction to programming, computers in business, or personal computing.

Machine manuals available from distributors also assist teachers in becoming familiar with the basics of computer operation. Some are easy to read; others may use too many technical terms.

Of late, the media is an important source of computer knowledge. Newspapers such as the *Financial Post* and the *Financial Times* are valuable resources. Some articles on computing are general, while others are designed specifically for the experts. Good TV and radio programs are presented, especially on the education channels.

Many journals carry in-service help for the teacher. They may be machine-oriented, business-oriented, or classroom-oriented. The uses made of these depend on the teacher. However, much of the software found in these journals may not have been adequately "debugged" and could create more problems than benefits. Professional journals are valuable in that they keep the teacher updated on the "state of the art" around the world.

There are numerous professional organizations which serve teachers—each one with a different purpose. They could be local, regional, national, or international. Typical examples are organizations for individuals who are interested in computers in education, special subject councils such as those formed by computer science teachers, computer user groups for those who own their own computers, as well as consortiums, university groups, general teachers groups, and, in some instances, computer clubs. In these groups a great deal of sharing takes place, including the sharing of software.

Teachers frequently use other people knowledgeable in computer studies to assist them in their classrooms. This includes students enrolled in their class, students in a more advanced class, graduates working in computer studies, experts in business, local dealers, computer store personnel, or fellow teachers.

Also, computer stores provide information on their own equipment and orientation programs for students. They motivate students by offering hands-on opportunities for using equipment.

What about the training course for teachers? Although teacher preparation courses have been available for a century or more, the specialized education offered in computer studies has not been available for long.

Courses in CAI and CAL have been offered in summer sessions since the 1960s. They were offered on university campuses by university professors and other experts in the field; then, when computer science was included in the school program, some courses were offered by businesspeople-turned-authors. These were popular for the teacher who was looking for a quick way to prepare for the coming semester.

Some courses, seminars, and workshops are available for administrators who want to learn more about CMI and other school management software packages. Many schools have adopted regionally or locally prepared school management systems which may have been written by some of their own teachers.

The informal training chosen by the teacher depends on his or her immediate need, the distance to be traveled, and the block of time required for it. Therefore, the background preparation of teachers presently teaching computing studies is varied.

COMPETENCIES FOR TEACHERS OF COMPUTER STUDIES COURSES

Competencies are required by a professional teacher and prospective teachers of computer studies. The teacher should recognize and deal with the social and intellectual needs of the computer studies student. This means drawing on the knowledge of human growth and development, learning theories, social/cultural foundations, assessment techniques, curriculum goals, and content. Recognize and deal with the instructional goals and objectives based on the learner's needs. These goals and objectives must coincide with the curricular and educational goals of the learner. The knowledge, skills, and attitudes needed to achieve these goals must also be identified so that they can be communicated to the student.

Design instruction appropriate to goals and objectives; and develop and utilize a variety of strategies and techniques to promote the fulfillment of the instructional objectives of the computer studies course. Implement instruction consistent with the course objectives and necessary strategies and techniques. Design and implement evaluation procedures which reflect learner achievement and objectives stated. The evaluation reports must be compared to the effectiveness of the instruction.

Integrate the various environments of the student into the classroom instruction. Select materials, illustrations, motivators, and reinforcers so that the student can relate more easily to the content, processes, and outcomes intended for the fulfillment of the computer studies objectives. Select strategies and techniques most appropriate for teaching specific concepts in the curriculum.

Promote effective patterns of communication. Communicate with students verbally, nonverbally, and in writing according to their mental and physical needs. Student ideas and expressions must be accepted and supported, and interaction between and among students and the teacher must be promoted and achieved.

Use resources appropriate to objectives. Be knowledgeable about the great variety of audio, visual, print, and nonprint resources available in computer studies and be able to operate the equipment and select those resources most appropriate to the concept being presented. Modify instruction on the basis of learner's verbal and nonverbal feedback. Maintain a classroom climate conducive to interaction between teacher and student. Be able to identify and react with sensitivity to the needs of all participants in the learning environment.

Use organizational and management skills to establish an efficient and effective learning environment. Organize and encourage productive group interaction and establish positive relationships with the learner. Computer studies laboratories must be such that student learning is enhanced.

Exhibit openness and flexibility. Recognize the need for improvement of instructional effectiveness in computer studies and listen critically to the ideas of others; be open to suggestion; base decisions and changes upon the best data available. Work effectively as a member of a professional team, analyze professional effectiveness, and continually strive to increase that effectiveness. Work with others to achieve shared goals; display behaviors consistent with the goals and ethics of the teaching profession.

Design and implement instruction which incorporates career education concepts. Career education is an important factor in the educational system; the computer studies course content and instructional objectives should incorporate these. Students need to learn about themselves, their environment and the roles played by individuals in society so they may cope successfully when venturing on a career in computing.

Competencies as They Are Reflected in Course Objectives

Each of the competencies can be reflected in the objectives set by the teacher and for the teacher in the classroom. Examples of suitable objectives for a teacher are to:

1. Develop programs in computer studies based on the literature and research of the field.
2. Organize the classroom activities to effectively use the time, instructional materials, and facilities.
3. Apply teaching strategies and techniques which best promote computer studies concepts.
4. Exhibit mastery of content in computing.
5. Demonstrate competency in evaluating student achievement, remediation, and program effectiveness.
6. Demonstrate competency in the principles of learning by offering instruction that will meet the needs of computer studies students.
7. Exhibit a personal pattern of behavior that encourages favorable public opinion of education.

Glossary*

*Important words for introductory computer students to know.

Abacus: An ancient Oriental calculator that uses movable beads threaded on a grid of wires.

Access Arm: A mechanical arm on a disk file storage unit which positions the reading and writing mechanism.

Access, Random: The process of obtaining information from or placing information in storage, such as primary memory, when the time required for such access is not dependent on the location of the data.

Access, Serial: The process of obtaining information from or placing information in storage when the time required for such access is dependent on waiting while non-desired storage locations are processed in sequential order.

ACM: Association for Computing Machinery.

Acoustical Coupler: Data communication device that converts electrical signals to/from tones for transmission over a telephone line using a conventional telephone headset.

Acronym: Group of letters formed from the initials of the words in a name or phrase. APL is an example.

A/D Converter: Analog-to-digital converter.

Address: The identification for a register or location in storage, represented by a name, label, or number.

ALGOL: ALGOrithmic Language—a programming language by which numerical procedures may be precisely presented to a computer in standard form.

Algorithm: Set of rules for solving a problem using a finite number of operations.

Alphanumeric Data: Data made up of both alphabetic characters and numbers.

ALU: Arithmetic and Logic Unit.

Analytical Engine: Device invented in the mid-1800s by Charles Babbage, a British mathematician, to solve mathematical problems—forerunner of the modern digital computer.

ANSI (American National Standard Institute): Acts as a national clearinghouse and coordinator for standards in the computing industry.

APL (A Programming Language): A mathematically-structured programming language developed by IBM Corporation.

Applications Software: Programs which are written by the users of a computer system—either of the computational type or the data processing type.

Arcade Games: Wide variety of games which computers have been programmed to play.

Architecture: Internal configuration of a computer, including its registers, instruction set, and input/output structure.

Argument (Parameter): Variable used to pass information back and forth between a subprogram and the main program.

Arithmetic/Logic Unit (ALU): That part of a central processing unit in which arithmetical or logical operations are performed.

Arithmetic Expression: Structure within a program which allows a combination of arithmetic operations such as addition, subtraction, multiplication and division.

Array: Series of related data items in a program. Examples include vectors, lists, and tables.

Artificial Intelligence (AI): The science, technology, and art of programming computers to do things that would require intelligence by human beings.

ASCII (American Standard Code of Information Interchange): Eight-bit code used for transmitting alphanumeric data between computing equipment.

Assembler: Computer program that takes low-level nonmachine language instructions prepared by a user and converts it into a form that may be used by the computer.

Atanasoff, John V.: Designed the first electronic digital computer; wanted to find faster ways of performing computations for physics problems.

Audio Response Terminal: Output device that produces spoken response.

Audit Trail: System of tracing items of data through processing, step by step, particularly from a machine-produced report or other machine output back to the original source data.

Automatic Data Processing: See DATA PROCESSING.

Automatic Teller Machine (ATM): Computer terminal used by depositors for fast banking services.

Automation: Implementation of processes by automatic means which take the place of manual human effort.

Auxiliary Storage/Secondary Storage: Storage, such as disks and tapes, that supplements the primary internal storage of a computer.

Babbage, Charles: See ANALYTICAL ENGINE.

Backspace: Key on a keyboard which is used to move backward one character at a time.

Backup: Procedures or equipment that are available for use in the event of failure or overloading of the normally used equipment or procedures.

Badge Reader: Terminal equipped to read credit cards or specially coded badges.

Bar Code/Universal Product Code: System of data coding used for input whereby bars of varying width and position represent data.

BASIC (Beginner's All-Purpose Symbolic Instruction Code): A computer language.

Batch Processing: Technique by which items to be processed are coded and collected into groups prior to processing.

Baud: Unit of signaling speed on data communications equipment which corresponds to a rate of one signal element per second.

Benchmark: Point of reference from which measurements can be made; the use of a program to evaluate the performance of a computer.

Bi-directional Printer: Printing device that moves in either direction as it types the characters.

Binary: A characteristic, property, or condition in which there are two possible alternatives. The binary system uses 2 as its base. Computers utilize binary values—either 0 or 1.

Binary Arithmetic: Arithmetic performed on binary numbers. The binary system is used as a base in computer processing.

Binary Coded Decimal (BCD): Computer coding system in which each decimal digit is represented by a group of four binary ones and zeros.

Binary Digit: See BIT.

Binary Number: A string of 1's and 0's representing a number.

Bit: A single binary value that carries the value of 0 or 1. A bit is the smallest unit of binary code.

Bit Check: A bit added to a group of binary digits in order to detect the alteration of any bit from the group during processing. Often called a parity bit.

Black Box: Electronic or mechanical device that functions in a predictable manner, but whose inner workings are often a mystery to the user.

Block: Group of words considered as a unit by virtue of being stored in successive storage locations.

Blocking: Combining two or more records into one block, such as on a magnetic tape, usually to increase efficiency of the computer input-output operations.

Block Diagram: Graphical representation of the logical connections within a computer system.

Board/Circuit Board: Flat board found inside computing equipment upon which the circuitry, integrated circuits, and other electrical components are located. Examples of boards are memory, processor, input/output, speech, or graphics.

Boolean Algebra: Binary system of algebra named after George Boole, an English mathematician, 1815–1864.

Boot: See BOOTSTRAP.

Bootstrap: Technique for automatically loading a program, usually the operating system, from the disk when the computer is turned on.

BPI: Bits per inch or bytes per inch.

BPS: Bits per second or bytes per second.

Branch: Term used to "jump" to another part of a computer program rather than to sequentially execute the code.

Bubble Storage/Memory: Memory that uses magnetic "bubbles" that move. The bubbles are locally magnetized areas that can move about in a magnetic material.

Buffer: Unit of computer memory that holds data awaiting input, processing, or output.

Bug: Error in a computer circuit or a computer program.

Bus: Cable or set of wires that acts as a major pipeline for electrical signals to go from one part of the computer to another.

Business Data Processing: Data processing for business purposes.

Business Form: Any document, usually preprinted, used to record or transmit business data including checks, invoices, statements, etc.

Byte: Unit of binary coding composed of eight bits that represents a number, symbol, or letter processed by the computer.

CAI: Acronym for Computer-Assisted Instruction—the use of a computer to provide instruction through interaction with individual learners.

CAL: Acronym for Computer-Augmented Learning—the use of a computer to augment or supplement more conventional instructional systems.

Call: Term used to activate a subroutine in a program.

Card: A punched card.

Card Punch: Machine which punches holes in a punched card.

Card Reader: Machine for reading information from a punched card.

Carry: Special condition that occurs when the results of a binary arithmetic operation is greater than the machine can handle.

Cashless Society: Computerized system in which monetary transactions are settled instantaneously by transferring credits from the customer's bank account to the store's account via a point-of-sale terminal.

Cassette Tape: Small plastic cartridge containing one-eighth inch magnetic tape used for long-term storage on microcomputers.

Catalog: Directory or a list of files residing on a user's disk storage.

CBL (Computer-Based Learning): Embraces all forms of educational computing.

CDP: An acronym for Certificate in Data Processing.

Central Processing Unit: See CPU.

Chain Printer: Line printer in which the type slugs are carried by the links of a revolving chain.

Character Code: Specific combination of binary elements (bits, or holes punched in cards) used to represent characters.

Character Printer: Printer in which only a single character is printed at a time.

Character Set: Comprises the numbers, letters, and symbols associated with a given device or coding system.

Check Bit: Binary check digit (parity check)—used for detecting errors.

Chip: Miniature electronic device using integrated circuits that performs processing, memory, and switching functions in a computer.

CIPS: Canadian Information Processing Society.

CMI: Computer Managed Instruction; the educational use of a computer to store student records and keep track of course information.

COBOL: Common Business Oriented Language—a computer programming language used mainly in business.

Code: Statements of a program.

Coder: Person whose primary duty is to write, not design, computer programs.

Coding: Writing a computer program.

Collating Sequence: An ordering assigned to the character set to be used for sequencing purposes.

Column: Vertical members of a two-dimensional array or table (cf. ROW).

COM: Acronym for Computer Output Microfilm wherein computer output is placed on microfilm or microfiche.

Comments: Statements within a program that do not trigger any computer processing but are helpful notes for future users who may attempt to understand or alter the program. Synonymous with REMARKS.

Communication Link: Medium of communication in an electronic telecommunication system.

Compatibility, Equipment: Characteristics of computers which enable one computer to accept and process data prepared by another computer without conversion or modification.

Compiler: Software package that accepts English-type programming statements, such as in FORTRAN and COBOL, and converts them to machine language for use by the computer.

Computer Graphics: Use of a computer to draw pictorial information on a screen or plotter.

Computer Literacy: Nontechnical study of the computer and its effect on society.

Computer Program: Ordered set of instructions written in a programming language which describes completely the operations required to solve a problem.

Computer Science: Field of knowledge embracing all aspects of the design, programming, and use of computers.

Computer System: Physical equipment and instructions; the hardware and software, used as a unit to process data.

Concatenate: To link together or join two or more character strings into a single character string.

Conditional Branch or Transfer: Program statement that may cause a departure from the sequence of instructions being followed depending upon the result of an operation, the content of a register, or the settings of an indicator.

Configuration: Assembly of computing machines that is interconnected and programmed to operate in a manner specific to the needs of the computing center.

Connect Time: In timesharing, the length of time you are "on" the computer. Usually measured by the duration between "sign-on" and "sign-off."

Console: Work station from which a computer is controlled: a typewriter which is on-line to the computer that allows communication between the machine and the computer operator.

Constants, Numeric and String: Values that do not change during the execution of the program.

Continuous Forms: Paper that is used on computer printers. The sheets are separated by perforations. Holes are used on the outer edges to advance the paper line by line.

Control Character: Special character on the keyboard, such as the program "STOP" key, whose function is to initiate controlling operations.

Control Unit: That part of a central processing unit which accesses instructions in sequence, interprets them, and initiates appropriate functions.

Conversational Mode: Mode of operation, in a program such as BASIC, in which the user is able to obtain immediate responses to input messages.

Copy: Reproduction of information in a new part of memory, usually leaving information unchanged at the original location.

Core Memory: Obsolete form of memory utilizing magnetic "donuts," usually strung through wires in the form of an array.

CPI: Characters per inch.

CPS: Characters per second.

CPU: Central Processing Unit; contains the arithmetic unit, the logic unit, the control unit, and special register groups.

Crash/Bomb: System shutdown caused by a hardware or software malfunction.

Cryptographic Techniques: Methods of concealing data by encrypting a character or group of characters.

CRT: Abbreviation for cathode ray tube, a TV-like display used in computer terminals.

Cursor: A moving or blinking symbol on a video terminal that indicates where the next character will appear.

Cycle: Any set of operations on a computer which is repeated as a unit.

Cylinder: Vertical column of tracks on a magnetic disk file unit.

Data: Numbers, symbols, or letters that have meaning and can be processed to produce information.

Data Bank: Collection of related data used and processed by a computer program and stored on a disk or tape.

Data Base Management System (DBMS): Systematic approach to the storing, updating, and retrieval of information stored as data items, usually in the form of records in a file, where many users, or even many remote installations, will use common data banks.

Data Capture: Gathering or collecting information for computer handling, the first step in job processing.

Data Conversion: Any method of converting data from human-readable form to a form readable by computers.

Data Entry: Act of entering data in some machine-readable form.

Data Preparation: Process of organizing information and storing it in a form that can be input to the computer.

Data Processing: Series of steps followed in accepting and processing data on a computer.

Data Set: Device that connects a data processing machine to a telephone or telegraph communication line.

Data Structure: Related set of items which is processed as a unit by a program.

Debug: To find and correct errors in the coding of a program.

Decision: The computer operation of ascertaining whether certain relationships exist between data values and taking alternative courses of action depending upon the result.

Decision Box: Flowchart symbol used to represent a decision or branch.

Declaration: An instruction written as part of a source program which is not executed when the program executes. Instructions which set up tables and arrays are examples of declarations.

Decryption: The translation of data back into regular text after being encrypted for security reasons.

Dedicated Computer: A computer whose use is reserved for a particular task, such as weather predictions.

Degradation: Refers to the operation of a computer system at a lower level of service as a result of failures or bottlenecks.

Delete: Operation to eliminate a record, group of records, or an entire file. The operation of deleting or erasing a character from the keyboard.

Density: Number of bits per unit area of a disk or tape.

Desk-Checking: Manual checking process in which representative sample data items, used for detecting errors in program logic, are traced through the program before the latter is executed on the computer.

Diagnostic Routine: Routine for locating and explaining errors in a computer routine or hardware component.

Difference Engine: Machine designed by Charles Babbage that was a precursor of the modern computer.

Digital Computer: Computer that processes data in binary form.

Digitize: To convert a measurement, such as temperature, into a digital value; automatically converting an electrical signal into a binary number.

Dimension: 1) The maximum size or the number and arrangement of the elements of an array. 2) A statement in a programming language used to declare the attributes of the array.

Directory: Dictionary or catalog of the files on a disk.

Disk/Diskette: A round, flat surface used for storage of data; the surface is coated with a ferrous material for magnetic recording of data.

Disk Drive: A data storage peripheral used for reading and writing on diskettes.

Disk Operating System (DOS): An organized collection of software that controls the overall operations of a computer.

Disk Pack: One or more magnetic disks built into a protective housing which can be inserted and removed from a disk drive.

Display: See VIDEO DISPLAY TERMINAL.

Document Reader: A general term referring to OCR or OMR equipment.

Documentation: 1) Manuals describing the use and operation of computers, programming languages, etc. 2) Any aids to understanding a program such as flowcharts or pseudocode.

Dot-Matrix Printer: Printer that forms characters by placing dots, end to end, on paper.

Double Density Disk: A disk which has twice the storage capacity of a single density disk.

Downtime: The period during which a machine is inoperable due to a hardware or software fault.

Drive: Any device which physically houses some recording medium such as a disk drive.

Drum/Magnetic Drum: A peripheral storage device consisting of a cylinder with a magnetizable surface on which data is stored.

Dumb Terminal: Input devices that are only used to input data and instructions into the computer and to receive the processed information from the computer. It consists of a display screen, a keyboard for data entry, and a communication link to the CPU.

Duplex: A communication system which allows transmission in both directions simultaneously.

EBCDIC: Acronym for Extended Binary Coded Decimal Interchange Code, an 8-bit code used to represent data in modern computers.

Echo Check: A check on the accuracy of data transmission—the computer sends back the character which the user typed on the keyboard.

Edit: To enter, correct, arrange, and change data or textual information on a computer.

Editor: A software package used for editing.

EDP: An acronym for Electronic Data Processing.

EDVAC: An acronym for Electronic Delayed Storage Automatic Computer, the first digital computer to feature the stored program concept.

Egoless Programming: A programming philosophy in which programs are no longer regarded as the personal property of a single programmer.

Electronic Cottage: A trend to have employees working at home on terminals tied into the company computer.

Electronic Book: Computers that act like books; they store information on "pages." You can turn the pages just by pressing a button.

Electronic Funds Transfer System (EFTS): A computerized system in which money is transferred electronically over communication lines thereby, for example, allowing a purchaser to pay for merchandise by the direct transfer of funds, thus eliminating a great deal of paperwork.

Electronic Mail: The transmission of messages at high speeds over telecommunication facilities.

Electronic Processing: Data and information are handled by electronic devices, including integrated circuit chips; digital computers do electronic processing.

Electronic Spreadsheet: A program that enables the user to create financial data consisting of columns and rows, to make calculations using these data, and to automatically change all other data depending upon these calculations.

Electrostatic Printer: Computer printout device that electronically charges spots on treated paper that correspond to letters or graphics. After being "charged," the paper is passed through a toner solution which sticks to the charged spots to produce the printed output.

Encryption: Transcription of data in a secret code for security reasons.

ENIAC: Electronic Numerical Integrator And Calculator; the first electronic digital computer.

End-of-File: A special character located at the end of a data file.

Erase: To remove data from storage without replacing it or to remove information from a CRT.

Error: Any problem in a computer program which causes any deviation of a computed or measured quantity from the theoretically correct or true value.

Execute: To interpret a machine instruction and perform the desired operation.

Expression: A source language combination of one or more operations, e.g. $(x + y)$.

Fair Credit Reporting Act: Federal (U.S.) legislation giving individuals the right to see and challenge credit data that is kept about them.

Fault: The failure of any physical component of a system to operate in an expected manner.

Feasibility Study: A projection of how a proposed computer system or software package might operate in a particular organization—it provides the basis for a decision to change the existing system.

Federal Privacy Act: A law enacted to protect rights of citizens from invasion of privacy.

Fiber Optics: Technology based upon fine strands of transparent material used for transmission of data and other signals at high rates of speed.

Field: A group of related characters treated as a unit in a record.

File: A collection of data records stored on a disk or tape for reference and use. Data files are stored, retrieved, and processed automatically within computer systems.

File Name: Alphanumeric characters used to identify a particular file on a disk.

File Organization: The manner in which the application programmer views the data in a file. Typical organizations are sequential, indexed, and random.

File Update: Additions, deletions, and changes against a master file.

Firmware: Software instructions or data that are permanently stored on an integrated circuit.

Fixed-Length Record: Pertaining to a file in which the record size is constant. Contrast with VARIABLE-LENGTH RECORD.

Floating Point: A form of number representation in which real numbers (whole part plus fraction) are represented.

Floppy Disk: A flexible plastic disk on which data are stored magnetically.

Flow: A general term to indicate the sequence of events in a flowchart or program.

Flowchart: A diagram to show the step-by-step procedures to be followed in a program or data processing system represented through the use of standard graphic symbols.

Flowline: On a flowchart, the line representing a connecting path between flowchart symbols.

Form Feed (FF): The standard ASCII character to cause a form feed to occur, which results in the movement of paper in a printer to the top of the next page.

FORTRAN: Acronym for FORmula TRANslator. A higher-level programming language used to perform mathematical, scientific, and engineering computations.

Freedom of Information Act: Federal legislation giving individuals the right to obtain data gathered about them by governmental agencies.

Function: A process that is performed on a number or character string; for example, squaring is the mathematical function of multiplying a number by itself.

Generation: A term usually applied to the progression of computers from those using vacuum tubes (first generation), those using transistors (second generation), those using integrated circuits (third generation), and those using VLSI circuits (fourth generation).

Gigabyte: 10^9 bytes.

Gigo (garbage in garbage out): Refers to the concept that incorrect input data will produce incorrect results even if the program works properly.

Graphics: Line figures or other illustrations produced by a computer.

Graphics Terminal: A computer keyboard and screen used for creating pictures; it may have a light pen for drawing on the screen, a graphics tablet for tracing outlines of pictures and maps, and a color palette.

Halt: A situation that arises when the sequence of operations in a program comes to a stop. Most programming languages have a command to do this.

Hands-On: An educational approach where the equipment is actually manipulated by the learner.

Hardcopy: Printed documents produced by output devices.

Hard Disk: A storage disk made of rigid material. Hard disk devices generally store more information and access it faster than floppy disk devices.

Hardware: Equipment that is part of a data processing system or computer installation.

Heuristic: Rule of thumb for solving a problem on a computer (cf. ALGORITHM).

Hexadecimal: Pertaining to a numeric system with a radix of 16. Digits greater than 9 are represented by letters of the alphabet.

High-Level Language: A programming language oriented toward the problem to be solved or the procedure to be used, like FORTRAN, COBOL.

Hollerith Code: The coding system used on 80-column cards to represent alphanumeric data on punched cards; named after Herman Hollerith, the originator of punched card tabulating.

Home Computer: A microcomputer used in the home.

Host Computer: The primary or controlling computer in a multiple-computer network.

Housekeeping: Computer operations that do not directly contribute toward the desired results: initialization, set-up, and clean-up operations.

IBM: Acronym for International Business Machines, the largest computer company in the world.

Identifier: A symbol whose purpose is to identify or name a body of data. A variable name is an identifier.

Illegal Character: A character or combination of bits which is not accepted as a valid input by the computer.

Immediate-Mode Commands: System and editing commands that are executed as soon as the carriage control key (RETURN, ENTER) is pressed.

Impact Printer: A data printout device that imprints by momentary pressure of raised type against paper, using ink or ribbon as a color medium.

Implementation: The process of installing a computer system. It involves choosing the equipment, installing the equipment, training the personnel, and establishing the computing center operating policies.

Increment: An amount added to or subtracted from the value of a variable during the execution of a loop in a program.

Indexed Sequential Access Method: A means of organizing data on a disk. A directory or index is created to show where the data records are stored.

Industrial Robots: Industrial machines that are controlled by computers, usually to do simple, repetitive tasks.

Information: Processed data. Computers accept raw data and process it into information.

Information Explosion: The exponential increase in the growth and diversification of all forms of information.

Information Revolution: The name given to the present era because of the impact of computer technology on society.

Inherited Error: 1) An error in the results of a computation attributed to some previous stage of processing. 2) An error arising initially from the inability to measure values with sufficient accuracy.

Initialize: To preset a variable or counter to a proper starting value before commencing the program.

Input: 1) Data put into a computer system for processing. 2) The activity of entering data into the computer.

Input Device: The mechanical unit designed to bring data into a computer.

Input Media: Materials or devices used to capture data and enter it into the computer, such as keyboards, punched cards, and joysticks.

Inquiry: A technique for interrogating the contents of a database.

Installation: A general term for a particular computing system in the context of the overall function it serves and the individuals who manage it, operate it, apply it to problems, service it, and use the results it produces.

Instruction: 1) A statement of a programming language. 2) A basic operation in the machine language of the CPU.

Instruction Set: The repertoire of commands available in the machine language of a particular computer or programming system.

Integer: A whole number that may be positive, negative, or zero. It does not have a fractional part.

Integrated Circuit (IC): The building block of computers consisting of tiny electrical circuits stored inside a small plastic block.

Intelligent Terminal: A computer terminal that has its own data processing capability.

Interactive Computer: The computer is responsive to inputs from people using terminals.

Interblock Gap/Interrecord Gap (IRG): The distance on a magnetic tape between the end of one block (record) and the beginning of the next. Such spacing facilitates tape start-stop operations.

Interpreter: A software package, such as BASIC, which executes the statements of a user's program without first translating them into machine language.

Iterate: Repeatedly execute a loop in a program.

Jacquard's Loom: A weaving machine invented near the beginning of the 19th century by Joseph Marie Jacquard, in which punched cards controlled the movements of the shuttles in order to produce tapestries of complicated designs.

JCL: Acronym for Job Control Language, a language used to specify the sequencing and operation of jobs on a mainframe.

Jetspray Printer: Uses a fine spray of ink at rapid speeds to produce printed output.

Job: A collection of specified tasks constituting a unit of work for a computer.

Joystick: A type of input device. It has a stick that is manipulated by the user, often used in conjunction with graphic terminals.

Jump: A departure from the normal sequence of executing instructions in computer, a branch.

Justify: To align printed characters in a field; to justify right or left margins.

K: An abbreviation for kilobyte.

Key: 1) The field or fields that identify a record. 2) One of the individual elements of a keyboard.

Keyboard: The standard input device upon which the user keys information.

Keypunch: A keyboard-operated device used to punch holes in cards to represent data.

Keystroke: The action of pressing one of the keys on a keyboard.

Keyword: 1) One of the significant and informative words in a title or document, residing in a database, that describe the content of that document. 2) A primary element in a programming language, such as the words LET or GOTO in the BASIC programming language.

Key-to-Disk: A keyboard unit used to store data directly on a magnetic disk.

Key-to-Tape: A keyboard unit used to store data directly on magnetic tape.

Kilobyte (K): Stands for 1024 or 2^{10} bytes.

Labor Displacement: The replacement of human labor with machines such as computers.

Language: See PROGRAMMING LANGUAGE.

Large-Scale Integration (LSI): The process of placing a large number of components on a single integrated circuit.

Letter Quality: Printed output equal to that produced by a good-quality typewriter.

Library, Computerized: 1) Application of computers to library operations and services. 2) Collection of standard, proven routines and other information available to a computer user, usually on magnetic tapes or disks.

Light Pen: A device, which resembles a pen, used to alter or enter data on the face of a video screen of a computer terminal.

Line Numbers: Line numbers are required for each statement in a BASIC program.

Line Printer: A printer which prints out the results from a computer one line at a time.

Line Speed: The maximum rate at which signals may be transmitted over a communications channel, usually measured in baud or bits per second.

List: 1) Any printing operation where a series of records on a file are printed one after another. 2) The printing of the source code of a program.

Listing: Printed version of the source code of a program.

Literal: Another name for a string constant.

Liveware: A misleading expression meaning computer people.

Load: To read a program into the main memory of a computer from secondary storage.

Log Off: To terminate a session on a timesharing system.

Log On: To initiate a session on a timesharing system.

Logic: The underlying meaning of a program as embodied in the programming language code.

Logic Error: An error in the logic of a program which makes it work differently than expected.

Logical Operation: A programming operation that is logical in nature, such as logical tests and decisions, in contrast with arithmetic and transfer operations which involve no decision.

LOGO: A higher level, interactive programming language that assumes the user has access to some type of on-line terminal—designed for students, and suited to students in the younger age group.

Loop: A sequence of instructions in a program that can be executed repetitively until certain specified conditions are satisfied.

Lovelace, Ada Augusta: A skilled mathematician and friend of Charles Babbage's. She developed the essential ideas of programming. ADA, a programming language to be used as a Department of Defense standard programming language, was named after her.

Lower Case: Small letters, in contrast to upper case or capital letters.

Low-Level Language: A language in which each instruction has a single corresponding machine code equivalent (cf. HIGH-LEVEL LANGUAGE).

LPM: An acronym for lines per minute to describe output of a line printer.

LSI: See LARGE-SCALE INTEGRATION.

Machine Language: The coding, in binary form, that directs the operation of the CPU. Programs must be translated into machine language before they can be run on a computer.

Machine Readable Information: Information recorded on any medium in such a way that it can be sensed or read directly by a computer input device without human intervention. Also called machine-sensible.

Magnetic Card: A storage device consisting of a tray or cartridge of magnetically coated cards.

Magnetic Core: A tiny doughnut-shaped piece of magnetizable material that is capable of storing one binary digit. An older form of primary memory.

Magnetic Disk: Light plastic or metal disk covered with a ferrous oxide coating on which data may be stored magnetically.

Magnetic Ink Character Recognition (MICR): The recognition of characters printed with a special magnetic ink such as that used on special lines on checks.

Magnetic Tape: A coated plastic tape used for magnetic recording of data. Tape is utilized for sequential storage of data.

Magnetic Tape Unit: A device containing a magnetic tape drive, which reads and writes on magnetic tape.

Mainframe: Medium or large-scale computer system. Refers to the CPU and main memory, not the peripherals.

Main Memory: Internal storage, holds the program and its data.

Main Program: The central or main portion of the program, in contrast to the subsidiary portions which are called subprograms.

Maintenance, Hardware: Checking and fixing of the hardware components of a computer system.

Maintenance, Programming: Fixing, updating, and improving existing programs.

Manual: A book containing documentation for the computer.

Mark I: The first electromechanical computer developed under the direction of Howard Aiken at Harvard University.

Master File: A file containing relatively permanent information that is used as a source of reference and is updated periodically.

Matrix Printer: See DOT MATRIX PRINTER.

Mauchly, John: Co-inventor of the ENIAC, an early electronic computer.

Megabyte: A million bytes.

Memory: A device within a computer system that records data and information and stores it. Synonymous with STORAGE.

Menu: A set of options listed on a terminal; the user selects one option.

Merge: A function in which two files containing ordered records are grouped into one file which still has all the records ordered.

MICR: See MAGNETIC INK CHARACTER RECOGNITION.

Microcomputer: A small computer, containing a microprocessor, that usually fits on a desk top. Processing capabilities are usually limited to the handling of one job at a time.

Microprocessor: A single integrated circuit which contains the circuitry of a complete CPU. Microprocessors are used in many electronic devices, including microcomputers.

Microsecond: One millionth of a second.

Millisecond: One thousandth of a second.

Minicomputer: A computer midway between a microcomputer and a large (mainframe) computer.

Mnemonic Code: A technique for assisting the human memory whereby the code resembles the original word and is usually easy to remember; for example, MPY is the code for MULTIPLY.

Modem: A device that transmits and receives binary signals over telephone and other communication circuits. The term is an acronym for modulate-demodulate.

Module: 1) An interchangeable plug-in item containing electronic components, such as a memory module or a CPU module. 2) A component of a program resulting from structured programming techniques.

Mouse: An input device which resembles a tiny box on two wheels; the computer senses the position of the mouse as it is moved around on a table top.

Multiprocessor: Computer equipped with multiple CPUs which operate simultaneously.

Multiprogramming: A technique for concurrently running several programs by interleaving their operations.

Nanosecond: One thousandth of a millionth of a second, or one billionth of a second.

Network: A complex of two or more interconnected computer systems, terminals and communication facilities.

Nibble: One-half of a byte (four bits), sometimes spelled *nybble.*

Node: Any terminal, station, or communications computer in a computer network.

Non-Impact Printer: The use of heat, laser technology, or photographic techniques to produce printed output.

Number Cruncher: A machine with great computational power, where the accent is on the ability to handle many numerical computations.

Number System: A system for representing numeric values or quantities, for example, the decimal system utilizes ten digits, 0 to 9.

Numeric Constant: A constant value in a program that is represented by a number.

Numeric Key Pad: A keyboard on a computer terminal similar to that on a calculator.

Numeric Variable: A variable which contains a numeric value.

Object Code: Output from a compiler or assembler that is essentially executable machine code.

Octal Number System: A number system that utilizes base 8.

Off-Line: A unit of equipment which is not connected directly to a computer.

On-Line: A unit of equipment which is connected directly to a computer.

Opcode/Operation Code: The machine language instruction used to specify the operation a computer is to perform.

Operating System: See DISK OPERATING SYSTEM.

Operation: The action specified by a single computer instruction or higher-level language statement.

Operator, Computer: A person who operates a large mainframe computer.

Optical Character Recognition (OCR): A system under which data are sensed and read, such as the characters in a book, by optical scanning equipment.

Optical-Mark Recognition (OMR): Mark sensing; a capability of devices with electronic scanners that reads marks placed on paper with a pencil; the marks are converted into 1's (mark) and 0's (no marks).

Optical Scanning: A process which permits machine recognition of printed or handwritten characters.

Output: 1) A result of computer processing which may be in the form of video display, printed material, or data recorded on storage media. 2) Information transferred from the internal storage of a computer to a secondary or external storage.

Output Devices: Any device capable of producing computer output, such as printed forms, punched cards, and magnetic writing on tape.

Overflow, Arithmetic: The condition that exists when the result of an arithmetic operation exceeds the maximum value allotted in a digital computer.

Page Printer: A printer in which an entire page of characters is composed and printed as a unit.

Paper Tape: A continuous strip of paper in which holes are punched to record numerical and alphanumerical information for computer processing.

Parameter: A quantity in a subprogram which is used to pass information back and forth from the calling program.

Parity Bit: An extra bit added to a byte, character, word, or set of words, to ensure that, if one bit is accidentally changed, the computer system will detect the error.

Pascal: A computer language named after the famous French mathematician Blaise Pascal. It is a popular language for small computers.

Password: A private sequence of letters and/or numbers provided to the users of a time-sharing system to prevent unauthorized access.

Peripheral Devices: The input/output units and auxiliary storage units of a computer system. The units are attached by cables to the central processing unit.

Picosecond: One thousandth of a nanosecond.

PILOT: Computer language originally designed as an authoring language for Computer-Assisted Instruction (CAI). It is also used for teaching beginners computer programming.

PL/I: A higher level programming language designed to process both scientific and business applications; it contains many of the best features of FORTRAN, COBOL, ALGOL and other languages as well as a number of facilities not available in previous languages.

Plot: To diagram, draw, or map with a plotter.

Plotter: A hardcopy device which produces graphical output on paper.

Point of Sale Terminal (POS): The computer terminal at which retail sales are completed—includes checkstands in supermarkets or sales counters in retail stores.

Portable Computer: Small microcomputer or minicomputer that can be carried from place to place.

Precedence: Rules that state which operators get executed first in an arithmetic expression.

Precision: The degree of exactness of a numeric quantity.

Primary Memory: Another name for main memory.

Printed Circuit Board: See BOARD.

Printer: A device that converts computer output to printed documents.

Printout: Output from a computer in printed form.

Privacy: An individual's right regarding the collection, processing, storage, dissemination, and use of data about his or her personal attributes and activities.

Problem Definition: A method of presenting a problem for computer solution in a formal and logical manner.

Procedure: A task or set of steps for the processing or use of data.

Process Control: The use of the computer to control industrial processes such as oil refining and steel production.

Processing: The handling of data to deliver information.

Processor: Short form of central processing unit.

Program: A set of instructions in a language the computer understands that direct a computer in completing a specific job or controlling the operations and functions of a computer.

Programmer: A person who prepares computer programs.

Programming: The art of writing programs.

Programming Language: A language that humans use to write programs.

Prompt: A character or message provided by the computer to indicate that it is ready to accept keyboard input.

Pseudocode: A design tool used to represent algorithms in English-like statements (cf. FLOWCHART).

Punched Card: A cardboard card used in data processing operations in which tiny rectangular holes denote numerical values and alphanumeric codes.

Quota: The maximum secondary storage space that a user is allowed on a time-sharing system.

Query: The request for specific data made by a user to a database.

Random Access Memory (RAM): Direct access is permitted to any storage location in a memory or storage device. Used synonymously with main memory. Information can be both read from and written into such a memory (cf. ROM).

Random Number: A patternless sequence of digits. An unpredictable number produced by a computer program that satisfies one or more of the tests for randomness.

Raw Data: Data which have not yet been processed.

Read: To obtain data from one form of storage or an input device, and transfer it to main memory or the CPU.

Read-Only Memory (ROM): High speed memory which cannot be altered (cf. RAM). ROM is usually used to store software routines such as monitors or operating systems. Once information is stored in ROM at the factory, it is frozen and will accept no new information.

Read/Write Head: A small electromagnet used to read, write, or erase data on a magnetic storage device.

Record: A set of related facts or fields of information related as a unit and stored in a file.

Relational Expression: A programming language expression that contains one or more relational operators.

Relational Operator: A symbol used in programming languages to compare two values; the operator specifies a condition that may be either true or false, such as =, <, >.

Relay: An electromagnetic switching device that was used in early computers.

Reliability: A measure of the ability of a system or individual hardware device to function without failure.

Remarks: Synonymous with COMMENTS.

Remote Job Entry (RJE): The submission of processing jobs from remote terminals.

Remote Terminal: A terminal located at a distance from a computer system and connected to the computer by communication lines.

Renumber: A programming language capability to assign new numbers to lines.

Repetition: To repeat a series of instructions more than once. See ITERATE.

Repeat Key: A key on the keyboard permitting a key stroke to be duplicated a number of times.

Reset: A switch on a computer which sets the hardware to an initial state.

Reserved Word: Certain words that, because they are reserved by operating systems, language translators, and so on for their own use, cannot be used in an application program.

Resolution (Low/High): The density and overall quality of a video display.

Response Time: The time it takes for a computer system to react to user input.

Retrieve: Records are read from memory or storage for use by a processor.

Return: A set of instructions at the end of a subroutine that permits control to return to the proper point in the main program.

Reverse Video: The ability to reverse standard display on CRT terminals to highlight characters, words or lines.

Rewind: To return a magnetic tape to its starting position.

Robot: A computer-controlled machine that interacts physically with the outside world. It is equipped with sensing instruments for detecting input signals or environmental conditions, with a calculating mechanism for making decisions and a guidance mechanism for providing control.

Robotics: An area of artificial intelligence related to robots.

Rounding: To truncate the rightmost digit of a number and to increase by one the now remaining rightmost digit if the truncated digit is greater than or equal to half of the number base.

Row: The horizontal members of a two-dimensional array or table (cf. COLUMN).

Run: To execute a program on a computer.

Run-Time Error: An error in a program which is detected when the program is being run or executed, causing an error message to be printed.

Saving a Program: Storing a program on a disk or cassette.

Scrolling: Moving the lines, up or down, of data displayed on a screen for user review.

Search: The process of looking through data records, seeking one or more which have certain characteristics.

Sector: The data on each track of a disk is divided up into fixed size segments called sectors.

Secondary Storage: Data storage located in a place other than in the central processor, like disk, tape.

Security: Protection of computer system equipment and data from unauthorized access.

Sentinel Value: A character or set of characters which is used to indicate the occurrence of a specified condition such as the end of the input to a program.

Sequential Access: A system in which data is recorded and read from a storage media in a linear order, such as magnetic tape.

Serial Access: See SEQUENTIAL ACCESS.

Sign Bit: One bit—usually the leftmost one—that represents the sign of a binary number.

Silicon Chip: See CHIP.

Simulation: A computer program that mimics some process or event in the real world; it might imitate the way a tornado is created or the way the economy works.

Single Density Disk: A diskette which contains half the number of bytes compared to a double density diskette.

Smart Terminal: A terminal that contains some capacity to process information being transmitted or received from a computer.

Softcopy: Data presented as a video image, in audio format, or in any other form that is not hardcopy (printed).

Software: All programs written to run on a computer.

Sorting: The automatic sequencing of records by a computer.

Source Document: The original information that is the basis for an entry into a data processing system.

Source Code: The form of a program that is understandable to humans, i.e. written in the programming language. It is processed by a compiler to become object code.

Source Program: A computer program written in source code such as BASIC.

Standards: Guides used to establish uniform practices and common techniques when developing software.

Stand-Alone/Self-Contained: A computer not connected to other devices and only used by one person at a time.

Statement: One line of a computer program.

Storage: Refers to the use of devices, such as disks, to retain information for future use.

Storage Media: A medium, such as disks or tapes, on which data can be stored and from which it can be retrieved at a later date.

Store: The process of transferring an element of information to a device, such as memory, disk, or tape, from which the information can be obtained at a later time.

Stored Program: The concept that programs can be saved on a secondary storage device, read into main memory, and then executed. This allows different programs to run on computing equipment.

String Constant/String Variable: A constant or variable containing a sequence of characters that is treated as a single data item.

Structured Programming: A technique for designing and writing computer programs that uses a limited number of basic statement types and a minimum of branching to produce programs that can be read from top to bottom. It also involves dividing the program into small, manageable modules.

Structured Walkthrough: The process of reviewing program design and program coding with other programmers by systematically working through the code.

Stub Testing: The process of testing a program one module at a time.

Subprogram: A segment of a program that can perform a specific function.

Subroutine: A set of statements which is external to the main program and performs some logical function required by the calling routine.

Subscript: A notation used to identify individual members of an array, list or table.

Subscripted Variable: Variables which use subscripts such as that found in arrays.

Substring: A portion of a character string.

Supercomputer: A large, expensive, fast computer which can perform hundreds of millions of operations a second.

Syntax: The grammatical and structural rules of a programming language.

Syntax Error: An error in the grammatical usage of a programming language.

Synthesizer: An electrical device that translates a computer's digital signal into an analog signal such as human speech, music, or sound effects.

System: A group of procedures, people, materials, and equipment that follow a pattern of activity to produce results.

Systems Analyst: A person who designs computer systems, usually software, required by users.

Tab: A key which allows a preset number of spaces between information on a line of type without using the spacebar.

Table: A collection of data in a form suitable for ready reference, stored in the form of an array of rows and columns.

Tape Deck: A device used for reading and writing data stored on cassette or tape.

Tape Drive: A peripheral device that reads data from or records onto magnetic tape.

Tape Library: A special room that houses a file of magnetic tapes under secure, environmentally-controlled conditions.

Tape Reel: A plastic reel used for storing magnetic tape.

Task: A unit of work for the computer.

Telecommunications: The transfer of data from one place to another over communication lines.

Telecommuting: Instead of going to work, people dial their office computer and plug it into their home computer, doing all their work using the computer and the telephone.

Teleconferencing: Holding a conference with people at different sites who usually can see each other on video terminals.

Teleprocessing System: The use of telephone lines to transmit data and commands between remote locations and a data processing center, or between two computer systems.

Teletype: A generic term referring to teleprinter equipment—used widely as an input/output unit in computer systems.

Telex: A teletype communications service that allows users to direct dial each other's teletype.

Template: A plastic device used to draw precise outlines of symbols used in flowcharting computer systems or programs.

Terminal: A user work station that may be connected to a computer system for input or output.

Test Data: A set of data developed specifically to test the adequacy of a computer program or system.

Text Editor: A program that facilitates changes to computer-stored information; assists in the preparation of text.

Text Processing/Word Processing: The use of computers to create, view, edit, store, retrieve, and print textual material such as letters and books.

Throughput: A term describing the productivity of a computer—the amount of work a computer can do per unit of time.

Time-Sharing: A technique which allows more than one user to interactively use a computer system at the same time.

Top-Down Design: A technique for designing a program or system according to its major functions and breaking these down into even smaller subfunctions.

Trace: A diagnostic technique which provides an analysis of the results of a computer run after each instruction is executed.

Track: A path along which data is recorded on a disk or tape.

Translator: A program which has input in the form of a sequence of statements in some language and which has output in the form of an equivalent sequence of statements in another language.

Truncation: The process of removing the fractional part of a number, leaving just an integer value. (cf. ROUNDING).

Turnaround Time: The time it takes for a job to get from the user to the computing center, to be run on the computer, and the results returned to the user.

Turnkey System: A computer system selected, designed, programmed, and checked out by a company, a service business or a computer store, then turned over to the user for immediate use.

TTY Terminal: See TELETYPE.

Unary Minus: The symbol in a programming language which is used to indicate a negative value.

Unconditional Transfer: Another name for a GOTO statement; an instruction that always causes a branch in program control away from the normal sequence of executing instructions.

Underflow: The condition when a computer computation yields a result that is smaller than the smallest possible quantity the computer is capable of storing.

Univac I: The first commercial digital computer. It was used by the Census Bureau for processing data from the 1950 census.

Universal Product Code (UPC): Developed by the supermarket industry for identifying products and manufacturers on product tags; optical scanning devices read the code during supermarket checkout.

Update: The process of placing in a master file the changes required by current information or transactions.

User: A person or organization using the results of computer processing.

User Friendly: A computer program or system that is easy for noncomputer people to learn and/or use.

User Group: A group of computer users who exchange information, share programs, and trade equipment. They usually all have the same brand of computing equipment.

Utility Routines: Software used to perform some frequently required process in the operation of a computer system, such as sorting, editing programs, and file transfer software.

Variable: A quantity, used in programming languages, that can assume any of a given set of values. Usually variables can hold either numeric values or strings.

Variable-Length Record: Pertaining to a file in which the records are not uniform in length (cf. FIXED-LENGTH RECORD).

Variable Name: The name given to a variable by the programmer.

Verify: The process of checking entered data by comparing it to the same data as entered by another person.

Videodisk: A disk that uses optical techniques to read and write data.

Video-Display Terminal (VDT): A video display terminal or monitor. A device for entering information into a computer system and displaying it on a screen; also called a videodisplay unit (VDU).

Videotext System: A general term used to describe personal computing/communications networks that permit interaction between people and stored data bases.

Video Output: Output in the form of a display on a cathode ray tube terminal.

VLSI (Very Large Scale Integration): The process of placing a very large number of integrated circuits on a single silicon chip.

Voice-Activated Input: A system in which data may be entered through voice commands.

Voice Input Devices: A device that allows vocal input to be accepted and interpreted in a form processable by a computer.

Voice Output Devices: A device enabling the computer system to deliver output by the spoken word.

Von Neumann, John: One of the most important early architects of computers, who first suggested the concept of the STORED PROGRAM.

Wand Reader: A device used in reading source data represented in optical bar-code form.

Winchester Disk: A nonremovable disk offering greater storage capacity and faster access speed than floppy disks. It is made from metal rather than plastic and is hermetically sealed to keep out dust and grease, minimizing the chance of error.

Word: A group of bits occupying one storage location and treated by the computer as a unit.

Word Processing (WP): A system for processing text materials, such as letters, in which input files are stored for later correction and use, eliminating rekeying the material.

Write: The process of transferring information from the computer to an output medium. To copy data, usually from internal storage to auxiliary storage devices.

References

ALBRECHT, ROBERT L., LEROY FINKEL AND JERALD R. BROWN, *BASIC A Self-Teaching Guide* (2nd ed.), New York: John Wiley & Sons Inc., 1978.

BUROS, OSCAR KRISEN, *The Eighth Mental Measurements Yearbook,* II. Highland Park, N.J., The Gryphon Press, 1978.

Canadian Classifications and Dictionary of Occupations, Department of Manpower and Immigration, Ottawa, Canada.

DATATECH SYSTEMS LTD., VICTORIA, B. C., advertising brochure.

Department of Education Computer Science Curriculum Guide, Government of Saskatchewan, 1985.

Dictionary of Occupational Titles, 4th ed. supplement: US Department of Labor, 1977, 1982.

Encyclopaedia Brittanica, 6. Chicago: 1980.

KELLEY, ROB, *The World of Computers and Information Processing,* Rexdale, Ont.: John Wiley & Sons, Limited, 1982.

MITCHELL, JAMES V. JR., ed., *Tests in Print III.* Lincoln, NE: The Buros Institute of Mental Measurement, 1983.

Office Administration and Automation, Willowdale, Ont.: Jan. 1982; Feb., Nov. 1983; Apr., Jun., Sept., Oct., Nov. 1984; Feb. 1985.

Saskatchewan Education, "A Curriculum Guide for Division III," Dept. of Education, Regina, Sask., 1984.

Secretary's Guide to Preparing Visuals, London, Ont.: 3M Canada.

UNIVERSITY OF REGINA, Regina, Saskatchewan: calendar, 1985.

Index

A

F

G

H

I

J

L

M

N

O

P

Q

R

S

T

U

V

W

Y